**SSADM VERSION 4
PROJECT MANAGER'S HANDBOOK**

THE McGRAW-HILL INTERNATIONAL SERIES IN SOFTWARE ENGINEERING

Consulting Editor
Professor D. Ince
The Open University

Titles in this series

Portable Modula-2 Programming	Woodman, Griffiths, Souter and Davies
SSADM: A Practical Approach	Ashworth and Goodland
Software Engineering: Analysis and Design	Easteal and Davies
Introduction to Compiling Techniques: A First Course Using ANSI C, LEX and YACC	Bennett
An Introduction to Program Design	Sargent
Object-Oriented Databases: Applications in Software Engineering	Brown
Object-Oriented Software Engineering with C++	Ince
Expert Database Systems: A Gentle Introduction	Beynon-Davies
Practical Formal Methods with VDM	Andrews and Ince
SSADM Version 4: A User's Guide	Eva
A Structured Approach to Systems Development	Heap, Stanway and Windsor
Rapid Information Systems Development	Bell and Wood-Harper
Software Engineering Environments: Automated Support for Software Engineering	Brown, Earl and McDermid
Systems Construction and Analysis: A Mathematical and Logical Framework	Fenton and Hill
SSADM Version 4: Project Manager's Handbook	Hammer
Knowledge Engineering for Information Systems	Beynon-Davies
Introduction to Software Project Management and Quality Assurance	Ince, Sharp and Woodman
Software System Development: A Gentle Introduction	Britton and Doake
Introduction to VDM	Woodman and Heal
An Introduction to SSADM Version 4	Ashworth and Slater
Discrete Event Simulation in C	Watkins
Objects and Databases	Kroha
Object-Oriented Specification and Design with C++	Henderson

SSADM
Version 4
Project Manager's Handbook

Martin J. Hammer

McGRAW-HILL BOOK COMPANY

London · New York · St Louis · San Francisco · Auckland
Bogotá · Caracas · Lisbon · Madrid · Mexico · Milan
Montreal · New Delhi · Panama · Paris · San Juan
São Paulo · Singapore · Sydney · Tokyo · Toronto

Published by
McGRAW-HILL Book Company Europe
Shoppenhangers Road, Maidenhead, Berkshire, SL6 2QL, England
Tel 0628 23432; Fax 0628 770224

British Library Cataloguing in Publication Data

Hammer, Martin J.
  SSADM Version 4 Project Manager's
Handbook. — (McGraw-Hill International
Series in Software Engineering)
  I. Title II. Series
  658.40380285421

ISBN 0-07-707659-1

Library of Congress Cataloging-in-Publication Data

Hammer, Martin J.
    The SSADM version 4 project manager's handbook/Martin J. Hammer.
      p. cm. — (The McGraw-Hill international series in software
engineering)
    Includes index.
    ISBN 0-07-707659-1
      1. Electronic data processing—Structured techniques. 2. System design.
  3. System analysis. I. Title. II. Series.
QA76.9.S84H35 1993   92-24292
005.1'2—dc20   CIP

Copyright © 1993 Martin J. Hammer. All rights reserved. No part of this publication may be reproduced, stored in a retrieval system, or transmitted, in any form or by any means, electronic, mechanical, photocopying, recording, or otherwise, without the prior permission of Martin J. Hammer.

12345 CUP 96543

Typeset by Alden Multimedia, Northampton
and printed and bound in Great Britain at the University Press, Cambridge

Contents

Preface   ix
Acknowledgements   xi

PART 1   SSADM Version 4 Overview   1

1 Introduction   3
    1.1 Why a 'Handbook' to SSADM Version 4?   4

PART 2   A Review of SSADM Version 4   7

2 Documentation Review   9
    2.1 Overview   9
    2.2 Volume 1   9
    2.3 Volume 2   11
    2.4 Volume 3   11
    2.5 Volume 4   12

3 Technique Reviews   14
    3.1 Business System Options   14
    3.2 Data Flow Modelling   14
    3.3 Dialogue Design   15
    3.4 Entity–Event Modelling   16
    3.5 Function Definition   18
    3.6 Logical Data Modelling   19
    3.7 Logical Database Process Design   20
    3.8 Physical Data Design   21
    3.9 Physical Process Specification   21
    3.10 Relational Data Analysis (RDA)   22
    3.11 Requirements Definition   23
    3.12 Specification Prototyping   23
    3.13 Technical System Options   24

4 Structural Model Review   25
    4.1 Stage 0 — Feasibility Study   25
    4.2 Stage 1 — Investigation of Current Environment   25
    4.3 Stage 2 — Business System Options   27
    4.4 Stage 3 — Definition of Requirements   28
    4.5 Stage 4 — Technical System Options   30

4.6	Stage 5 — Logical Design	31
4.7	Stage 6 — Physical Design	32
4.8	Quality Reviews	34

PART 3   A Detailed Representation of the Design of SSADM Version 4 (The Structural Model)   35

5 Overview and Notation Used   37

6 Project Planning — A New Technique   41
6.1 Phase 1 — Define Products to be Delivered   45
6.2 Phase 2 — Create Module/Stage   49
6.3 Phase 3 — Check, Agree and Publish Plans   52

7 Feasibility Study Module   55
Stage 0 — Feasibility Study Structural Model   58
7.1 Step 010: Prepare for the Feasibility Study   60
7.2 Step 020: Define the Problem   63
7.3 Step 030: Select Feasibility Options   69
7.4 Step 040: Assemble the Feasibility Report   71

8 Requirements Analysis Module   74
Stage 1 — Investigation of Current Environment   77
8.1 Step 110: Establish Analysis Framework   79
8.2 Step 120: Investigate and Define Requirements   82
8.3 Step 130: Investigate Current Processing   85
8.4 Step 140: Investigate Current Data   89
8.5 Step 150: Derive Logical View of Current Services   92
8.6 Step 160: Assemble Investigation Results   95
Stage 2 — Business System Options   98
8.7 Step 210: Define Business System Options   100
8.8 Step 220: Select Business System Option   103

9 Requirements Specification Module   106
Stage 3 — Definition of Requirements   109
9.1 Step 310: Define Required System Processing   111
9.2 Step 320: Develop Required Data Model   115
9.3 Step 330: Derive System Functions   118
9.4 Step 340: Enhance Required Data Model   121
9.5 Step 350: Develop Specification Prototypes   124
9.6 Step 360: Develop Processing Specification   128
9.7 Step 370: Confirm System Objectives   132
9.8 Step 380: Assemble Requirements Specification   135

10 Logical System Specification Module   139

    Stage 4 — Technical System Options   142

    10.1 Step 410: Define Technical System Options   144

    10.2 Step 420: Select Technical System Options   148

    Stage 5 — Logical System Specification   151

    10.3 Step 510: Define User Dialogues   153

    10.4 Step 520: Define Update Processes   157

    10.5 Step 530: Define Enquiry Processes   160

    10.6 Step 540: Assemble Logical System Specification   163

11 Physical Design Module   166

    Stage 6 — Physical Design   168

    11.1 Step 610: Prepare for Physical Design   169

    11.2 Step 620: Create Physical Data Design   173

    11.3 Step 630: Create Function Component Implementation Map   176

    11.4 Step 640: Optimize Physical Data Design   179

    11.5 Step 650: Complete Function Specification   182

    11.6 Step 660: Consolidate Process Data Interface   184

    11.7 Step 670: Assemble Physical Design   188

Appendix 1 Techniques — where they are used and described   191

Index   192

Preface

SSADM is probably the most popular systems analysis and design method in use in the UK—arguably in Europe—and is gathering a considerable following around the world. It is the recommended method for UK government departments, and is in extensive use within the public sector. It is the only method in the UK for which a practitioner can take a public examination and obtain a certificate of proficiency, a qualification that is increasingly becoming a mandatory requirement for the employment of practitioners. It is supported by a wide variety of CASE tools, for which there is a formally controlled conformance testing scheme. In September 1990 SSADM Version 4 was released. It is this version that is now forming the basis for the development of the British Standard for SSADM, the first time in the UK that a British Standard has been created for a systems analysis and design method. This will lay the foundations for a family of standards for SSADM that will ensure its continued growth and development. SSADM is now a mature method, it is successful, and it has passed the most difficult test of all, the test of time.

Version 4 will be seen as a major milestone in SSADM's life, for two reasons. Technically it is a vast improvement over Version 3, it is truly an SSADM for the 1990s. The creation of a British Standard for it places it firmly in the public domain—its future has been assured.

This book has been designed for practitioners and project managers of all levels of experience, with two specific purposes in mind: to provide a clear understanding of the method to assist practitioners in its use, and to provide the basic building blocks to demonstrate how it can and should be implemented to suit the profile of any particular project.

Martin J. Hammer

Note

This publication has been assessed by the Technical Committee of the SSADM Users Group as conformant to core SSADM Version 4 and this has been endorsed by the Design Authority Board.

Acknowledgements

Although this book is all my own work, many people have provided valuable assistance by way of discussion of the various aspects, and reviewing the manuscript. My grateful thanks go to the Ministry of Defence DGITS Directorate and the Department of the Environment PINS Project for giving me the opportunity to research SSADM Version 4 and use the results as the basis for this book. In particular my thanks go to Keith Robinson of the Ministry of Defence, John Rendall of the PINS project team, and my colleagues Dr Arthur Haynes, Andrew Wallington and Andrew Hamilton. No less important, my thanks go to my wife Christine, her parents John and Joy Smith, and my four children Wayne, Sheree, Brian, and Michael, for their patience, forbearance and encouragement during the spring and summer of 1991.

PART 1
SSADM
Version 4 Overview

1 Introduction

SSADM Version 4 is a major step forward from Version 3. Existing techniques have been revised; new techniques have been included; the design of the Structural Model has been thoroughly overhauled; and a Dictionary Volume has been included for the first time, introducing the concept of Product Breakdown Structures and containing a full set of over 100 Product Descriptions and a comprehensive Glossary.

Version 3 had attracted some criticism for being too prescriptive, with insufficient explanation of some of the techniques. Version 4 has certainly answered these criticisms; however, the pendulum may have swung too far the other way. In Version 4 the emphasis is clearly on text, with little diagrammatic support for the Structural Model, and as a result there are a number of places where the method is open to interpretation. The following table provides a brief comparison between Version 3 (as described in the first two volumes of the NCC reference manuals) and Version 4, illustrating the change in emphasis.

Comparison of Version 3 and Version 4

	Version 3	Version 4
Volumes	2	4
Phases/Modules	3 (phases)	5 (modules)
Stages	8	7
Steps	41	33
Tasks	228	149
Structural Model Diagrams	52	7
Supporting Text (pages)	31	161
Reference Text (pages)	423	1261

One of the areas where SSADM has been improved is its interface to project management methodologies. Version 4 follows, perhaps not surprisingly, the PRINCE approach (PRINCE being the UK Government's project management method, recommended by the CCTA for use by all government departments) in that it is a 'Product'-oriented approach. In SSADM Version 4 the essential planning documents and the relationships between them are as follows:

Product Breakdown Structure (PBS)

This identifies the products that are to be delivered. It describes them in a hierarchical way, decomposing compound products through a number of levels down to elementary products.

Product Descriptions

These describe the purpose, form and derivation of each product, and list the quality criteria that apply to them. Each product in the PBS has a Product Description.

Product Flow Diagram (PFD)

This shows the logical sequence of production of the deliverable products. The PFD enables the identification of the transformations required to develop the products.

Activity Network

This shows the activities required to carry out the product transformations identified on the PFD, and thereby produce the deliverable products. It includes activities for quality reviewing to ensure that products meet the quality criteria defined in the Product Descriptions. It arranges the activities in a logical sequence and identifies any inter-activity dependencies.

Having produced a precise description of the products to be produced, and the activities required to produce them, the resources required can be identified, both in terms of skill and quantity, and then work can be scheduled.

Quoting from the section in the PRINCE manuals on producing an activity network, concerned with the size of activities:

> 'At the lowest level activities should not be subdivided to an unnecessary level. The 8 to 80 hour rule is a good general guideline, i.e. activities at the lowest level should last between 1 day (8 hours) and two weeks (80 hours).'

This supports the author's cardinal rule of project management, i.e. that 'A project should be broken down into activities that are small enough to be estimated with confidence'.

This product-oriented approach requires the production of a Product Flow Diagram, which is the essential stepping stone to an Activity Network. However, it should not be forgotten that it is the Activity Network that is the end-product upon which all planning is based.

In terms of the essential planning documents, SSADM Version 3 did not include the concept of Product Breakdown Structures and was very weak in Product Descriptions, but did include a detailed Structural Model in diagrammatic form down to the step level, showing each individual task. This Structural Model provided good support for producing an Activity Network, although not necessarily via a Product Flow Diagram.

Conversely, SSADM Version 4 includes an almost mirror image of the PRINCE Product Breakdown Structures, detailed Product Descriptions, but no detailed Structural Model in diagrammatic form, no Product Flow Diagram, and no Activity Network. In fact, producing the Product Flow Diagram and Activity Network is identified as one of the initial tasks. However, producing the Product Flow Diagram directly from the manuals — which do not contain a detailed structural model in a diagrammatic form — would be difficult under ideal circumstances. The Version 4 manuals, being the first issue of a major technical piece of work, inevitably contain some inconsistencies and ambiguities which only serve to compound the problem.

1.1 Why a 'Handbook' to SSADM Version 4?

In reviewing the planning aspects of a project from the SSADM Version 4 point of view I found that, despite acknowledging that SSADM is not a Project Management method, insufficient emphasis has been placed on the creation of the planning products. At the beginning of the Feasibility Study, Requirements Analysis and Physical Design Modules, there is a single task in the first step that produces all the SSADM-related planning products with no detailed explanation of how to create them. In practice, I have found this to be a significant, and not always easy, task. In particular, creating the Product Breakdown Structures and obtaining agreement as to what should and what should not be deliverable products from any given module, is a fundamentally important aspect to the successful planning of a project that is to use SSADM Version 4.

I therefore came to the conclusion that, to aid understanding of the method in general and for planning purposes in particular, the manuals needed to be supplemented by a handbook. Such a handbook would need to contain detailed Product Breakdown Structures for each module, showing both the normal deliverable and working products, a detailed version of the Structural Model in diagrammatic form, and detailed guidance on how to tailor the Product Breakdown Structures and Structural Model to suit any particular project's circumstances.

This handbook provides all the detailed information necessary for the understanding of the structure of SSADM Version 4, and for planning a project that is to use it. It contains a detailed Product Breakdown Structure and Product/Task Matrix (except Stage 6) for each module; the Structural Model in detailed diagrammatic form — which I find serves adequately as the Product Flow Diagram — supported by rewritten Step Descriptions in a more precise form; and a detailed Activity Network for each stage (except Stage 6), derived from the model.

It also contains a new technique of my own creation to be used at the beginning of every module/stage to create Project Plans. How to use this technique is described in the same style as the stages, and a detailed description of it is included in Part 3. As a result, I have excluded the project planning activities from the beginning of the Feasibility Study, Requirements Analysis and Physical Design Modules, so that they are now concerned only with the application products and related activities.

In summary, this handbook reviews the SSADM Version 4 manuals in terms of the documentation, the Structural Model and the techniques used. It provides a precise description of the Structural Model of SSADM Version 4, and detailed material and guidance on how to adapt the structure of SSADM Version 4 to the user's requirements. It therefore enables the practitioner to understand SSADM Version 4, and plan a project that is to use it, at the right level and with confidence.

PART 2
A Review of SSADM
Version 4

2 Documentation Review

2.1 Overview

The reference manuals for the core method are produced as a boxed set containing four volumes. The volume contents are as follows.

- Volume 1 — *Foundation and Feasibility*. Foundation is a new section that gives an introduction and includes an overview of the method for the benefit of management, and two technique descriptions. Feasibility is equivalent to Version 3 Stages 01 and 02.

- Volume 2 — *Requirements Analysis and Requirements Specification*. These two modules are equivalent to Version 3 Stages 1, 2, part of 3, and 4.

- Volume 3 — *Logical System Specification and Physical Design*. Logical System Specification is equivalent to Version 3 Stages 3 and 5. Physical design is equivalent to Version 3 Stage 6.

- Volume 4 — *Dictionary*. This is equivalent to the Version 3 Manual, Volume 2, Documentation section, but in a much more comprehensive form.

Note that the Technique Descriptions, which in Version 3 were in the first part of Volume 2, are in the Version 4 manuals interspersed throughout Volumes 1, 2 and 3. Each technique description has been placed by the authors where they think it most appropriate, although it does state in the Introduction that, due to its loose-leaf format, the user may restructure the manual as required. Appendix 1 gives a breakdown by technique, showing where each one is described and used.

2.2 Volume 1

This volume is divided into two basic sections, Foundation and Feasibility. The Foundation section contains the following chapters:

Introduction

This is an introduction to the reference manuals, not the method. It explains the structure of the manuals and hence where to find things, and is very useful in this respect. It does, however, state that:

> 'A key characteristic of SSADM is its modular structure. Each SSADM module can be considered as a self-contained set, or black box, of project activities to produce a structured set of end-products.'

In practice, readers of the manuals will find that, because the Structural Model is heavily dependent on the Technique Descriptions and the Product Descriptions, they will usually need to be reading two, and frequently three, volumes simultaneously.

It does state that due to the loose-leaf format the manuals may be restructured as required, which would appear to contradict the concept of each module being a black box. In practice, particularly on large projects where there may be several copies of the manuals in use, restructuring them could give rise to confusion, unless it was strictly controlled and everyone was aware of how they had been restructured.

However, in conjunction with this handbook, if all the Technique Descriptions (with the exception of Physical Data Design and Physical Process Specification) are sited in one volume, then the user should find the method relatively easy to follow: i.e. one volume for the techniques, one volume for the Product Descriptions, and this handbook for the Structural Model and general guidance.

Overview

This is an overview of the method, and by and large quite useful for that purpose. It does, however, focus on what I consider to be the Achilles heel of SSADM Version 4: in describing the approach to the Structural Model it stresses the need for accuracy, precision and understandability — principles I wholeheartedly agree with, but in practice, these are the areas where I find the manuals most wanting, hence the need to write this handbook.

Concepts

This chapter contains a more detailed expansion of some of the theory behind SSADM, the key word being theory. In practice I have found that the concepts as explained are not always supported by the method itself, for example, it states that in Stage 1: Investigate the Current Environment, if there is no current system then the Requirements Definition will be supported by models of the future business, but there are no products or activities in Stage 1 to do this. This chapter is probably best viewed as being full of good intentions.

Project Procedures

This is quite a long and useful chapter on the general principles of overall project management. However, due to its general nature and breadth of coverage it tends to lose the focus on SSADM-related activities. Hence the section in the introduction to this book on SSADM's relationship with Project Management methodologies, and my creation of a new project planning technique.

Dialogue Design

This is the Technique Description for Dialogue Design, which is used in Stages 1, 3 and 5. A detailed review of the technique is contained in Chapter 3, Technique Reviews.

Requirements Definition

This is the technique description for the Requirements Definition, which is used throughout the method. A detailed review of the technique is contained in Chapter 3.

Introduction to the Structural Model

This chapter describes how the Structural Model is presented, the notation used for the diagrams, and contains a diagram for the whole method with a description for each module. In practice, the author has found that the Structural Model, as presented, is extremely difficult to understand and follow. It only has one high-level diagram per stage, giving an overall ratio of seven diagrams to approximately 1500 pages of text. It is heavily dependent on the Product Breakdown Structures, Product Descriptions and Technique Descriptions, which are not always consistent. Being so heavily dependent on text makes it particularly difficult to use for the purposes of planning anything but the smallest project.

Feasibility Section

This section contains the Structural Model for the Feasibility Study Module, a chapter on feasibility laid out in a format similar to that of a Technique Description, and a brief annexe on information strategy planning inputs.

2.3 Volume 2

This volume contains two modules, Requirements Analysis and Requirements Specification.

Requirements Analysis Module

This consists of the activity description and structure diagram for the module; the activity description and diagram for Stage 1: Investigation of Current Environment; the detailed descriptions of the six Steps in Stage 1; the activity description and structure diagram for Stage 2: Business System Options; the detailed descriptions of the two steps in Stage 2; and the Technique Descriptions for Data Flow Modelling, Logical Data Modelling and Business System Options.

Requirements Specification Module

This consists of the activity description for the module (one line that states that the module consists of one stage); the activity description and diagram for Stage 3: Definition of Requirements; the detailed descriptions of the eight steps in Stage 3; and the Technique Descriptions for Function Definition, Relational Data Analysis, Specification Prototyping and Entity–Event Modelling.

2.4 Volume 3

This volume contains two modules, Logical System Specification and Physical Design.

Logical System Specification Module

This consists of the Activity Description and Structure Diagram for the module; the Activity Description and Structure Diagram for Stage 4: Technical System Options; the detailed descriptions of the two steps in Stage 4; the Activity Description and Structure Diagram for Stage 5: Logical Design; the detailed descriptions of the four steps in Stage 5; and the Technique Descriptions for Technical System Options, and Logical Database Process Design.

Physical Design Module

This consists of the activity description for the module (one line that states that the module consists of one stage); the Activity Description and Structure Diagram for Stage 6: Physical Design; the detailed descriptions of the seven steps in Stage 6; a chapter on the Introduction to Physical Design; and the Technique Descriptions for Physical Data Design and Physical Process Specification. This last Technique Description includes five annexes on the Processing System Classification Form, Processing System Classification Issues, Physical Design Strategy Issues, Example Program Specification Standards, and Distribution of Processing.

2.5 Volume 4

This volume contains the dictionary, which is divided into three sections — Product Breakdown Structure, Product Descriptions and a Glossary.

Product Breakdown Structure

This section provides a complete structured model of all the products that are produced in the analysis and design phase of a project using SSADM. The top level of the structure divides the products into three categories: management, technical and quality. One of the elements within the technical category includes all the application products that are produced using SSADM. The Product Breakdown Structures provided for each of the SSADM modules identify the products to be delivered by that module, and therefore should not include working products produced during the course of a module that are not deliverables. However, this principle has not always been adhered to. In some places some working products have been depicted as deliverables.

In practice, the author has found that there is a rather grey overlapping area between the lowest elements of a Product Breakdown Structure and a product's composition as defined in its description, which gives rise to a degree of inconsistency. Furthermore the Product Breakdown Structures for the modules are not always contained in a single diagram on a single page.

Having found the concept extremely useful I have included in this handbook a Product Breakdown Structure for each module, containing in a single diagram all the products produced during the course of a module. The notation used makes it easy to distinguish between deliverable products and working products. (Author's note: The Product Breakdown Structures contained in this handbook are used by the SSADM User Groups Technical Committee as baseline material when reviewing publications on SSADM Version 4.)

Product Descriptions

This section contains the individual SSADM product descriptions in alphabetical order. Every SSADM product within the application products substructure of the technical category should be included, not just the products at the bottom of the structure, although there are some omissions. By doing this the dictionary supports the Structural Model. The only slight difficulty is that when looking at a high-level product description — the Requirements Specification for example, — and then wishing to look at its constituent products, the user has to flick backwards and forwards through the alphabetically ordered Product Descriptions.

There are 102 products described in this section. The descriptions all have a standard format comprising purpose, composition, derivation, quality, external dependencies and references. The derivation and external dependencies again help support the Structural Model. Not all of the products described are actually produced by SSADM activities:

some are generic products that support other Product Descriptions, and others are products that are referred to.

Glossary

This section is a glossary of all the SSADM terms used in the manuals. Each entry gives the name of the term, its type (product, object, technique, Structural Model element or general), and a brief description. There may also be cross-references to associated entries in the Glossary and/or the Product Descriptions.

3 Technique Reviews

3.1 Business System Options

This technique supports the Business System Option Stage which consists of two Steps: Define Business System Options and Select Business System Options. It is directly equivalent to the part of the User Options Technique in Version 3 that addressed Business Options. In Version 3, the identification and selection of Business Options was a single step within Stage 2. To all intents and purposes the combination of step and technique in Version 4 is no different from the equivalent combination in Version 3. It has expanded text and is modified as required to match the new product descriptions. The techniques' purpose, and the relative position of the related steps within the method, are the same as for Version 3.

3.2 Data Flow Modelling

The Data Flow Modelling (DFM) Technique is particularly useful in that at the high level it is an effective way of communicating with users and developing an understanding of the basic areas of a business and the functions that it carries out; while at the low level it is an effective way of initially identifying events.

The technique is virtually unchanged from Version 3, although it now takes 55 pages to describe it rather than the previous 27. There are only two changes to the technique: the first is the simple addition of an asterisk in the bottom right-hand corner of a process box used to identify a bottom-level process; the second is in the part of the technique concerned with grouping bottom-level processes during logicalization. In Version 4 the grouping is done by entity, whereas in Version 3 it was done by datastore. This should produce a more 'accurate' grouping of processes that will be a sounder basis for defining the required system processing.

The section of the Technique Description covering the relationship to other techniques is rather imprecise, and the guidelines for Data Flow Diagram (DFD) decomposition are somewhat vague. However, SSADM Version 4 is much more rigorous in its approach to Process Specifications and Dialogue Specifications. Because of this extra rigour it is necessary to ensure that practitioners take a consistent approach to the use of the technique, with a clear understanding of what they are trying to achieve — an approach that will make it easier to develop the products of later stages, and considerably reduce the risk of developing incompatible products.

The main purpose of DFDs is defined in the Technique Description as:

'to facilitate the identification of the events and functions of the required system, in Function Definition. The DFDs should be constructed so that functions can be readily identified. At the top level, the model reflects the user's perception of the system's functionality, while at the bottom level the Required System DFDs are the basic components of Function Definitions.'

The Technique Description also states that:

'Within SSADM there are two vehicles for discovering data input to the system. Firstly, data flows are identified and drawn on DFDs. Secondly, the events which update entities are identified in Entity Life History analysis and documented in ELH diagrams. Both may be described in terms of data items.'

What needs to be understood is that data flows on the bottom level of the Required System DFDs that cross the system boundary are documented as the Required System I/O Descriptions, and it is these that define the start-up set of events used in Entity–Event Modelling.

Bearing this in mind, two observations can be made. First, after the Required System DFM has been completed, there are two paths that lead to the development of the Logical System Specification, one being the development of Dialogues and Enquiry Process Models. I/O Descriptions are developed into I/O Structures, which are developed into Dialogues and Enquiry Process Models. The second path is the development of Update Process Models. The Entity–Event Matrix is used in the creation of Entity Life Histories, from which Effect Correspondence Diagrams are derived, which in turn are developed into Update Process Models. Secondly, there is no technique within the method that ensures that the products of the two paths are developed in a manner consistent with each other, or that provides any sort of cross-checking. Furthermore, the task of putting operations on to the Dialogue Structures, as is clearly required by the Product Description, is missing from Step 510: Define User Dialogues.

The Function Definition technique is used to ensure that all the components of a function are created and cross-referenced, but it does nothing to ensure that they are technically consistent with each other. It is therefore imperative that each Required System I/O Description identifies one, and only one, event. Further, it is admissible when using the technique to create the Current Logical DFM and Required System DFM that all events known about at that time should be documented on the DFDs. There is a great temptation with Data Flow Modelling for practitioners to stop developing the model when they feel they have a sufficient understanding of the required functionality, and to identify multiple events on a single data flow for the sake of expediency. If the technique was being used in isolation, such an approach would be acceptable. However, if that approach is taken with SSADM Version 4, the practitioner will find that developing I/O Structures and completing the specification of Dialogues becomes extremely difficult, if not actually impossible.

3.3 Dialogue Design

This chapter states that Dialogue Design is really two techniques: Dialogue Identification and Dialogue Design. However, a detailed analysis of the chapter and where the technique is used shows that, if the method is followed rigidly, there are four distinct phases used at specific points in the method. In Step 120 (and Step 020 if a feasibility study is carried out) it is used to produce the User Catalogue. In Step 310 it is used to identify the User Roles. In Step 330 it is used to identify the Dialogues. Finally, in Step 510 it is used to specify the Dialogues.

If circumstances permit, it may be possible and desirable to start identifying User Roles and Dialogues as early as Step 120, when the User Catalogue is being created. However, if this is done they should be reassessed for the required system when the Selected Business System Option is created.

Within the technique six pages are used to describe the tasks of creating the User Catalogue, identifying User Roles and identifying Dialogues, these Tasks being relatively simple and straightforward. The majority of the Technique Description is devoted to Dialogue Design.

Within the technique there is one obvious inconsistency and one omission that need to be understood and resolved. The inconsistency is in the identification of dialogues; this is described in Section 8.3 where a User Role/Function Matrix is created, and every cross-reference point identifies a Dialogue. The paragraph at the end of the section indicates that not every cross-reference point will require the creation of a separate Dialogue because some User Roles using the same Function will require the information presented in the same way. The implication of this is that there is some sort of technique and/or activity that analyses the order of information presented to a Function by a particular User Role. Detailed examination of the technique description and the Steps involved show that there is no such technique or activity. The order of transformations of products into Dialogue Structures is that I/O Descriptions are developed into I/O Structures (curiously, done in Function Definition), which in turn are developed into Dialogue Structures. Nowhere in this series of transformations are User Roles involved. One is therefore led to the inevitable conclusion that regardless of the User Role involved, the Dialogue Structure will be the same. What the User Role/Function Matrix does do is provide a very good way of identifying the dialogues required by a particular User Role, which is used in the construction of menu hierarchies in Step 510, Task 30.

The omission in the technique concerns the inclusion of operations in the Dialogue Structure Diagrams. These are produced using a Jackson-like notation described in the SSADM Structure Diagram and Dialogue Structure Product Descriptions. Both these Product Descriptions indicate that operations detailing data manipulations should be included in the diagram. However, neither the Technique Description nor the Step Description (Step 510: Define User Dialogues), where they are created, include this activity. This perhaps is not surprising. If one accepted the manual's definition of a Dialogue, there would have to be a technique that enabled one to put the operations from more than one Process Model on to a single Dialogue Structure — which would be extremely difficult, if not actually impossible. An additional task has therefore been included in Step 510: Define User Dialogues to put operations on the Dialogue Structures, with a detailed description of how to do it included in the step description.

3.4 Entity–Event Modelling

This technique is an expansion of the Version 3 Entity Life History technique, enhanced by the addition of a supplementary technique, Effect Correspondence Diagramming

(ECD), plus the addition of operations to Entity Life Histories. These combined provide a more rigorous definition of required processing before starting Logical System Specification.

Effect Correspondence Diagramming is a relatively straightforward step from Entity Life Histories. An ELH takes an individual entity and examines its life by analysing the effects on it caused by events. The ECD takes an individual event and examines the effects that it has on entities. This then provides a firm basis for developing the logical specification of processes.

Although the Entity Life History technique is shown as being used in two Steps, 360 and 520, there is in fact no structural reason for its being in Step 520, as the only part of the technique used is to add state indicators. This could easily be done during Step 360.

There is an apparent omission from the technique, in that the concept of an Event Catalogue has been dropped. The more rigorous documentation of required processing may make it an unnecessary end-product of Requirements Specification. However, it will be an almost indispensable working document and is well worth retaining.

Because of its greater rigour it is probably worth reviewing the concepts of Entity Roles, Parallel Lives and Quits and Resumes with separate substructures.

Entity Roles

If a single event affects more than one occurrence of an entity, and the effects for each one are different, they must be identified on the Entity Life History separately, as separate processing has to be specified for each one. This is achieved by having a separate box for each effect, with the event name being qualified by the 'role' that the entity is assuming in this particular case. Hence the concept of an Entity Role.

Parallel Lives

During the life of an entity it is possible to know that certain events will definitely happen, but not in what sequence. In this case, the normal SSADM Structure Diagram notation is insufficient to model the situation correctly. Entity Life History notation includes parallel structures to cater for this situation, and is the only SSADM Structure Diagram to use it. The notation is quite simple, using a structure box representing parallelism separated from the next level down by a parallel bar. The best description of this in the reference manuals is found in the SSADM Structure Diagram Product Description.

Quits and Resumes with separate substructures

In Section 7.3.2 of the technique description, Random Events are defined as events that may occur at any stage during the life of an entity, or during a particular stage of its life, and by their very nature, for any particular occurrence of an entity they may not occur at all. These Events are modelled on the Entity Life History by creating a separate substructure not attached to the main life structure, and using the Quit and Resume notation. Note that although this is described in Section 7.3.2, the only figure that provides an example is Figure 13 at the end of Section 6.2.1.

3.5 Function Definition

Function Definition is described as a technique, a product, and a step, but in reality it is not really any of these. It is a procedure that identifies Functions, and then references all the SSADM products that provide the detailed specification for their components. It does contain a subtechnique to produce I/O Structures, but logically that fits more easily as part of Dialogue Design.

As a product, apart from description, classification and volumetrics, it is built up as a set of cross-references to other products. It is in this aspect that some confusion arises. SSADM Version 4 does not include activities to maintain the deliverable products from one module in succeeding modules, unless they are deliverables of the succeeding module. However, the Function Definition product includes references to products produced in one module as well as references to the products from which they were derived in earlier modules. There is therefore an implicit assumption that all of the products that a Function Definition references are complete, consistent and up to date, which may not in fact be the case.

As a single step, Step 330: Derive System Functions, in Stage 3, is a rather awkward fit. It is carried out in parallel with Step 340: Enhance Required Data Model, Step 350: Development Specification Prototypes, and Step 360: Develop Processing Specification, which gives rise to a rather circular Activity Network for that stage, and yet it cross-refers to products created as early as Stage 1, and provides cross-referencing to products produced as late as Stage 6 via the products they were derived from in Stage 3. Given Function Definition's position in the Structural Model, it makes an interesting contrast with the following quote from the Concepts chapter in the Foundation section of Volume 1, viz:

> 'This means that the detailed activity of function specification is not undertaken in one step alone — it is described in a group of steps which each contain the tasks of the separate techniques.'

The following table shows in which steps the technique is used, and the products involved.

Step technique	Product
330 Function Definition	Function Definitions
	I/O Structures
360 Logical Data Modelling	Enquiry Access Paths
Entity/Event Modelling	Effect Correspondence Diagrams
510 Dialogue Design	Dialogue Structures
520 Logical Database Process Design	Update Process Models
	Enquiry Process Models
630 Physical Process Specification	Function Component Implementation Map

The body of the Technique Description is really a discussion document to help the practitioner identify, classify and document functions, produce I/O Structures, and establish the sequence of processing.

3.6 Logical Data Modelling

This technique has been enhanced and is described more fully, with some useful sections on naming relationships, informal use of Relational Data Analysis when producing the model, and defining Enquiry Access Paths.

The technical changes are that the concept of Operational Masters has been dropped; the technique now recognizes that resolving m:m relationships does not have to be done at the very beginning; the entity boxes now have rounded corners; and the definition and notation for showing optionality have been changed. In Version 3, optionality was shown by writing an 'o' on the relationship line, simply to indicate that a detail could exist before its master. Without the 'o', a master had to exist before a detail, and therefore could exist without a detail for some time. In Version 4, optionality is shown by using a dotted relationship line; if the entire line is dotted then the relationship is optional from the point of view of both master and detail. If it is half solid and half dotted, then it is mandatory from the point of view of the entity attached to the solid half, but optional from the point of view of the entity attached to the dotted half. If the relationship line is completely solid, then it is mandatory from the point of view of both master and detail. Note that this has altered the meaning of the solid relationship line from Version 3. In Version 4, mandatory means that an entity occurrence must *always* be associated with an entity occurrence at the other end of the relationship line.

The technique does now recognize the concept of entity subtypes, but only the briefest description is given and a rather 'narrow' point of view is taken as to how to represent them. They are depicted as being modelled as a set of exclusive relationships that are mandatory at both ends. However, reading Section 7.3 of the Entity–Event Modelling technique description makes it clear that the relationship may be optional from the master (super-type) end. Furthermore, there may be more than one group of exclusive relationships. It is particularly unfortunate that they are not more comprehensively described, because the use of entity subtypes, and their subsequent effect in Entity–Event Modelling, is important to the successful development of Update Process Models.

If entity subtyping has not been used when it could have been, this will cause the Entity Life History to become much more complex, with an increased use of Entity Roles, Parallel Lives and Quits and Resumes. The inevitable consequence is that the inexperienced or unwary practitioner may not get the use and combination of these aspects of Entity–Event Modelling quite right. Should this happen, the results are likely to be carried forward into the Effect Correspondence Diagrams, thence to the Update Process Models, and probably not discovered until operations are put on to the Dialogue Structures.

There is one aspect of the technique that may cause confusion, that is, the collecting of information concerning User Roles and Access Rights. The product descriptions for Entity, Relationship and Attribute/Data Item support the collection of this information, although the notes at the end of the guidance for completion of the forms in Annexe

A do not encourage it. However, the Function Definition Product Description does not include Access Right information: it only names the User Roles that use a function. Whether it is collected or not, no use is made of Access Right information in any technique or activity in the method.

3.7 Logical Database Process Design

Logical Database Process Design is one of two techniques (the other being Dialogue Design) used in Logical Process Design. The technique is concerned with producing Enquiry Process Models from Enquiry Access Paths and I/O Structures, and producing Update Process Models from Entity Life Histories and Effect Correspondence Diagrams. The technique is fairly straightforward in producing Structure Diagrams, using Jackson notation plus an operations list for each diagram.

Enquiries seem to be more complex because there is an additional task of resolving data structure clashes, but little advice is given. A better discussion of structure clashes will be found in the Physical Process Specification Technique. This Technique Description also contains the first reference to the Universal Function Model, which is supposed to help in the resolution of structure clashes, but no indication is given of how it achieves this. It is defined in the glossary (as an object, not a product) as 'a standard model used to identify the components of an SSADM function', but no use is made of it until Stage 6. As a concept it does not fit at all well with Jackson Structures; this is discussed further in the reviews of Stage 6 and the techniques involved.

There is also a curious statement in Section 6.11 on modelling enquiry processes, which states that 'Clashes between the structures of input and output data may be identified but their resolution will be delayed until Physical Design'. This is clearly an erroneous statement, in complete conflict with the rest of the Technique Description and the description of Step 530, where the technique is used. If structure clashes are identified but not resolved, Enquiry Process Models cannot be produced!

There are two references, one in Section 6.5 on merging data structures and one in Section 6.7 on recognition problems, that refer to 'the guide on the interface between SSADM and 3GLs', which at the time of writing is unavailable.

Included in the Technique Description is an interesting discussion (Section 6.8) on logical success units, which, however, are not used or referred to anywhere in the application of the technique.

One of the inconsistencies in this technique is fairly obscure and could cause a considerable degree of confusion in the unwary practitioner. The Enquiry and Update Process Models use the standard SSADM Structure Diagram notation, but there is one fundamental difference: the Enquiry Process Model diagram is produced using the Jackson technique of combining input and output data structures, and therefore supports the concept of sequence; the Update Process Model diagram is produced by converting the Effect Correspondence Diagram, and therefore, despite using the same notation, it does *not* support the concept of sequence. In Update Process Models the concept of sequence is supported solely by the sequence numbers of the operations.

These are derived by reference to the Entity Life Histories and the I/O Structure for the process to respond to the event.

3.8 Physical Data Design

Like Physical Process Specification, this technique contains a lot of discussion about related topics; it is, however, more specific about what the practitioner has to do. The main concepts are to gain a thorough understanding of the implementation environment, for which a database management system (DBMS) classification scheme has been devised. An environment-independent physical design is produced, from which an environment-specific one is then created using the appropriate product interface guide; the design is then optimized to meet preset performance objectives.

However, as with Physical Process Specification, this technique must be viewed in the context of who does the Physical Design. Physical Data Design is a highly specialized area that must be carried out by someone experienced in the implementation environment. Given the level of detail achieved by the end of Logical System Specification, such an individual is not likely to need to classify the DBMS, or want to bother with the extra stage of a non-environment specific design.

3.9 Physical Process Specification

This is not really a technique or a set of defined steps. Included in the Purpose section of the technique are the following two sentences:

> 'While designers are generally confident of their ability to transform a (correct and complete) Logical Data Model (LDM) into a physical database, many designers are unsure how to implement a Logical Design in a specific programming environment. The aim of this chapter is to help them.'

Rather than give a detailed and lengthy review of the technique, I think it is more useful to examine two of its fundamental concepts in the context of the rest of the method.

The first is the concept of the Universal Function Model. In the beginning of the description of this concept is the statement 'each function is viewed as a series of input/output processes (with no access to database) and database processes (with no access to user interface), communicating via intermediate data streams'. This may be valid in isolation, but in practice it would require detailed guidance on how the communication via intermediate data streams was specified, and no such guidance is given. It is also in complete conflict with the Jackson technique of Structure Diagrams, with operations detailing data manipulation that are used throughout the rest of the method!

The second is the concept of the Function Component Implementation Map. This is described as 'a system network diagram showing how the elements of the processing within Physical Design fit together, and showing the mapping of logical function components on to the physical'. Given its title and description it is rather disappointing to find that its Product Description does not include a diagram or proforma of any sort. The Product Description states that it cross-refers function components to fragments, but a fragment is not defined. There is no guidance given of how the logical components of a function produced in Stage 5 are cross-referred to the physical components produced in Stage 6, which in any case are difficult to identify. As well as the cross-reference, its composition includes detailed specifications of fragments that can be written using anything the practitioner cares to use. This may apparently include formal languages based on predicate calculus, such as Z. I find this comment particularly unhelpful, as in practice I have never worked with a practitioner that has heard of Z. Furthermore, the product's derivation does not conform to the standard composition for a Product Description because it does not identify where in the method the product is created or updated.

Bearing in mind that, by the time that the Logical System Specification is completed there is a detailed specification of dialogues, processes, etc., very little practical prescriptive guidance is given on how to develop these specific products into their physical equivalents. The Product Descriptions in the dictionary for the outputs of this technique are rather vague, and of little help to the practitioner in trying to deduce what he should actually produce. This technique is best viewed in the context of who does Physical Design. Physical Design is a specialist area that has to be carried out by experienced practitioners knowledgeable in the implementation environment. Any technique to support such a process that is not environment-specific will inevitably be of the nature of general guidance, as indicated in the overview in the Technique Description.

3.10 Relational Data Analysis (RDA)

This technique is very well known and has been described in many publications. Its basic principles are fixed, although different authors emphasize different aspects. The description within Version 4 has a greater emphasis on understanding dependencies; this is taken to the extent that it is described as a separate task between conversion to First Normal Form and conversion to Second Normal Form; and 5 of the 13 pages of the Concepts section are devoted to functional dependencies. It also has some useful supporting text concerning Domains (a 'pool of values' from which the actual values appearing as attribute values are drawn), and Fourth and Fifth Normal Forms.

As for all Technique Descriptions, the relationship to other techniques is described. However, within the RDA description there are extra sections: Section 10 on Representing 3NF Relations as Logical Data Models; Section 11 on Representing Logical Data Models as 3NF Relations; and Section 12 on Comparing the RDA models and a Logical Data Model. Section 12, and Section 3 on the use of the technique, do, however, create a slight conflict with the Structural Model. The Structural Model is quite specific about the use of the technique in Step 340: Enhance Required Data Model, whereas these sections within the technique description refer to the informal use of the technique in Step 140: Investigate Current Data and Step 320: Develop Required Data Model.

This informal use of the technique supports the changes to the Structural Model whereby RDA in Version 4 is now a complementary validation technique supporting Logical Data Modelling, and not a 'mainstream' analysis technique, as it was in Version 3. From a Project Management point of view this could give rise to the problem of expending resources on unplanned activities, because they do not appear in the

Structural Model. However, if a Relational Data Design is required and the technique is intended to be used in these steps, the Product Breakdown Structures, Structural Model, Step Descriptions and Activity Networks should be amended accordingly, as described in the Project Planning Technique in Section 3.2, to ensure that the activities are properly planned, estimated, scheduled and monitored.

3.11 Requirements Definition

This is not a technique in the same way that Relational Data Analysis is, for instance. It is an ongoing iterative procedure that builds the Requirements Catalogue and expands upon its entries. The Requirements Catalogue itself is a development of the Version 3 concept of a Problems Requirements List (PRL). There is a proforma for catalogue entries in the dictionary that is more comprehensive than its equivalent in Version 3 for PRL entries. The main difference is that the catalogue entry proforma now caters specifically for differentiating between functional and non-functional requirements. Reasonably good guidance is given within the body of the Technique Description for identifying and defining non-functional requirements.

Emphasis is placed on the fact that the Requirements Definition is a driving technique, and that the Requirements Catalogue is used throughout the method and should be under constant review and revision. However, although it is accepted that, as a concept, this is so, it is very much a matter of emphasis. From a structural point of view, Requirements Definition cannot be a driving technique because the Requirements Catalogue is always updated as the result of some other activity — usually using one of the other techniques.

3.12 Specification Prototyping

The Structural Model includes Step 350 in Stage 3, Requirements Specification, which is there to prototype aspects of the Requirements Specification, the intention being to identify any errors in the specification in advance of detailed design; it does not, however, make it clear that it can be regarded as an optional step.

The Technique Description gives some fairly commonsense advice about prototyping in general, and points out that only specification prototyping is included in the core method; any other sort of prototyping will be covered in a separate subject guide. However, the technique then becomes rather specific about menu structures and command structures etc. to be prototyped.

Prototyping is undoubtedly a valuable technique during analysis, to gain a thorough understanding of the user's requirements and, as importantly, for the user to gain a thorough understanding of the implications of what he has asked for. However, it can be very expensive in resources, particularly if it is in addition to other techniques and not a replacement for them. Projects should therefore be very specific about what is required to be prototyped and why. They should not spend any more resources than is required to gain the benefit of using the technique.

Prototyping is dependent on the technical environment and therefore the technique is concerned with what has to be produced; it cannot address the 'how'. The Product Descriptions for Menu Structures, Command Structures and Prototype Pathways should therefore be regarded as suggestions, and will almost inevitably need adapting to the technical environment to be used.

3.13 Technical System Option

This technique supports the Technical System Options Stage, which consists of two Steps — Define Technical System Options and Select Technical System Options. It is directly equivalent to the part of the User Options Technique in Version 3 that addressed Technical Options. In Version 3, the identification and selection of Technical Options was the first of two steps of Stage 3, Selection of Technical Options. The remaining two steps were concerned with the completion of the Required System Specification, and defining Performance Design Objectives.

In Version 4, Performance Objectives (termed Service Level Requirements) are defined for each Function as it is developed during Step 330: Derive System Functions in the Requirements Specification Module. This is feasible in Version 4 because the Version 3 equivalent of Stage 4 — Data Design is now done in Step 340: Enhance Required Data Model, in parallel with Step 330: Derive System Functions during Requirements Specification. The Select Technical System Options stage is now the first of two stages in the Logical System Specification Module, producing products that are used both in the second stage of the module, Logical Design, and in the Physical Design Module.

Note, however, that it does miss out any necessary rework to the Requirements Specification if this has been constrained by the chosen technical option.

4 Structural Model Review

4.1 Stage 0 — Feasibility Study

This stage is the only stage in the Feasibility Module and consists of four steps. In essence it is equivalent to a high-level pass through Stages 1, 2, 3 and 4 to produce a Feasibility Report. The report assesses whether a proposed information system can meet a specified business requirement, and if so whether there is a business case for such a system.

Step 010: Prepare for the Feasibility Study (3 Tasks)

This step, as described in the reference manuals, consists of three tasks, the second and third of which are project planning activities that produce management products. The presentation of the Structural Model in Part 3 of this handbook is concerned only with the technical products, and therefore these two tasks are not shown; the step as presented here consists of the one remaining task, which contains the SSADM application product-related activities that review the input documents for the study. They use the SSADM techniques only so far as is necessary to establish that there are no inconsistencies or errors that would prevent a feasibility study from proceeding.

Step 020: Define the Problem (6 Tasks)

These tasks develop an understanding of the business and its information needs; identify any problems with the current environment that are to be resolved with the new system; identify any additional services to be provided by the new system; and identify the users of the new system.

Step 030: Select Feasibility Options (8 Tasks)

These tasks develop a range of options which are a combination of Business and Technical Options; present the options to the Project Board and select one, which may be a composite of those presented; and develop an Action Plan.

Step 040: Assemble the Feasibility Report (2 Tasks)

The two tasks of this step check the completeness and consistency of the products of the Feasibility Report, and assemble and publish the Feasibility Report.

4.2 Stage 1 — Investigation of Current Environment

This stage is the first of two stages in the Requirements Analysis Module and consists of six steps. Although Requirements Definition is supposed to be the driving technique for this Stage, it is a matter of emphasis rather than structure. In practice it has been found that, from a structural point of view, Data Flow Modelling is the driving technique. The emphasis placed on the techniques depends upon the relative importance of the current system: at one extreme, if there is no current system, Steps 130, 140 and 150 would not be used, and all the emphasis would be on Requirements Definition in Step 120, and greater importance would be attached to the context diagram produced in Step 110. On the other hand, if the project were a straightforward replacement for an existing system, due to an updated hardware platform, then there would be far less emphasis on Requirements Definition.

Step 110: Establish Analysis Framework

This step, like Step 010 in the Feasibility Module as described in the manuals, consists of three tasks, the second and third of which are project planning activities. As for the Feasibility Module these two tasks are not shown in the presentation of the Structural Model in Part 3 of this handbook. The step as presented here consists of the one remaining task, which contains the SSADM application product-related activities to review the input documents to ensure that there are no inconsistencies or errors that would prevent a full study proceeding. It creates a Context Diagram, the Physical Level 1 Data Flow Diagram and an Overview Logical Data Structure, and initiates the Requirements Catalogue.

Step 120: Investigate and Define Requirements (4 Tasks)

This step is carried out largely in parallel with Steps 130 and 140. As the Physical Data Flow Model and Logical Data Model are developed, problems with the current system will become apparent and ideas will be generated for additional functions and data required, all of which are documented in the Requirements Catalogue. It includes a task, not structurally dependent on the others, that creates the User Catalogue. Note that although this step is shown as being in parallel with Steps 130 and 140, the last task of prioritizing the Requirements Catalogue has to be done after the other steps are complete.

Step 130: Investigate Current Processing (5 Tasks)

This step develops the Physical Data Flow Model from the Physical Level 1 Data Flow Diagram created in Step 110, and in so doing identifies deficiencies in the current processing. It is this step that, from the structural point of view, is the driving step for this stage. The first two tasks are optional ones that develop Resource Flow and Document Flow diagrams should they be necessary or useful. The next two tasks develop the Data Flow Diagrams and supporting products, and the last task updates the Requirements Catalogue with the results of the investigation; this is essentially the same activity as Tasks 10 and 30 of Step 120.

Note that the extent to which the Current Physical Data Flow Model should be developed depends upon the relevance of the current system to the required system. If there is little relevance, then not too much effort should be expended on this activity and Data Flow Models supporting the Business System Options become much more important. Conversely, if the required system is little more than a rewrite of the current system, then a detailed Current Physical Data Flow Model will be required.

Step 140: Investigate Current Data (4 Tasks)

The first two tasks develop the Logical Data Model from the Overview Logical Data Structure created in Step 110, using data as they are identified during the course of the development of the Physical Data Flow Model in Step 130. The next task checks to ensure that the model supports the Elementary Process Descriptions created in Step 130. The last task identifies any deficiencies in the current data and records them in the

Requirements Catalogue; as for Step 130, this is essentially the same activity as Tasks 10 and 30 of Step 120.

Step 150: Derive Logical View of Current Services (4 Tasks)

This step consists of four (not five as indicated in the manual) tasks that convert the Physical Data Flow Model into the Logical Data Flow Model. A comparison of the Task Descriptions with the activities of logicalization in the Data Flow Modelling Technique Description in the reference manual, shows that the initial Task 10 is, in fact, a summary of the activities in Task 20 and the first part of Task 30. These first two tasks develop the Logical Data Flow Model and the supporting products. The next task checks that the elementary Process Descriptions are still supported by the Logical Data Model. The final task ensures that any remaining valid physical constraints are recorded in the Requirements Catalogue, so that they may be taken into account when building the Required System Data Flow Model in Stage 3.

Step 160: Assemble Investigation Results (2 Tasks)

This step consists of two tasks. The first is a straightforward review of all the products of Stage 1, checking for completeness and consistency, and the second is a more thorough and rigorous review of the Requirements Catalogue conducted with users, including a review of the priority levels.

Note that, although the compound product produced by Stage 1 is called the Current Services Description (not a particularly good name, because there may not be any current services), it consists solely of its constituent products. It is created implicitly not explicitly: there is no activity that refers to it. In practice, an end-of-stage management report will be required that includes a textual Current Services Description and cross-refers to its constituent products.

4.3 Stage 2 — Business System Options

This is the second of the two stages in the Requirements Analysis Module; it completes the Analysis of Requirements, and consists of two steps.

Step 210: Define Business System Options (5 Tasks)

The first two tasks identify the minimum requirements that must be satisfied by any option, and develop a range of possible options. The third task produces a shortlist of the options in discussion with the users. The next task develops the options from a systems point of view; the option may be supported by Logical Data Models and Data Flow Diagrams. Note that if there is little or no emphasis on the current system, the creation of these supporting models and diagrams becomes a particularly important activity. In the last task, each option is developed from a business point of view by adding a Cost/Benefit Analysis and outlining the organizational implications.

Step 220: Select Business System Option (2 Tasks)

The first task is the selection process itself, presenting the options to the Project Board, discussing the implications and recording the reasons for decisions taken. The second task finalizes the documentation for the selected option, which may well be an amalgam of those presented, and contains the reasons for the selection of the particular option and the rejection of others.

Note that, similarly to the end of Stage 1, this is the end of the Requirements Analysis Module that produces the compound product — the Analysis of Requirements — which also consists solely of its constituent products. As for the Current Services Description it is created implicitly, not explicitly: there is no activity that refers to it. In practice, an end-of-module management report will be required that includes a textual Analysis of Requirements, and cross-refers to its constituent products.

4.4 Stage 3 — Definition of Requirements

This is the only stage in the Requirements Specification Module and consists of eight steps. In outline these steps comprise three phases. The first phase involves developing the Logical Data Flow Model into the Required System Data Flow Model, and the Logical Data Model into the Required System Data Model using information provided by the Selected Business Option. The second phase develops these models in a detailed manner using a variety of techniques. The third phase involves checking the products, confirming objectives and assembling the Requirements Specification.

Step 310: Define Required System Processing (6 Tasks)

The first task identifies any requirements that are not part of the Selected Business Option, annotating the entries in the Requirements Catalogue with their reason for exclusion. The next two tasks develop the Required System Data Flow Diagrams, taking into account additional processes identified in the Business System Option, and excluding those no longer in the Business System Option; the Requirements Catalogue is annotated to describe the inclusion of any new requirements on the Data Flow Diagrams. The fourth task develops the supporting products of the diagrams to create the Required System Data Flow Model. The fifth task cross-checks the datastores on the Required System Data Flow Diagrams against the entities on the Required System Logical Data Model (which has been developed in parallel), ensuring consistency. The last task defines the User Roles of the required system, ensuring that they can be mapped on to the external entities of the Required System Data Flow Model.

It is difficult to know how far to develop Data Flow Models. In the author's experience this comes about for two reasons, the first being due to the technique itself. At the high level it is very useful for developing an understanding of the users' business and communicating that understanding to the users, whereas at the low level it is an essential analysis technique for identifying events. The transition from one to the other is inevitably blurred, and frequently the purpose of the technique gets lost in the process. The second reason is that frequently the inexperienced practitioner does not understand the importance of the concept of events, or has difficulty in identifying them. Understanding this concept has become even more important in SSADM Version 4, due to the rigorous way the products of Data Flow Modelling are developed.

Step 320: Develop Required Data Model (3 Tasks)

The first task reviews the Selected Business System Option, identifies any aspects of the Logical Data Model that are not required, removes them from the model, and annotates any relevant entries in the Requirements Catalogue with the reason for exclusion; the model is then extended to incorporate any additional requirements of the new system and is cross-checked with the Data Catalogue to ensure that each Entity is fully defined with all of its Attributes, each of which must also be fully defined; the Requirements Catalogue is then annotated to reference the inclusion of any new requirements. The second task is a consistency check with the Required System Data Flow Model: as each Elementary Process Description is created/revised in Step 310 Task 40, it is cross-checked against what is now the Required System Logical Data Model, to ensure that all the required Entities and Attributes are present and that all required navigation paths are supported by the Relationships; the access paths are not formally documented at this step. The last task reviews the Requirements Catalogue for all non-functional requirements and revises the model as necessary to incorporate them.

Step 330: Derive System Functions (5 Tasks)

The first two tasks are concerned with the identification of Update Functions and Enquiry Functions. Initially this is done primarily using information derived from the Required System Data Flow Model created in Step 310; however, this is an iterative process carried out in parallel with Steps 340, 350 and 360: after the first iteration, the information used is the new events identified and defined using the Entity–Event Modelling technique in Step 360. The third task creates I/O Structures for each Function, derived from the I/O Descriptions on the Required System Data Flow Model, and for any enquiries that are not part of an update function. For enquiries not on the Required System Data Flow Model the enquiry interface will have to be established in consultation with the users, as part of creating the I/O Structures. The fourth task creates a User Role/Function Matrix which is used to identify which User Roles will use which Functions, and hence Dialogues; the critical Dialogues within the system are then identified. The last task defines the service level requirements for each Function.

Step 340: Enhance Required Data Model (4 Tasks)

This step applies the Relational Data Analysis technique to selected I/O Structures created in Step 330, to create data submodels which are then compared with the Required System Logical Data Model, and any differences are resolved. The first task examines the functions and selects those I/O Structures to which the technique will be applied. The second task applies the RDA technique to the selected I/O Structures and produces a set of normalized relations for each one. The third task converts the normalized relations into Logical Data Model-style submodels. The last task compares the submodels with the Required System Logical Data Model, identifies any differences, resolves those differences, and amends the Required System Logical Data Model as required.

Step 350: Develop Specification Prototypes (8 Tasks)

This step is used to identify any errors in the Requirements Specification so that they may be eliminated in advance of detailed design, and to help establish any presentational requirements for the user interface. The first task selects the Dialogues and reports to be prototyped. The second task creates prototype Menus and Command Structures, demonstrates them to the users and modifies them as necessary. The third task identifies the screen and report components to be prototyped, and creates Prototype Pathways for them. The next four Tasks are repeated for each Prototype Pathway, and involve implementing the pathway, preparing for the prototyping session, demonstrating the prototypes, and reviewing the results of the session. The final task assesses the results of the prototyping exercise, identifies any errors in the Requirements Specification, updates the Requirements Catalogue with any user interface requirements that have been identified, and completes the Prototype Report.

Step 360: Develop Processing Specification (6 Tasks)

This step is principally concerned with using the Entity–Event Modelling technique to develop the processing specification by producing Entity Life Histories and Effect Correspondence Diagrams. It is carried out in parallel with Step 330 after the first iteration. As new events are identified and their effects defined, they are fed back into Step 330 to update the Function Definitions. The first task is an initial pass through the Required System Logical Data Structure to create an Entity–Event Matrix. The next three tasks are concurrent activities: the first creates the Entity Life Histories, the second creates the Effect Correspondence Diagrams, and the third updates the Required System Logical Data Model and Requirements Catalogue with the results of the analysis before the information is fed back into Step 330. The next task creates an Enquiry Access Path for each Enquiry Function, and the last task updates the Required System Logical Data Model with volumetric information.

Step 370: Confirm System Objectives (4 Tasks)

This step is concerned with ensuring that all functional and non-functional requirements are fully addressed and described, and that there are proper objective measures of how well the functional requirements will be met. The first task checks the Requirements Catalogue to ensure that each functional and non-functional requirement is fully defined, and that each functional requirement is fully satisfied in the Requirements Specification products. The second task identifies any outstanding non-functional requirements and ensures that they are fully defined. The third task reviews the Function Definitions to ensure that they all contain objective measures defined in service-level requirements. The last task reviews the Required System Logical Data Model to ensure that all non-functional requirements are fully included.

Step 380: Assemble Requirements Specification (2 Tasks)

The first task is concerned with a complete review of all the products of the Requirements Specification, checking for completeness and consistency and making any amendments as necessary. The second task is the assembly and formal publication of the Requirements Specification Document.

Note that, although the Requirements Specification is explicitly referred to, it consists solely of its constituent products, one of which — the Processing Specification — is not explicitly referred to in this stage. In practice, an end-of-module management report will be required that includes a textual Requirements Specification, that, depending on installation standards, may include a textual Processing Specification and that cross-refers to its constituent products.

4.5 Stage 4 — Technical System Options

This is the first of two stages in the Logical System Specification Module, and consists of two steps. Its purpose is to identify the possible technical environments that could be used to implement the required system, and to select the most appropriate one.

Step 410: Define Technical System Options (6 Tasks)

The first two tasks identify all the constraints of the environment and produce up to six Outline Technical System Options that satisfy all of the constraints. The third task involves reviewing the options with the users to produce a shortlist of two or three options. The fourth task expands the outline options to include a Technical Environment Description and System Description. The next task assesses the capacity planning aspects of each option, ensuring that service-level requirements can be met or that variances are highlighted in the Technical Environment Description. The last task completes each option by adding an Impact Analysis, Outline Development Plan and Cost/Benefit Analysis.

Step 420: Select Technical System Options (4 Tasks)

The first task involves presenting the Technical System Options to the Project Board and assisting in the selection process; the selected option may well be a hybrid of those presented. The next task consists of reworking any of the elements of the selected option, which may come about as a result of selecting a hybrid. The third task is to check that service-level requirements can still be met by the selected option, and the last task is to develop an Application Style Guide for the system based on the Installation Style Guide.

4.6 Stage 5 — Logical Design

This is the second stage in the Logical System Specification Module, and consists of four steps. The first three steps are concerned with developing the dialogues and Logical Process Models. In the reference manuals these three steps are depicted as being carried out in parallel, as there are no interstep dependencies. However, Step 510 does not include an activity to put operations on the Dialogue Structures, as is required by the Dialogue Structure Product Description. This activity has been included in the presentation of the Structural Model in Part 3 of this handbook, which creates a dependency between Step 510 and Steps 520 and 530. In practice, therefore, Steps 520 and 530 are carried out first and in parallel, and are followed by Step 510. The last step reviews and publishes the Logical Design.

Step 510: Define User Dialogues (4 Tasks)

The first task is concerned with converting the I/O Structures into Dialogue Structures by identifying the Logical Groupings of Dialogue Elements. The next task identifies the navigation paths within each dialogue and creates a Dialogue Control Table. The third task defines a Menu Hierarchy for each User Role, including the valid control paths on completion of each Dialogue. The last task defines the requirements for Dialogue-Level Help facilities.

Note that, in the Structural Model as presented in Part 3 of this handbook, there is an additional activity in the first task in this step that is an extension to the Step Description in the manuals, but is consistent with the Dialogue Structure and SSADM Structure Diagram Product Descriptions. After the Update and Enquiry Process Models in Steps 520 and 530 are completed, this additional activity is used to put the operations defining the data manipulation requirements on to the Dialogue Structures.

Step 520: Define Update Processes (5 Tasks)

The first task in the step is concerned with adding the state indicator values to the Entity Life Histories produced in Step 360. The next four tasks are carried out for each event: the first is used to convert the Effect Correspondence Diagram for an event into a Jackson-like Processing Structure Diagram. Note that, although the notation used is the same for similar diagrams in other parts of the method, these diagrams *do not* support the concept of sequence. The second is concerned with listing the operations for each Entity affected by the event, by reference to the Entity Life Histories. The third task allocates the operations to the processing structure. Note that the sequence of the operations is worked out by reference to the I/O Structure for the processing for the Event, and thus the sequence of operations within the Update Process Model is contained solely within the operations sequence numbers. Conditions to govern selection and iteration are then added to the structure. The last task is used to specify the error outputs.

Step 530: Define Enquiry Processes (5 Tasks)

Each of the five tasks are performed for each enquiry. The first task is used to convert the Enquiry Access Path into a processing structure representing the input data structure. The second task creates an output data structure for the enquiry based on the output data identified in the I/O Structure. The next task then merges the two structures to form a single processing structure. The fourth task lists the operations and allocates them to the processing structure, and then allocates conditions to govern each selection and iteration. The last task is to specify error outputs.

Step 540: Assemble Logical Design (2 Tasks)

The first task carries out a complete review of all the products of Logical Design, checking for completeness and consistency and making any amendments as necessary. The second task assembles and publishes the Logical Design.

Note that, although the Logical Design is explicitly referred, the compound deliverable product that is deliverable from this module is the Logical System Specification, which is not explicitly referred to. Both of these products consist solely of their constituent products. In practice, an end-of-module management report will be required that includes a textual Logical System Specification, may include a textual Logical Design (depending on installation standards), and that cross-refers to its constituent products.

4.7 Stage 6 — Physical Design

This is the only stage in the Physical Design Module and consists of seven steps. Note that, although a precondition to beginning this stage is the existence of the Logical System Specification, in practice many of the activities within the first step are not dependent upon it, and therefore can and should be started well before the end of Stage 5. If, as is often the case, the technical environment is predefined, many of these activities can be started as early as the beginning of Stage 3, and sometimes as early as the beginning of Stage 1.

Furthermore, if the development is to be carried out using a 4GL, it has been found in practice that the best approach to Physical Specification is to modify the products, activities and techniques of Stages 3, 4 and 5, rather than as a separate stage after Stage 5.

The approach to Physical Design as depicted in Steps 620 to 670 is a theoretical one that, technically, would work even if the design team had no experience of the development environment. However, that situation should be avoided at all costs. In practice, practitioners carrying out physical design must be experienced in the development environment, or be advised by people who are, in which case it is highly unlikely that the approach described would be adopted.

Step 610: Prepare for Physical Design (8 Tasks)

This step, as described in the reference manuals, consists of eight tasks. However, if a product-specific guide exists the fourth task should be unnecessary, and much of the information produced by the first three tasks may already be in the guide. The sixth task is solely concerned with project planning activities. The presentation of the Structural Model in Part 3 of this handbook is concerned only with technical products and therefore this task is not shown.

The first task is concerned with classifying the processing system, the DBMS data-structuring facilities, and the DBMS performance characteristics. The next five tasks are concerned with specifying various forms and standards to be used in the rest of the stage. The seventh task is used to initiate the preparation of user, operation and training manuals. Note that this is somewhat inconsistent with the products of Stage 4, where these products have already been initiated. The last task is to agree the Physical Design Strategy with the Project Board.

Step 620: Create Physical Data Design (8 Tasks)

The first task identifies the features of the Required System Logical Data Model that are required for Physical Data Design. The second task identifies the required entry points. The next five tasks are concerned with identifying the physical hierarchies and splitting them into groups that fit the required block size. The last task is used to apply product-specific design rules.

Step 630: Create Function Component Implementation Map (8 Tasks)

The first two tasks are concerned with the removal of duplicate processing and the identification of common processing. The next six tasks are performed for each Function: the first five define success units; specify syntax error handling; specify controls and control error handling; specify the physical input and output formats; and specify the Physical Dialogue Design. The last task describes to the physical processing systems those function components that can be specified non-procedurally, except for database access components.

Step 640: Optimize Physical Data Design (2 Tasks)

The first task restructures the data design, as necessary, to fit in with any storage constraints. The second estimates the resource times of major Functions, compares them with the performance objectives and tunes the design as necessary.

Step 650: Complete Function Specification (2 Tasks)

The two tasks distinguish the logical processes of a Function and combine them into physical programs or run units.

Step 660: Consolidate Process Data Interface (6 Tasks)

The first three tasks are concerned with identifying any mismatches between a Function component to handle data access according to the Required System Logical Data Model and the Physical Data Design, and resolving how they will be handled in the Physical Design. The next task identifies any duplicate processing components thus formed. The fifth task fully documents the interaction of all access mechanisms within the Function Component Implementation Map. The last task annotates the Requirements Catalogue to show any design decisions that limit the extent to which requirements have been met.

Step 670: Assemble Physical Design (2 Tasks)

The first task carries out a complete review of all the products of the Physical Design, checking for completeness and consistency and making any amendments as necessary. The second task assembles and publishes the Physical Design.

Note that the composition of the Physical Design is dependent on the target environment and installation standards.

4.8 Quality Reviews

One of the differences between Version 4 and Version 3 is the approach to quality management. Version 3 had a fairly simple system of specifically identified quality review (QR) points within the Structural Model, where a major product set would be formally reviewed. In Version 4 there are no specific QRs identified, apart from an implied QR of the final result of each module. However, all the Product Descriptions in the dictionary volume include quality criteria. This enables projects to apply QR procedures according to their particular project management method, using formal and informal reviews as appropriate.

PART 3

A Detailed Representation of the Design of SSADM Version 4 (The Structural Model)

5 Overview and Notation Used

SSADM's greatest strength is not, as some people believe, the techniques it employs, but rather the way it employs them. The key word is, in fact, to be found in its very title — it is a 'structured' method. The way in which it uses the techniques — some of which are industry-standard ones that predate the method itself — is unique. Using tried and tested techniques, as well as new ones specific to itself, in this structured way, provides a robust method that produces rigorous and complete specifications. Crucial to its success, therefore, is a thorough understanding of the Structural Model of the method.

The representation of the Structural Model in this part of the book is complete, precise and concise. It is presented in a fully diagrammatic form that includes a complete Product Breakdown Structure and Task/Product Matrix for each module, an Activity Network for each stage, and a full-page diagram for each step that clearly identifies all the tasks and the products they create, amend and/or refer to. Each step diagram is supported by a comprehensive description of the step, with clear cross-references that identify where products are created, amended and referred to, as well as which individual tasks use which techniques.

The notation used for the step diagrams is similar in general concept and layout to that used in SSADM Version 3, and therefore should be familiar to any practitioner acquainted with that version of the method. It has, however, been developed to distinguish clearly between products and tasks; between working products and deliverable products; between compound products and elementary products; to provide forward and backward links between products and tasks from one step diagram to the next; and to indicate in the diagrams themselves where products are created, amended and referred to.

Furthermore, the notation and conventions used are consistent throughout all the diagrams and text, thereby eliminating any possibility of confusion or misunderstanding. In particular, the new project planning technique offered in this handbook is described in the same way, using the same notation as the Steps of the method to provide a consistency of approach.

SSADM VERSION 4 - MODULE PRODUCT BREAKDOWN STRUCTURE NOTATION

The notation used for the Product Breakdown Structures is a simple hierarchical structure using the standard six-sided product boxes, either drawn with solid or dotted lines to indicate deliverable and working products respectively.

Products that include other products in the hierarchy are known as compound products. Products at the bottom of the hierarchy, that do not include any other products, are known as elementary products.

The compound product at the top of the hierarchy is the overall deliverable product of the module.

Working products and optional deliverable products are connected in the hierarchy with dotted lines.

The elementary products are the ones, that in the majority of instances, are worked on by the tasks in the Structural Model Diagrams. On occasions within the Structural Model Diagrams tasks are depicted as working on compound products. Where this is done it means that all of the compound product's component products are used by the relevant task.

To aid the clarity of both the Product Breakdown Structures and the Structural Model Diagrams different styles of text are used within the six-sided product boxes. For consistency, the same styles of text are used throughout the Step Descriptions.

⬡ LOGICAL DATA MODEL — Standard typeface, upper case, in a solid box indicates a compound product that is a module deliverable.

⬡ Logical Data Structure — Standard typeface, lower case, in a solid box indicates an elementary product that is a module deliverable.

⬡ *REQUIRED SYSTEM DATA FLOW MODEL* — Italic typeface, upper case, in a dotted box, indicate a compound product that is not a module deliverable.

⬡ *I/O Descriptions* — Italic typeface, lower case, in a dotted box indicates an elementary product that is not a module deliverable.

Overview and Notation Used 39

NOTATION USED FOR STRUCTURAL MODEL DIAGRAMS

Symbol	Description
Rectangle with xxx.nn	An SSADM task where xxx.nn define the step and task number.
Solid hexagon	An SSADM product that is a deliverable product of the module
Dashed hexagon	An SSADM working product, i.e. an intermediate product that is created/amended by a task, but is not a deliverable product of the module
Solid downward pentagon	A link for products and tasks between diagrams where the product is created/modified
Dashed downward pentagon	A link for products and tasks between diagrams where the product is for reference only
Rounded shape	A non-SSADM product
Ellipse	An SSADM activity/task that doesn't produce a product but relates to Project Management issues
Solid line	Joins tasks/products where the product (on input) is going to be amended, or (on output) is created or amended.
Dotted line	Joins tasks/products where the product is for reference only
Dashed line (— — —)	Joins products to products to indicate where component products of a compound product are included to form the compound product.
Double vertical lines	N.B. A column on the right-hand side separated by two vertical lines is used where necessary to indicate products and/or tasks that interface to SSADM-related Project Management issues.
Circle with (A)	Used to show links on a single diagram where too many lines would cause confusion.

NOTATION USED FOR ACTIVITY NETWORK DIAGRAMS

The notation used for Activity Network diagrams is simple, and the layout straightforward. The same rectangualr box as in the Structural Model diagrams is used to represent the individual tasks. The tasks are connected by solid lines to indicate where a task has to be completed before the succeeding task can be started, and by dotted lines to indicate where a task has to be started before a succeeding task can be started.

The flow is from the top of the page to the bottom, except where indicated by arrows on the connecting lines.

Using this simple notation and layout the intertask dependencies and tasks that can largely be carried out in parallel are easily identified.

6 Project Planning — A New Technique

This technique does not appear in the reference manuals, but is offered as a new technique of the author's own creation, produced to pull together all the SSADM-related project management issues. A project plan can be seen as a contract between the Project Manager and the Project Board to deliver a defined product within a specified timescale using specified resources. This technique is laid out as three phases to reach that 'contractual' arrangement, and should be used at the beginning of every module/stage to create the module/stage plans.

Phase 1 — define products to be delivered (4 Tasks)

The first two tasks identify what are to be the working products and the deliverable products for each module/stage. The second two tasks modify the Product Breakdown Structures and Product Descriptions accordingly, and obtain agreement from Management/the Project Board.

Phase 2 — create Project Plans (5 Tasks)

The first three tasks modify the structural Model Diagrams, Step Descriptions and Activity Networks, as required, according to the changes made to the Product Breakdown Structures and Product Descriptions in the previous phase. The fourth task produces a Quality Plan to ensure that they will be produced to the required degree of quality. The last task estimates the resources required to carry out the activities, and produces a Resource Plan that shows how they will be produced and when they will be delivered.

Phase 3 — check, agree and publish plans (2 Tasks)

The two tasks of this phase check the products of the Stage Plan for consistency and completeness; obtain Management/Project Board approval of the plan; identify any required resources; and carry out any necessary activities to initiate the project.

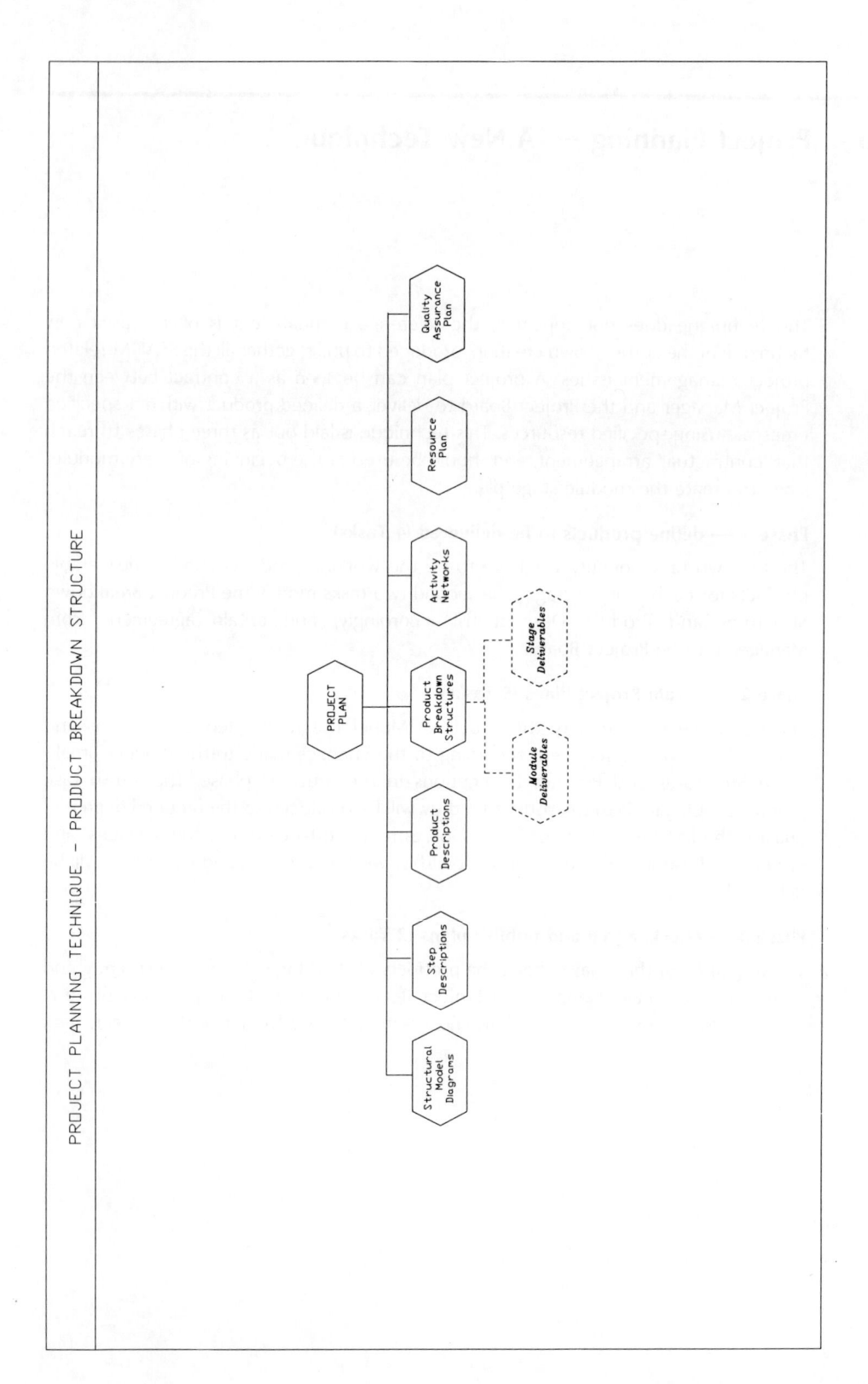

PROJECT PLANNING TECHNIQUE – PRODUCT BREAKDOWN STRUCTURE

- PROJECT PLAN
  - Quality Assurance Plan
  - Resource Plan
  - Activity Networks
  - Product Breakdown Structures
    - *Stage Deliverables*
    - *Module Deliverables*
  - Product Descriptions
  - Step Descriptions
  - Structural Model Diagrams

PROJECT PLANNING TECHNIQUE - TASK/PRODUCT MATRIX

	Module/Stage Deliverables	Redundant Products	Working Products	Additional Products	Product Breakdown Structures	Product Descriptions	Structural Model Diagrams	Step Descriptions	Activity Networks	Resource Plan	Quality Assurance Plan	PROJECT PLAN
001.10	C	C	C		R	R						
001.20				C	R	R						
001.30	R	R	R	R	A							
001.40					R	A						
002.10					R		A					
002.20					R	R	R	A				
002.30							R		A			
002.40									R	R	C	
002.50					R	R	R		R		C	
003.10			.	.	A	A	A	A	A	A		
003.20					I	I	I	I	I	I	I	C

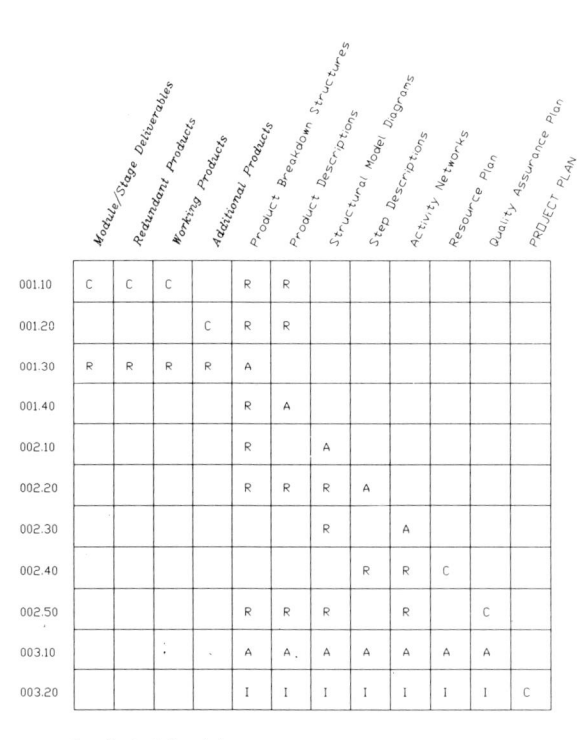

C — Product Created
A — Product Amended
R — Product Referenced
I — Product Included as part of a Compound Product

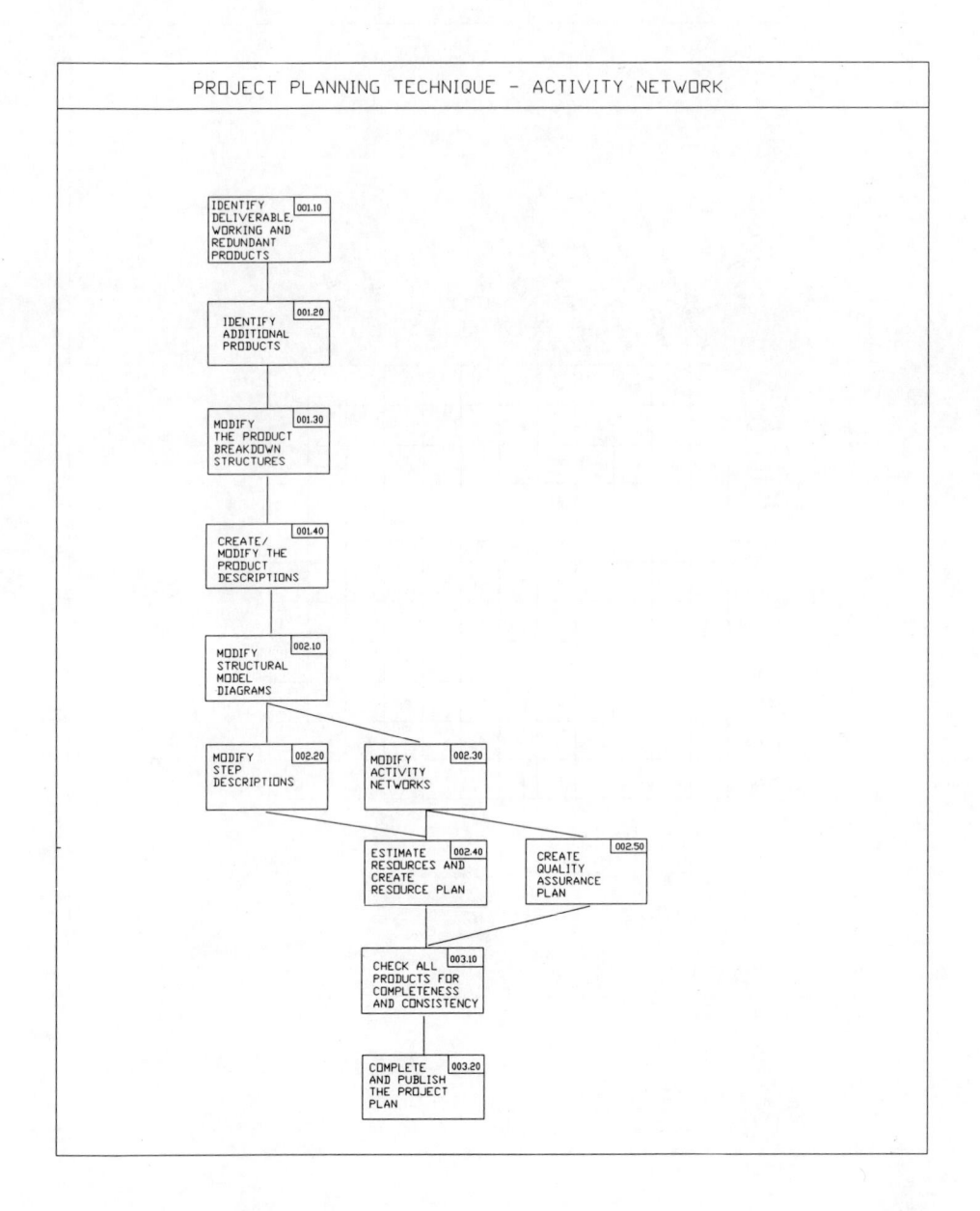

PROJECT PLANNING TECHNIQUE – ACTIVITY NETWORK

```
┌─────────────────────┐
│ IDENTIFY     001.10 │
│ DELIVERABLE,        │
│ WORKING AND         │
│ REDUNDANT           │
│ PRODUCTS            │
└──────────┬──────────┘
           │
┌──────────▼──────────┐
│ IDENTIFY     001.20 │
│ ADDITIONAL          │
│ PRODUCTS            │
└──────────┬──────────┘
           │
┌──────────▼──────────┐
│ MODIFY       001.30 │
│ THE PRODUCT         │
│ BREAKDOWN           │
│ STRUCTURES          │
└──────────┬──────────┘
           │
┌──────────▼──────────┐
│ CREATE/      001.40 │
│ MODIFY THE          │
│ PRODUCT             │
│ DESCRIPTIONS        │
└──────────┬──────────┘
           │
┌──────────▼──────────┐
│ MODIFY       002.10 │
│ STRUCTURAL          │
│ MODEL               │
│ DIAGRAMS            │
└──────┬───────┬──────┘
       │       │
┌──────▼──┐ ┌──▼──────┐
│ MODIFY  │ │ MODIFY  │
│ STEP    │ │ ACTIVITY│
│ DESCRIP-│ │ NETWORKS│
│ TIONS   │ │  002.30 │
│ 002.20  │ └────┬────┘
└─────────┘      │
         ┌───────┴────────┐
         │                │
┌────────▼─────┐  ┌───────▼──────┐
│ ESTIMATE     │  │ CREATE       │
│ RESOURCES AND│  │ QUALITY      │
│ CREATE       │  │ ASSURANCE    │
│ RESOURCE PLAN│  │ PLAN  002.50 │
│       002.40 │  └──────┬───────┘
└──────┬───────┘         │
       └────────┬────────┘
                │
┌───────────────▼─────┐
│ CHECK ALL    003.10 │
│ PRODUCTS FOR        │
│ COMPLETENESS        │
│ AND CONSISTENCY     │
└──────────┬──────────┘
           │
┌──────────▼──────────┐
│ COMPLETE     003.20 │
│ AND PUBLISH         │
│ THE PROJECT         │
│ PLAN                │
└─────────────────────┘
```

6.1 Phase 1 — Define Products to be Delivered

Objectives

- To identify the products to be delivered by the SSADM Version 4 module/stage to be undertaken, in accordance with the organization's technical policies.
- To produce accurate Product Descriptions, according to installation standards, for the products identified.

Summary

This phase is concerned with understanding and tailoring the SSADM Version 4 Product Breakdown Structures contained in this handbook, and reviewing and modifying the Product Descriptions as the first phase in producing the PROJECT PLAN.

A review of the Product Breakdown Structures and technical policies is conducted to ensure that products to be delivered by the module/stage are clearly identified. The Product Descriptions are then reviewed in the light of installation standards to ensure that they will be produced in the required format.

Agreement is then obtained to the identified products and their descriptions before proceeding to detailed planning of the project. Depending upon the organization's policies and the Project Management method employed, this agreement may or may not require formal approval by the Project Board.

References

- *Task 10:* Project Initiation Document
  (when this technique is used prior to starting Stage 0 or 1)
  Product Breakdown Structures
  Product Descriptions
  Technical policies

- *Task 20:* Project Initiation Document
  (when this technique is used prior to starting Stage 0 or 1)
  Product Breakdown Structures
  Product Descriptions
  Technical policies

- *Task 30:* Module/Stage Deliverables
  Redundant Products
  Working Products
  Additional Products

- *Task 40:* Product Breakdown Structures
  Installation standards

Products created

- *Task 10:* Module/Stage Deliverables
  Redundant Products
  Working Products

- *Task 20:* Additional Products

46 *Project Planning — A New Technique*

Phase 1 – DEFINE PRODUCTS TO BE DELIVERED

Inputs:
- Technical Policies
- Product Breakdown Structures
- Project Initiation Document
- Product Descriptions
- Installation Standards

Activities:
- **001.10** IDENTIFY DELIVERABLE WORKING AND REDUNDANT PRODUCTS
- **001.20** IDENTIFY ADDITIONAL PRODUCTS
- **001.30** MODIFY THE PRODUCT BREAKDOWN STRUCTURES
- **001.40** CREATE/MODIFY THE PRODUCT DESCRIPTIONS

Intermediate products:
- Module/Stage Deliverables
- Working Products
- Redundant Products
- Additional Products
- Product Breakdown Structures
- Product Descriptions

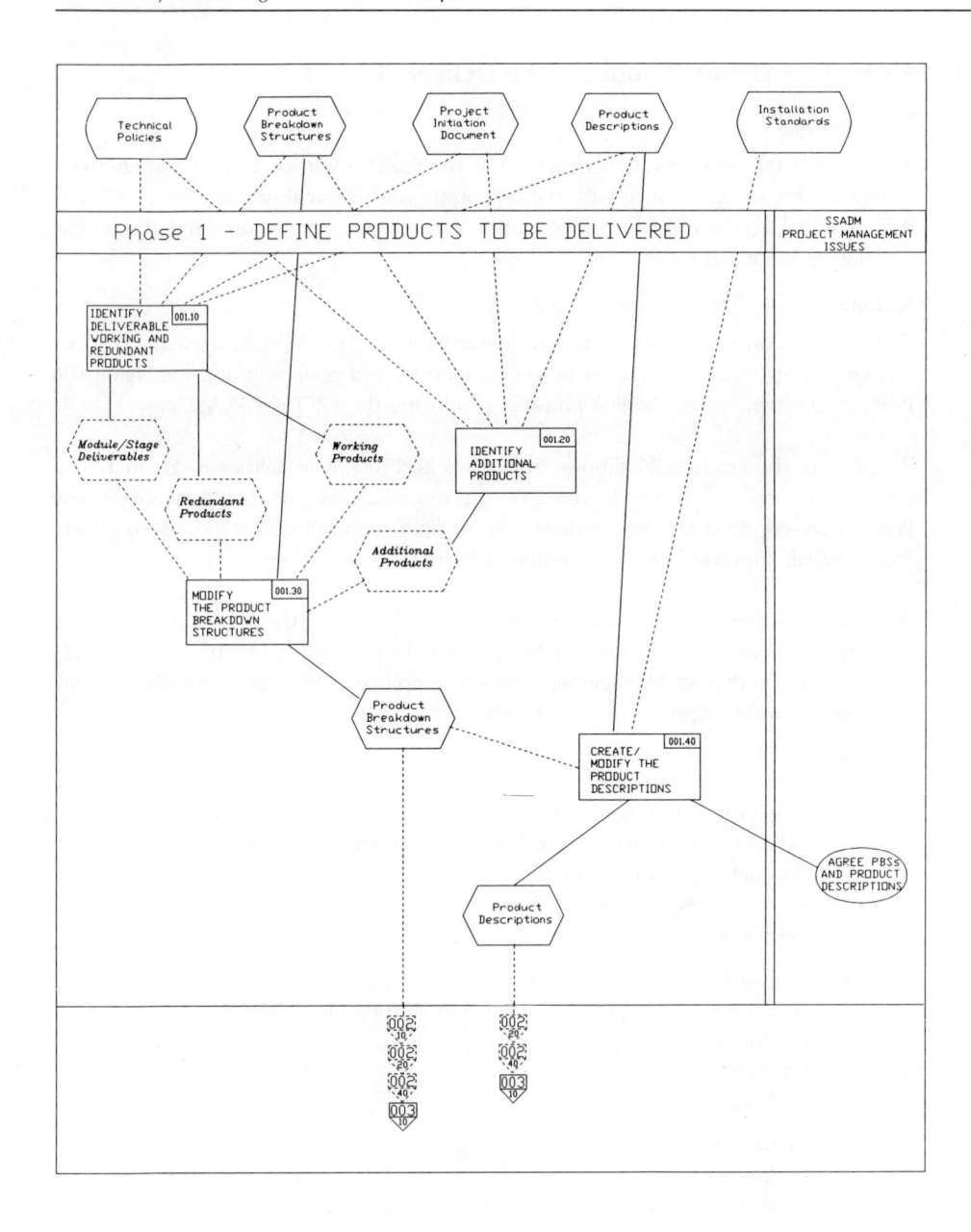

SSADM PROJECT MANAGEMENT ISSUES: AGREE PBSs AND PRODUCT DESCRIPTIONS

Outputs to: 002.10, 002.20, 002.40, 003.10 and 002.20, 002.40, 003.10

Products amended

Task 30:   Product Breakdown Structures

Task 40:   Product Descriptions

Activities

Task 10

10.1 The Product Breakdown Structures contained within this handbook clearly identify those products that are deliverables (solid box and standard typeface) and those products that are created as working products during the course of the module/stage but are not required as deliverables at the end of the module/stage (dotted box and italic typeface).

The Product Breakdown Structures and Product Descriptions are reviewed according to the technical policies to identify any *Redundant Products* that are not required by the module/stage. Care should be taken in this process not to eliminate any products that may be required in later modules/stages.

10.2 Each working product is carefully checked to identify those that are required as *Module/Stage Deliverables* according to the technical policies of the organization.

10.3 Each deliverable product is carefully checked and evaluated according to the technical policies to identify any that are required as *Working Products*, but are no longer deliverable products.

Task 20

20.1 The Product Breakdown Structures and Product Descriptions are reviewed according to the technical policies to identify any *Additional Products* required by the module/stage, and whether they should be deliverable or working products.

Task 30

30.1 Remove any *Redundant Products* from the Product Breakdown Structure.

30.2 On the Product Breakdown Structure, for each *Working Product* that has been identified as becoming a deliverable product, change the dotted box to a solid one, and the typeface from italic to standard.

30.3 On the Product Breakdown Structure, for each *Module/Stage Deliverable* that has been identified as being no longer required as a deliverable product, change the solid box to a dotted one and the typeface from standard to italic.

30.4 Modify the Product Breakdown Structures to include any *Additional Products* required by the project, taking care to use the correct notation according to whether the product is a working or deliverable one.

Task 40

40.1 For every product on the Product Breakdown Structures that has a description in the SSADM reference manuals, check the description and modify if necessary to ensure that it meets the installation standards.

40.2 For every *Additional Product,* write a Product Description in accordance with the installation standards

Obtain agreement from the Management/Project Board that the definition of the products to be produced, in terms of the Product Breakdown Structures and Product Descriptions, is correct. This is in effect the first half of a 'contract' between the Project Manager and the Project Board, defining what is to be delivered. The second half of the 'contract', the elapsed time and resources required, is created in the next phase.

6.2 Phase 2 — Create Module/Stage Plans

Objectives

- To create the Activity Networks required to produce the products to be delivered.
- To create the Resource Plan and Quality Plan based on the Activity Networks.

Summary

This phase is concerned with understanding and tailoring the SSADM Version 4 Structural Model Diagrams and Step Descriptions contained within this handbook, and reviewing and modifying them to match the Product Breakdown Structures and Product Descriptions created in the previous phase.

The Activity Networks are then modified to match the revised Structural Model.

Referring to the Activity Networks and Step Descriptions, the resources for the activities are then estimated and input to a proprietary project planning tool to produce the Resource Plan.

Referring to the Product Breakdown Structures, Product Descriptions and Activity Networks, a quality assurance strategy is worked out and a Quality Plan produced.

References

Task 10: Product Breakdown Structures

Task 20: Product Breakdown Structures
Product Descriptions
Structural Model Diagrams

Task 30: Structural Model Diagrams

Task 40: Step Descriptions
Activity Networks
Project Initiation Document

Task 50: Product Breakdown Structures
Product Descriptions
Activity Networks
Project Initiation Document
(when this technique is used prior to starting Stage 0 or 1)
Structural Model Diagrams

Products created

Task 40: Resource Plan

Task 50: Quality Assurance Plan

Products amended

Task 10: Structural Model Diagrams

50 *Project Planning — A New Technique*

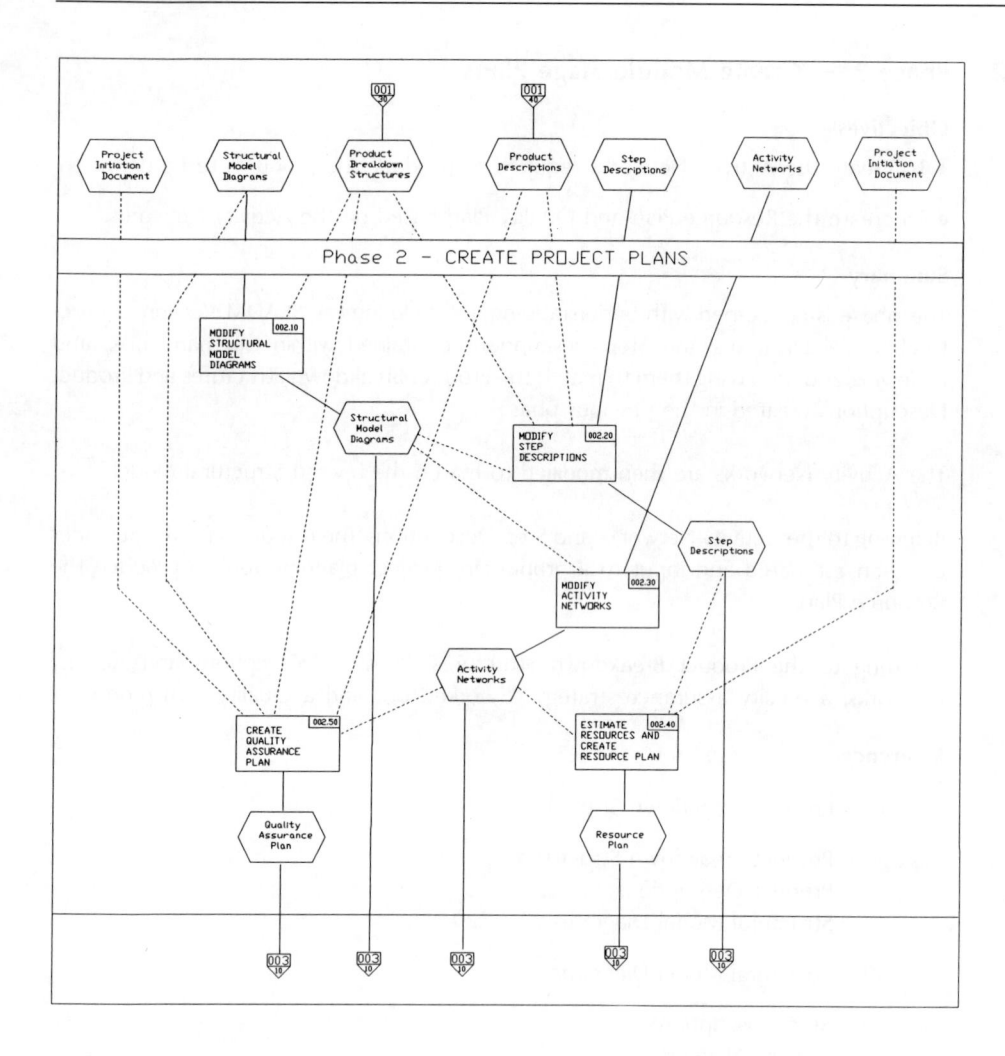

Task 20: Step Descriptions

Task 30 Activity Networks

Activities

Task 10

10.1 The Structural Model Diagrams are reviewed, in conjunction with the updated Product Breakdown Structures, and updated as required to reflect any changes. Care should be taken in this task to ensure that the correct notation is used, and that the products are created and transformed in the correct sequence.

Task 20

20.1 The Step Descriptions are reviewed, in conjunction with the updated Structural Model Diagrams, Product Breakdown Structures and Product Descriptions, and updated as required to reflect any changes. Again, care must be taken with this task to ensure that the Step Descriptions accurately reflect the activities to be carried out, including any additional or modified techniques required.

Task 30

30.1 The Activity Networks are reviewed in conjunction with the updated Structural Model Diagrams, and updated as required to reflect any changes. Particular care should be taken to ensure that the intertask dependencies are correctly identified.

Task 40

40.1 The Activity Networks and Step Descriptions are reviewed to produce estimates of the resources required for each task. As a guide, if any individual task is estimated as taking longer than two weeks it should be broken down into smaller subtasks where possible. The tasks in the Step Descriptions are broken down into separately numbered paragraphs, where appropriate, to aid the estimating process.

40.2 The estimates should then be fed into a proprietary project planning tool to produce the Resource Plan.

Task 50

50.1 The Product Breakdown Structures, Product Descriptions, Activity Networks and Structural Model Diagrams should be reviewed in the light of the quality policy, as defined in the Project Initiation Document, to produce a Quality Assurance Plan. This plan should identify which products are to be reviewed, and whether the review should be formal or informal.

As a guide, all stage deliverables should be subjected to formal review. All working products should be informally reviewed. As soon as any deliverable product ceases to be developed further and is only used for reference to develop other products, it should be reviewed, formally or informally, depending on the relative importance of the product.

NB: When products cease to be developed can easily be identified from the Structural Model Diagrams, because all forward links to subsequent tasks will be for reference only, i.e. dotted lines and dotted link boxes.

6.3 Phase 3 — Check, Agree and Publish Plans

Objectives

- To ensure that all the constituent parts of the PROJECT PLAN are complete and consistent.
- To obtain formal agreement to the PROJECT PLAN and the resources required to carry out the project.
- To create a support environment for the project team members.
- To identify and brief the users to be involved.

Summary

This step is concerned with the completion of and agreement to the PROJECT PLAN, and ensuring that the infrastructure is suitable for a project using SSADM Version 4.

Products created

Task 20:   PROJECT PLAN

Products amended

Task 10:   Product Breakdown Structures
Product Descriptions
Structural Model Diagrams
Step Descriptions
Activity Networks
Quality Assurance Plan
Resource Plan

Products included

Task 20:   Product Breakdown Structures
Product Descriptions
Structural Model Diagrams
Step Descriptions
Activity Networks,
Quality Assurance Plan
Resource Plan

Activities

Task 10

10.1 The Product Breakdown Structures and Product Descriptions should be checked to ensure that there is a description for every product that appears on the structure, and that every product appears on the structure.

10.2 The Product Breakdown Structures, Structural Model Diagrams and Step Descriptions should be checked to ensure that every product on the structure at least appears as being created on the model, and that there is a Task Description that describes how the product is created.

Project Planning — A New Technique

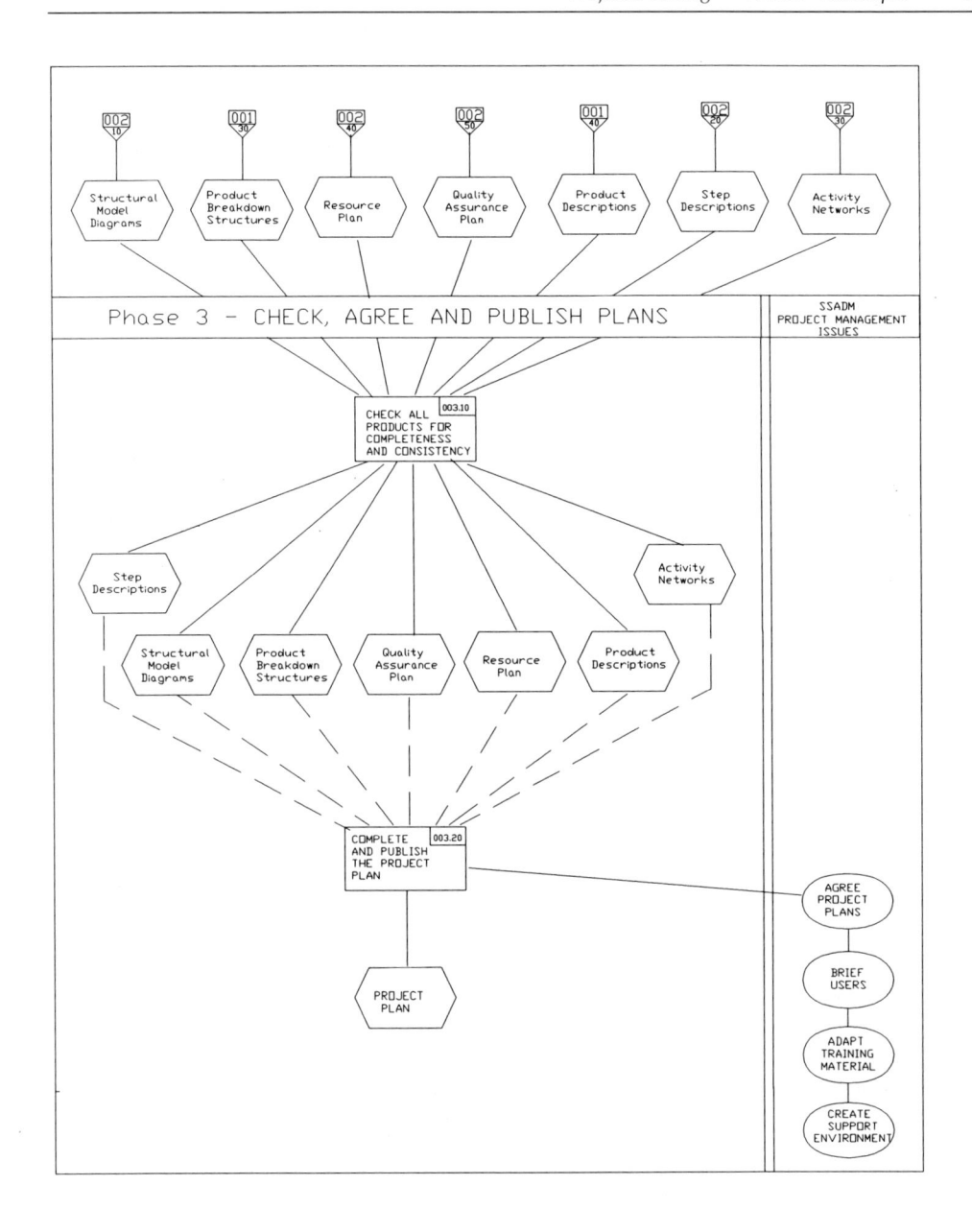

Phase 3 - CHECK, AGREE AND PUBLISH PLANS

10.3 The Product Descriptions should be checked to ensure that they are all complete. In particular, the quality criteria should be checked to ensure that they are a valid measure of quality, as well as a measure of completeness and consistency. Note that it can be quite difficult to write down criteria for the subjective assessment of quality, and these criteria are the vitally important foundations of quality management.

10.4 The Activity Networks and Structural Model Diagrams should be checked to ensure that every task appears on the network and that the intertask dependencies have been correctly identified.

10.5 The Activity Networks and Resource Plan should be checked to ensure that every task appears on the plan in the right sequence, and that the resources required to carry out each task have been realistically estimated.

10.6 The Quality Plan, Product Breakdown Structures and Product Descriptions should be checked to ensure that the correct products are being reviewed; and for each review the type of review is defined and the required skills of the reviewers are identified.

Task 20

20.1 Identify the users responsible, particularly those with budgetary control and the policy makers, for the business area under study and establish how they are to be involved in the project.

20.2 Identify all the necessary skills and resources required to carry out the project. It is quite likely that not all the necessary personal skills in relation to SSADM Version 4 will be available, and that some training will be required. If this is the case, it is vital to ensure that the training material will be adapted where necessary to match any adaptations that you have made to SSADM Version 4.

A support environment will need to be created for the project team to use SSADM Version 4. As a minimum, some sort of proprietary CASE tool will be required, with, as a guide, one workstation per 2/3 analysts; and word processing facilities with a similar or higher ratio of workstation to analyst. It is also quite likely that a bespoke dictionary will need to be created, using a proprietary DBMS, to support the CASE tool and provide cross-referencing.

20.3 Assemble the PROJECT PLAN and obtain the Project Board's approval. Obtain approval to acquire any necessary resources identified in **20.2**.

20.4 Publish the PROJECT PLAN

20.5 Brief the user representatives on their involvement in the project.

20.6 Ensure that any necessary adaptations are made to training material.

20.7 Create the support environment.

7 Feasibility Study Module

This module consists of one stage, Stage 0 — Feasibility Study, that produces the FEASIBILITY REPORT.

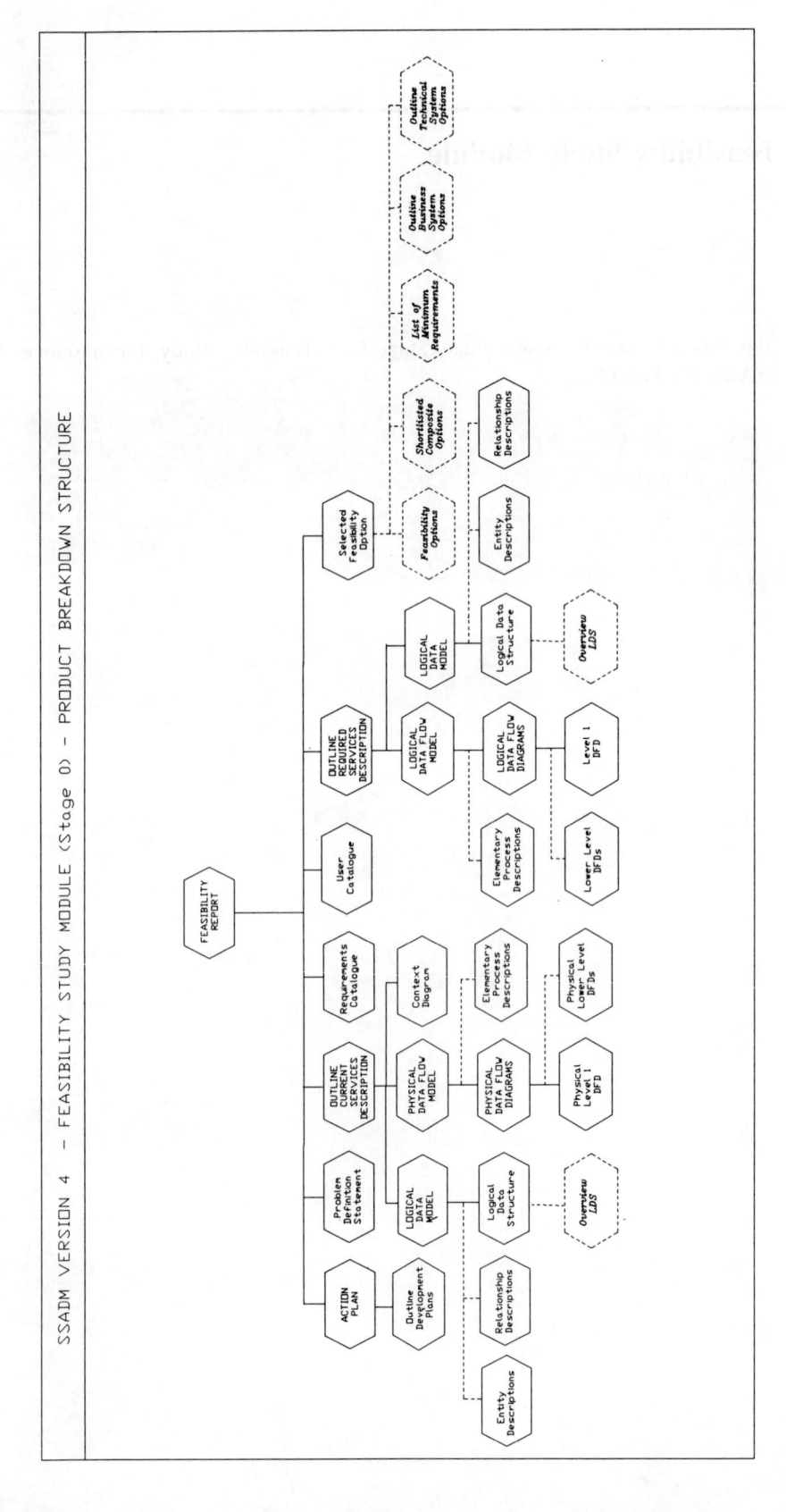

SSADM VERSION 4 - FEASIBILITY STUDY MODULE (Stage 0) - PRODUCT BREAKDOWN STRUCTURE

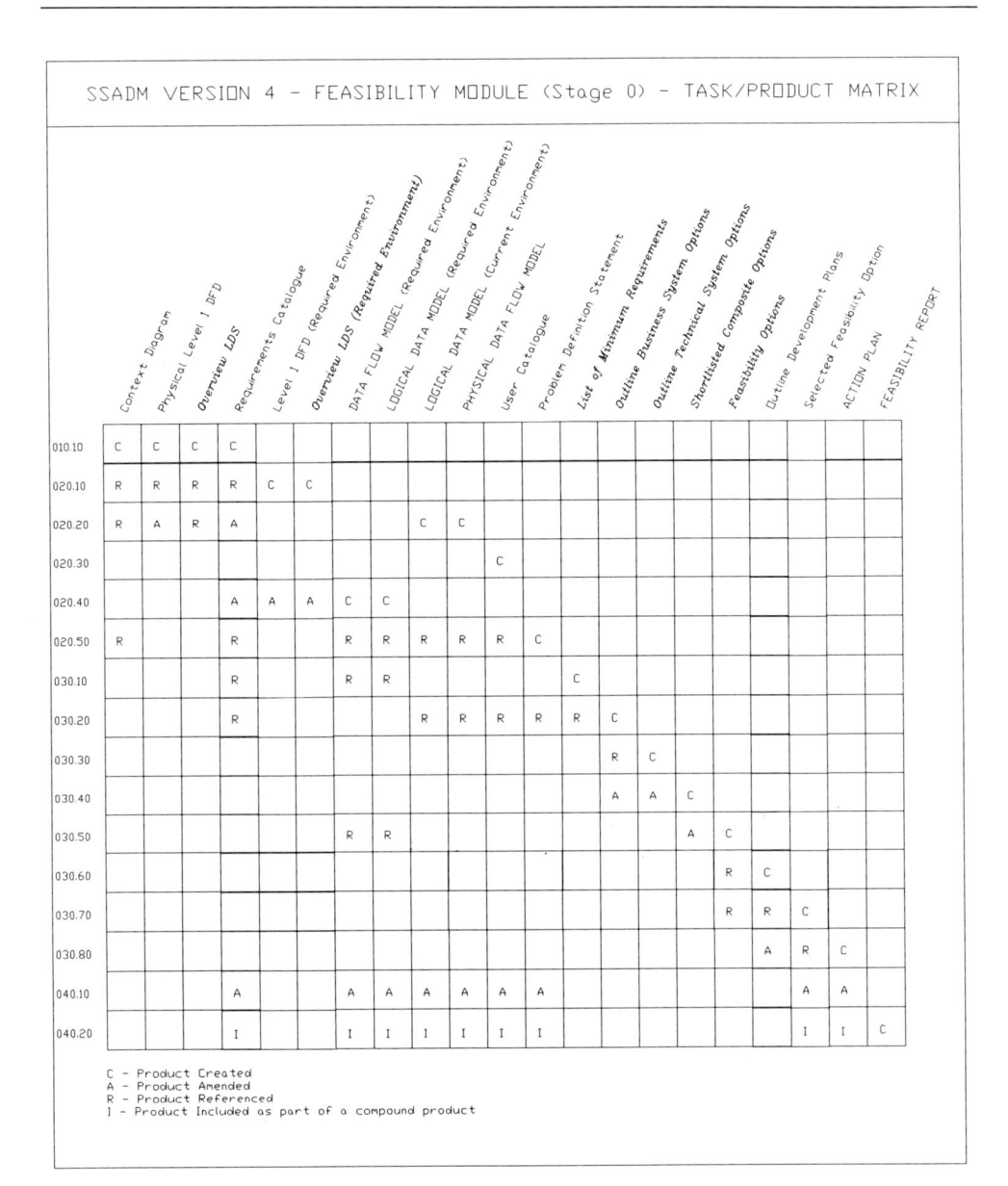

SSADM VERSION 4 - FEASIBILITY MODULE (Stage 0) - TASK/PRODUCT MATRIX

	Context Diagram	Physical Level 1 DFD	Overview LDS	Requirements Catalogue	Level 1 DFD (Required Environment)	Overview LDS (Required Environment)	DATA FLOW MODEL (Required Environment)	LOGICAL DATA MODEL (Required Environment)	LOGICAL DATA MODEL (Current Environment)	PHYSICAL DATA FLOW MODEL	User Catalogue	Problem Definition Statement	List of Minimum Requirements	Outline Business System Options	Outline Technical System Options	Shortlisted Composite Options	Feasibility Options	Outline Development Plans	Selected Feasibility Option	ACTION PLAN	FEASIBILITY REPORT
010.10	C	C	C	C																	
020.10	R	R	R	R	C	C															
020.20	R	A	R	A			C	C													
020.30									C												
020.40			A	A	A	C	C														
020.50	R		R		R	R	R	R	R	C											
030.10			R		R	R					C										
030.20			R				R	R	R	R	R	C									
030.30													R	C							
030.40													A	A	C						
030.50					R	R										A	C				
030.60																	R	C			
030.70																	R	R	C		
030.80																		A	R	C	
040.10			A		A	A	A	A	A	A									A	A	
040.20			I		I	I	I	I	I	I									I	I	C

C - Product Created
A - Product Amended
R - Product Referenced
I - Product Included as part of a compound product

Stage 0 — Feasibility Study Structural Model

This stage consists of the following steps:
- Step 010: Prepare for Feasibility Study (1 Task)
- Step 020: Define the Problem
- Step 030: Select Feasibility Options
- Step 040: Assemble the Feasibility Report

Feasibility Study Module 59

STAGE 0 - ACTIVITY NETWORK

- **010.10** REVIEW INPUT CREATE CONTEXT DIAGRAM, LEVEL 1 DFD, REQUIREMENTS CATALOGUE, LDS
- **020.10** IDENTIFY REQUIRED ACTIVITIES AND INFORMATION
- **020.20** INVESTIGATE CURRENT ENVIR'MT AND UPDATE THE REQUIREMENTS CATALOGUE
- **020.30** DEFINE INTENDED USERS OF THE NEW SYSTEM(s)
- **020.40** IDENTIFY NEW FUNCTIONS, DATA AND NON-FUNCT'NL REQUIREMENTS AND UPDATE AS REQ'D
- **030.10** COMPILE A LIST OF MINIMUM FUNCTIONAL AND NON-FUNCTIONAL REQUIREMENTS
- **020.50** PREPARE A PROBLEM DEFINITION STATEMENT
- **030.20** DEFINE UP TO SIX OUTLINE BUSINESS SYSTEM OPTIONS
- **030.30** DEFINE OUTLINE TECHNICAL SYSTEM OPTIONS
- **030.40** DEFINE COMPOSITE OPTIONS AND PRODUCE A SHORT LIST
- **030.50** DEVELOP DESCRIPTIONS OF SHORTLISTED OPTIONS
- **030.60** IDENTIFY PROJECTS AND PRODUCE OUTLINE DEVELOPMENT PLANS
- **030.70** SELECT FEASIBILITY OPTIONS
- **030.80** DEVELOP AN ACTION PLAN
- **040.10** CHECK THE COMPLETENESS AND CONSISTENCY OF FEASIBILITY STUDY PRODUCTS
- **040.20** ASSEMBLE AND PUBLISH THE FEASIBILITY STUDY

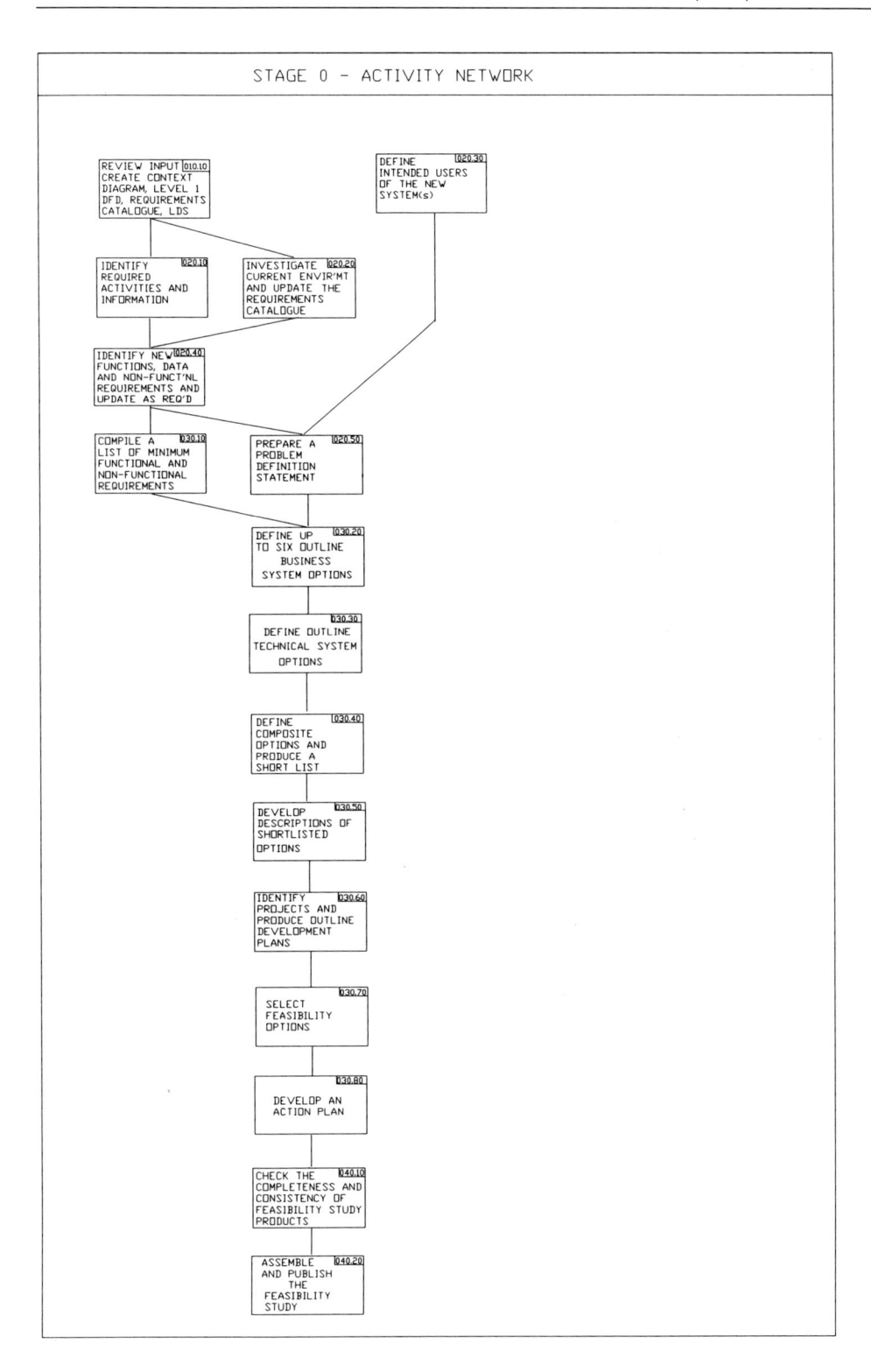

7.1 Step 010: Prepare for the Feasibility Study

Objectives

- To ensure that the terms of reference are complete and accurate.
- To undertake an initial assessment of the scope and complexity of the proposed information system.

Summary

This step is concerned principally with assimilating information contained within the Project Initiation Document, and preparing for more detailed analysis. The Project Initiation Document should contain the terms of reference for the study, describe the scope of the investigation and identify any relevant constraints.

A review of the step inputs is conducted to ensure that the study requirements are understood, clearly defined and capable of being achieved. Any significant problems should be resolved with the Project Board before proceeding beyond this step. This may entail some initial investigation work, but this should be kept to a minimum in advance of Step 020: Define the Problem.

References

Task 10: Relevant background material, e.g.
Business Objectives, Business Plans, IS/IT Strategy Statement, Data Administration Policies,
Corporate Business Models
Project Initiation Document

Products created

Task 10 Context Diagram
Physical Level 1 DFD
(of the current environment)
Overview LDS
(of the current environment)
Requirements Catalogue

Techniques

Project planning — used at the beginning of this step to create the Module/Stage Plans for the Feasibility Study Module.
Data Flow Modelling — used in Task 10
Logical Data Modelling — used in Task 10
Requirements Definition — used in Task 10

Activities

Task 10
10.1 Review the contents of the Project Initiation Document, or the equivalent terms of reference for the project, and any relevant background material.

10.2 Create a Context Diagram and a Physical Level 1 DFD of the current environment.

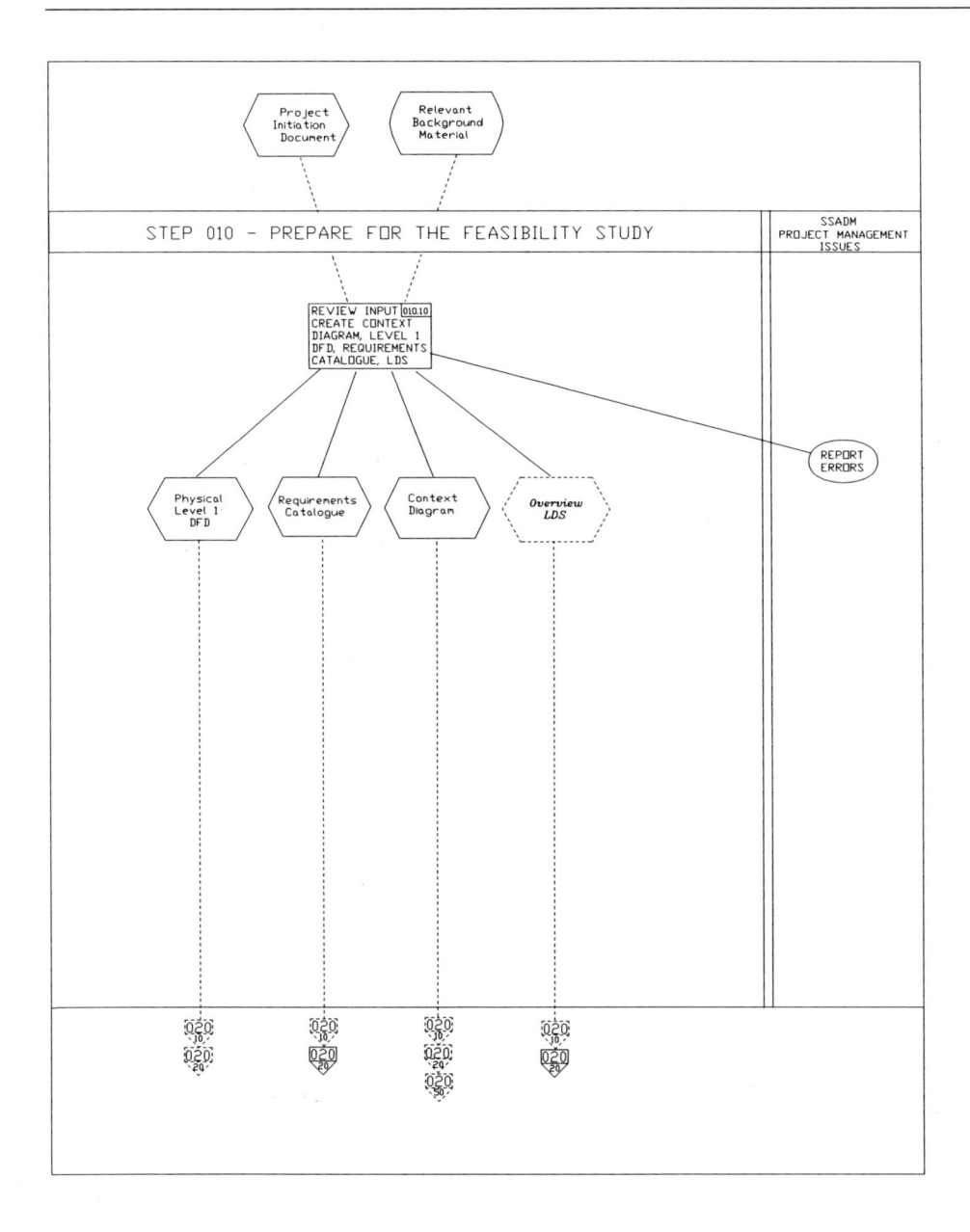

Feasibility Study Module

STEP 010 – PREPARE FOR THE FEASIBILITY STUDY

Inputs:
- Project Initiation Document
- Relevant Background Material

010.10 REVIEW INPUT, CREATE CONTEXT DIAGRAM, LEVEL 1 DFD, REQUIREMENTS CATALOGUE, LDS

Outputs:
- Physical Level 1 DFD
- Requirements Catalogue
- Context Diagram
- *Overview LDS*

SSADM PROJECT MANAGEMENT ISSUES: REPORT ERRORS

10.3 Create an *Overview LDS* of the current environment.

10.4 Identify specific system requirements described in the Projection Initiation Document or background material, and describe them in the Requirements Catalogue.

10.5 Report any errors or inconsistencies in the input documents that prevent the analysis proceeding as planned.

7.2 Step 020: Define the Problem

Objectives

- To obtain a more detailed understanding of the business and its information needs.
- To identify the problems associated with the current environment that are to be resolved by the new system(s).
- To identify the additional services to be provided by the new system(s).
- To define the users of the new system(s).

Summary

This step is concerned with gaining a good understanding of the business under consideration and its information needs. The emphasis is placed firmly on future requirements, and the study team begins by considering the processes and information that they believe ought to exist for the business area to meet its objectives.

The current environment is modelled at a high level to assess its efficiency and effectiveness. This activity highlights unsatisfactory service within the current environment and additional functions and data required in the new environment. A Problem Definition Statement in plain English is prepared and presented to the Project Board for approval.

SSADM techniques such as Requirements Definition, Data Flow Modelling and Logical Data Modelling are relevant. It is not, however, recommended that detailed data and process models be constructed. The purpose is to investigate to a level of detail that allows the key requirements that determine the options to be defined. Other techniques, such as those used by management services for organizational analysis and operational impact analysis, will also be relevant.

References

- *Task 10:* Context Diagram
  Requirements Catalogue
  Overview LDS
  (of the current environment)
  Physical Level 1 DFD
  (of the current environment)

- *Task 20:* Context Diagram
  Overview LDS
  (of the current environment)

- *Task 30:* Project Initiation Document

- *Task 50:* LOGICAL DATA FLOW MODEL
  (of the required environment)
  LOGICAL DATA MODEL
  (of the required environment)
  PHYSICAL DATA FLOW MODEL
  (of the current environment)

64 Feasibility Study Module

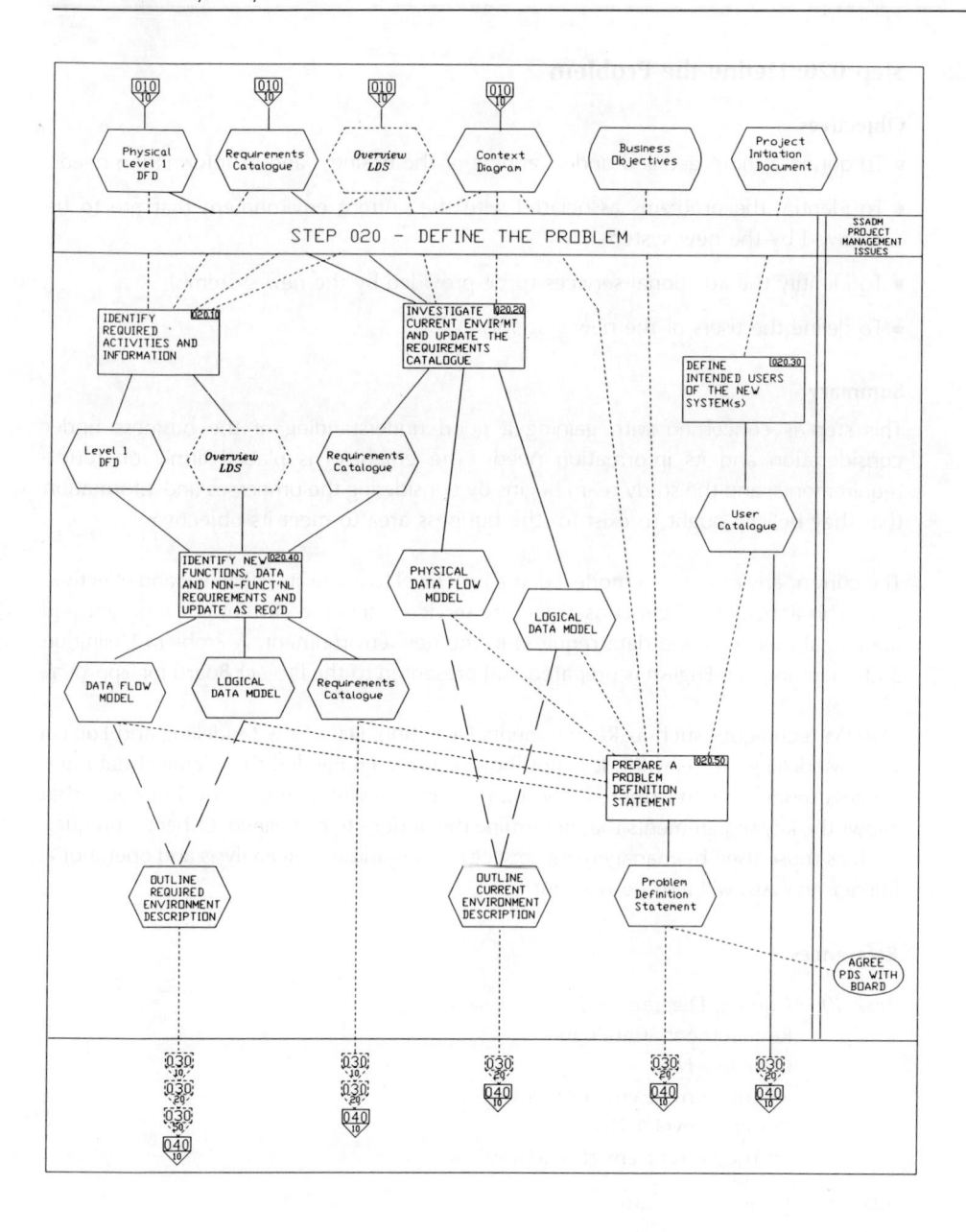

LOGICAL DATA MODEL
(of the current environment)
Requirements Catalogue
User Catalogue
Context Diagram
Business Objectives

Products created

Task 10:   Level 1 DFD
(of the required environment)
Overview LDS
(of the required environment)

Task 20:   LOGICAL DATA MODEL
(of the current environment, developed from the *Overview LDS*)
PHYSICAL DATA FLOW MODEL
(of the current environment, developed from the Physical Level 1 DFD)

Task 30:   User Catalogue

Task 40:   LOGICAL DATA FLOW MODEL
(of the required environment, developed from the Level 1 DFD)
LOGICAL DATA MODEL
(of the required environment, developed from the *Overview LDS* of the required environment)

Task 50:   Problem Definition Statement

Products amended

Task 20:   Requirements Catalogue
Physical Level 1 DFD
(developed to form the PHYSICAL DATA FLOW MODEL of the current environment)
Overview LDS
(developed to form the LOGICAL DATA MODEL of the current environment)

Task 40:   Level 1 DFD
(developed to form the LOGICAL DATA FLOW MODEL of the required environment)
Overview LDS
(of the required environment, developed to form the LOGICAL DATA MODEL of the required environment)
Requirements Catalogue

Techniques

Data Flow Modelling — used in Tasks 10, 20 and 40
Logical Data Modelling — used in Tasks 10, 20 and 40
Dialogue Design — used in Task 30 (see the reference manual technique description, section 8)
Requirements Definition — used in Tasks 20 and 40

Activities

Task 10

10.1 Identify the activities and information in the area of study that are necessary for the organization to meet its business objectives.

10.2 Referring to the Physical Level 1 DFD for the current environment, draw a Level 1 DFD for the required environment.

10.3 Referring to the *Overview LDS* for the current environment, draw an *Overview LDS* containing the major entities in the required environment.

Task 20

20.1 Investigate the operation of the current environment. Develop the Current System PHYSICAL DATA FLOW MODEL for selected processes that are critical, complex or unclear.

20.2 Develop the LOGICAL DATA MODEL for the current environment from the *Overview LDS*, containing the major entities.

20.3 Identify with the users the aspects of the current environment where the service is unsatisfactory or needs improvement, and describe appropriate requirements in the Requirements Catalogue.

Note that the PHYSICAL DATA FLOW MODEL and the LOGICAL DATA MODEL for the current environment combine to form the OUTLINE CURRENT ENVIRONMENT DESCRIPTION.

Task 30

30.1 Define the intended users of the new system(s) in the User Catalogue.

Task 40

40.1 Identify with the users the additional functions and data required from the new system(s) but not provided by the current environment.

40.2 Develop the Level 1 DFD for the required environment into a LOGICAL DATA FLOW MODEL to reflect the additional functions and data.

40.3 Develop the *Overview LDS* for the required environment into a LOGICAL DATA MODEL to reflect the additional data.

40.4 Identify additional non-functional requirements and record these in the Requirements Catalogue.

Note that the LOGICAL DATA FLOW MODEL and the LOGICAL DATA MODEL for the required environment combine to form the OUTLINE REQUIRED ENVIRONMENT DESCRIPTION.

Task 50

50.1 Prepare a Problem Definition Statement summarizing the requirements and assessing priorities in relation to business objectives.

Task 60

60.1 Agree the Problem Definition Statement with the Project Board.

7.3 Step 030: Select Feasibility Options

Objectives

- To develop a range of *Feasibility Options* that meet the defined requirements, from which a selection can be made by the users.

- To ensure user ownership of the results of the study by presenting the *Feasibility Options* to the Project Board and assisting in the selection of the preferred option.

- To recommend a preferred project or projects to implement each *Feasibility Option*

- To produce an ACTION PLAN containing Outline Development Plans for the Selected Feasibility Option.

Summary

The *Feasibility Options* defined in this Step are possible logical solutions to the requirements described in the Problem Definition Statement. Each *Feasibility Option* is a combination of the *Business System Options* and *Technical System Options* that would be defined during a full study, but in less detail. Although strategic direction may have been given by an IS Strategy Study, the purpose of the *Feasibility Options* is to limit the range of possible business and technical solutions that have to be examined in more detail later.

Up to six *Outline Business System Options* are identified initially, and possible *Outline Technical System Options* are then applied to them to produce a range of composite options. These are discussed with the users and a set of *Shortlisted Composite Options* is described in more detail. At this point it may become clear that the direction of the project is in conflict with either the Project Initiation Document or with the results of the IS Strategy Study. For each *Shortlisted Composite Option* the projects necessary to implement the option are identified. The options are developed into *Feasibility Options* and presented to the Project Board. After the Project Board has chosen a Selected Feasibility Option, an Outline Development Plan for each of the associated projects is defined.

References

Task 10: OUTLINE REQUIRED ENVIRONMENT DESCRIPTION
  Requirements Catalogue
  Strategy Documents

Task 20: OUTLINE CURRENT ENVIRONMENT DESCRIPTION
  OUTLINE REQUIRED ENVIRONMENT DESCRIPTION
  Requirements Catalogue
  Problem Definition Statement
  User Catalogue
  List of Minimum Requirements

Task 30: *Outline Business System Options*

Task 50: OUTLINE REQUIRED ENVIRONMENT DESCRIPTION

Task 60: *Feasibility Options*

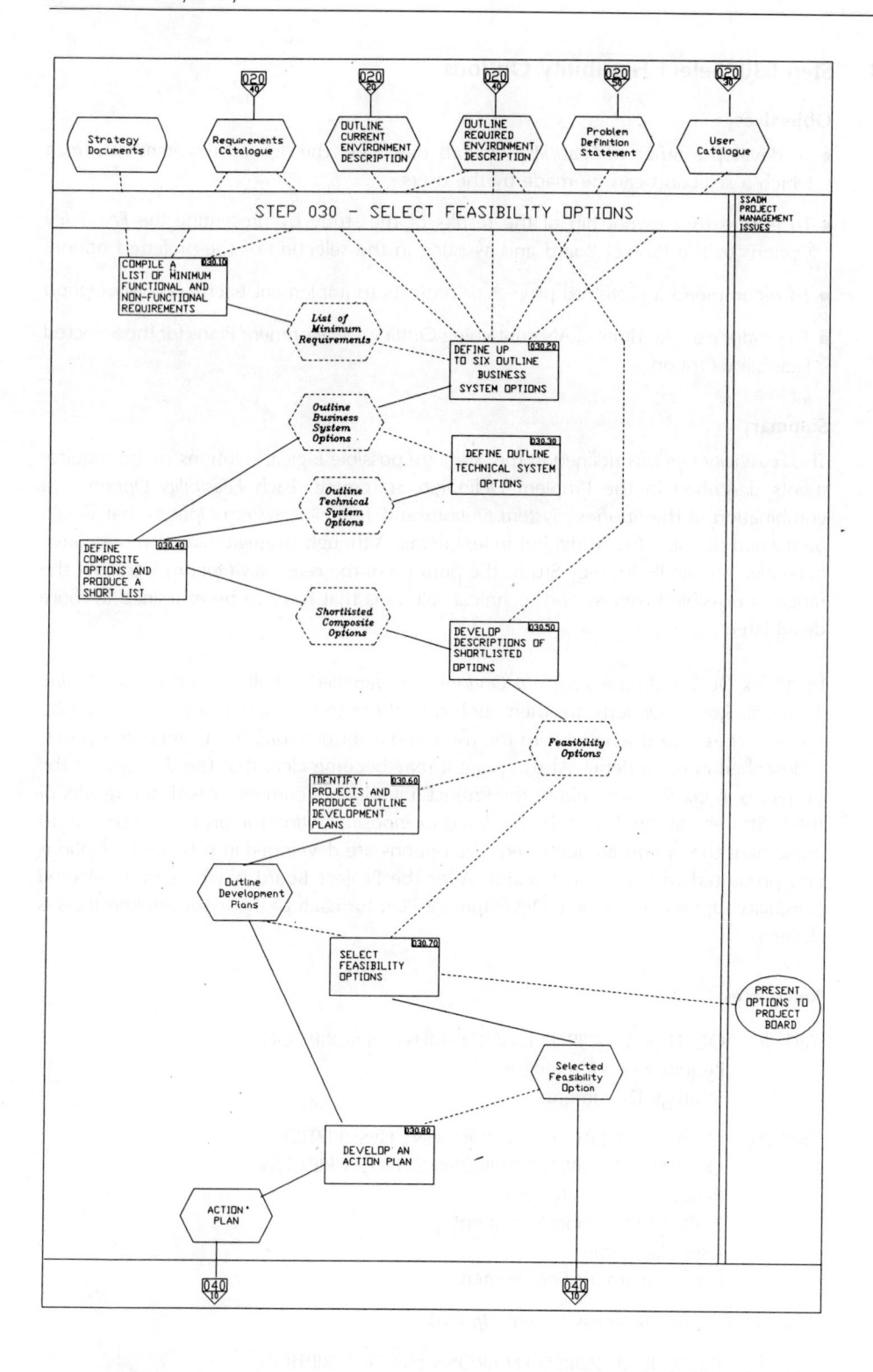

Feasibility Study Module

STEP 030 – SELECT FEASIBILITY OPTIONS

Inputs:
- Strategy Documents (020/40)
- Requirements Catalogue (020/20)
- Outline Current Environment Description (020/40)
- Outline Required Environment Description (020/50)
- Problem Definition Statement (020/30)
- User Catalogue (020/30)

SSADM PROJECT MANAGEMENT ISSUES

Tasks:
- 030.10 COMPILE A LIST OF MINIMUM FUNCTIONAL AND NON-FUNCTIONAL REQUIREMENTS → *List of Minimum Requirements*
- 030.20 DEFINE UP TO SIX OUTLINE BUSINESS SYSTEM OPTIONS → *Outline Business System Options*
- 030.30 DEFINE OUTLINE TECHNICAL SYSTEM OPTIONS → *Outline Technical System Options*
- 030.40 DEFINE COMPOSITE OPTIONS AND PRODUCE A SHORT LIST → *Shortlisted Composite Options*
- 030.50 DEVELOP DESCRIPTIONS OF SHORTLISTED OPTIONS → *Feasibility Options*
- 030.60 IDENTIFY PROJECTS AND PRODUCE OUTLINE DEVELOPMENT PLANS → *Outline Development Plans*
- 030.70 SELECT FEASIBILITY OPTIONS → *Selected Feasibility Option*
- 030.80 DEVELOP AN ACTION PLAN → *Action Plan*

PRESENT OPTIONS TO PROJECT BOARD

Outputs to: 040/10, 040/10

Task 70: Feasibility Options
Outline Development Plans

Task 80: Selected Feasibility Option
Outline Development Plans

Products definitely created

Task 10: List of Minimum Requirements

Task 20: Outline Business System Options

Task 30: Outline Technical System Options

Task 40: Shortlisted Composite Options
(developed from the Outline Business System Options and Outline Technical System Options)

Task 50: Feasibility Options

Task 60: Outline Development Plans

Task 70: Selected Feasibility Option

Task 80: ACTION PLAN

Products definitely amended

Task 40: Outline Business System Options
Outline Technical System Options
(the above are combined and developed to form the Shortlisted Composite Options)

Task 50: Shortlisted Composite Options
(to form the Feasibility Options)

Task 80: Outline Development Plans

Techniques

Business System Option — used in Tasks 20 and 40
Technical System Option — used in Tasks 30 and 40
Logical Data Modelling — used in Task 50
Data Flow Modelling — used in Task 50

Activities

Task 10

10.1 Compile a *List of Minimum Requirements* (both functional and non-functional and including any constraints imposed by the strategy documents). All of the options must satisfy these.

Task 20

20.1 Define up to six *Outline Business System Options* representing a range of possible functional solutions to the requirements, but satisfying the minimum requirements.

Task 30

30.1 Define *Outline Technical System Options* representing a full range of technical solutions. Each *Outline Technical System Option* should satisfy the constraints and meet the needs of at least one *Outline Business System Option*.

Task 40

40.1 Define up to six composite (*Business* and *Technical*) Options. Discuss the composite options with users and produce a shortlist, ideally of three *Shortlisted Composite Options*.

Task 50

50.1 Develop a description of each *Shortlisted Composite Option* to create the *Feasibility Options*. The description must be expressed textually but can be supported by subsets of the LDS and DFDs, illustrating the differences. The description also includes an approximate investment appraisal and impact analysis.

Task 60

60.1 Identify and define the preferred project or projects to be implemented.

60.2 Produce an Outline Development Plan for each recommended project.

Task 70

70.1 Present the *Feasibility Options* and associated Outline Development Plans to the Project Board. Assist the decision-making process by further explanation and discussion of the implications of the options if required. Create the Selected Feasibility Option, which may be one of those presented or a combination of different elements of those presented. Record the reasons for the decisions made.

Task 80

80.1 Develop an ACTION PLAN, containing a description of the technical approach for the selected project(s) within the Selected Feasibility Option, and develop the Outline Development Plans for each project.

7.4 Step 040: Assemble the Feasibility Report

Objectives

- To ensure the integrity of the feasibility study.
- To publish the FEASIBILITY REPORT document.

Summary

This step is the completion of the Feasibility Study Module and is concerned with checking the consistency of the products of the module and assembling them into the FEASIBILITY REPORT.

Each of the SSADM steps represents a transformation which takes a starting set of products, performs some tasks, and applies quality control to produce a target set of products. Quality management procedures are not part of SSADM, but each of the SSADM products that transports information between steps has quality criteria defined as part of the Product Description (Dictionary Volume). These quality criteria are only those that can be applied to the individual products. The cross-checking of products for consistency is part of this step. The review methods to be used are defined within the quality management procedures.

This step also publishes the formal FEASIBILITY REPORT document, according to the organization's standards.

References

Task 10: Project Initiation Document

Products created

Task 20: FEASIBILITY REPORT

Products amended

Task 10: Requirements Catalogue
User Catalogue
ACTION PLAN
Problem Definition Statement
Selected Feasibility Option
OUTLINE CURRENT ENVIRONMENT DESCRIPTION
OUTLINE REQUIRED ENVIRONMENT DESCRIPTION

Products included

Task 20: Requirements Catalogue
User Catalogue
ACTION PLAN
Problem Definition Statement
Selected Feasibility Option
OUTLINE CURRENT ENVIRONMENT DESCRIPTION
OUTLINE REQUIRED ENVIRONMENT DESCRIPTION

Feasibility Study Module

STEP 040 – ASSEMBLE THE FEASIBILITY REPORT

Inputs:
- Requirements Catalogue (020/40)
- User Catalogue (020/30)
- ACTION PLAN (030/80)
- Project Initiation Document
- Problem Definition Statement
- Selected Feasibility Option (020/50)
- OUTLINE CURRENT ENVIRONMENT DESCRIPTION (030/50)
- OUTLINE REQUIRED ENVIRONMENT DESCRIPTION (020/20)

040.10 CHECK THE COMPLETENESS AND CONSISTENCY OF FEASIBILITY STUDY PRODUCTS

Products flowing into step:
- Requirements Catalogue
- User Catalogue
- ACTION PLAN
- Problem Definition Statement
- Selected Feasibility Option
- OUTLINE CURRENT ENVIRONMENT DESCRIPTION
- OUTLINE REQUIRED ENVIRONMENT DESCRIPTION

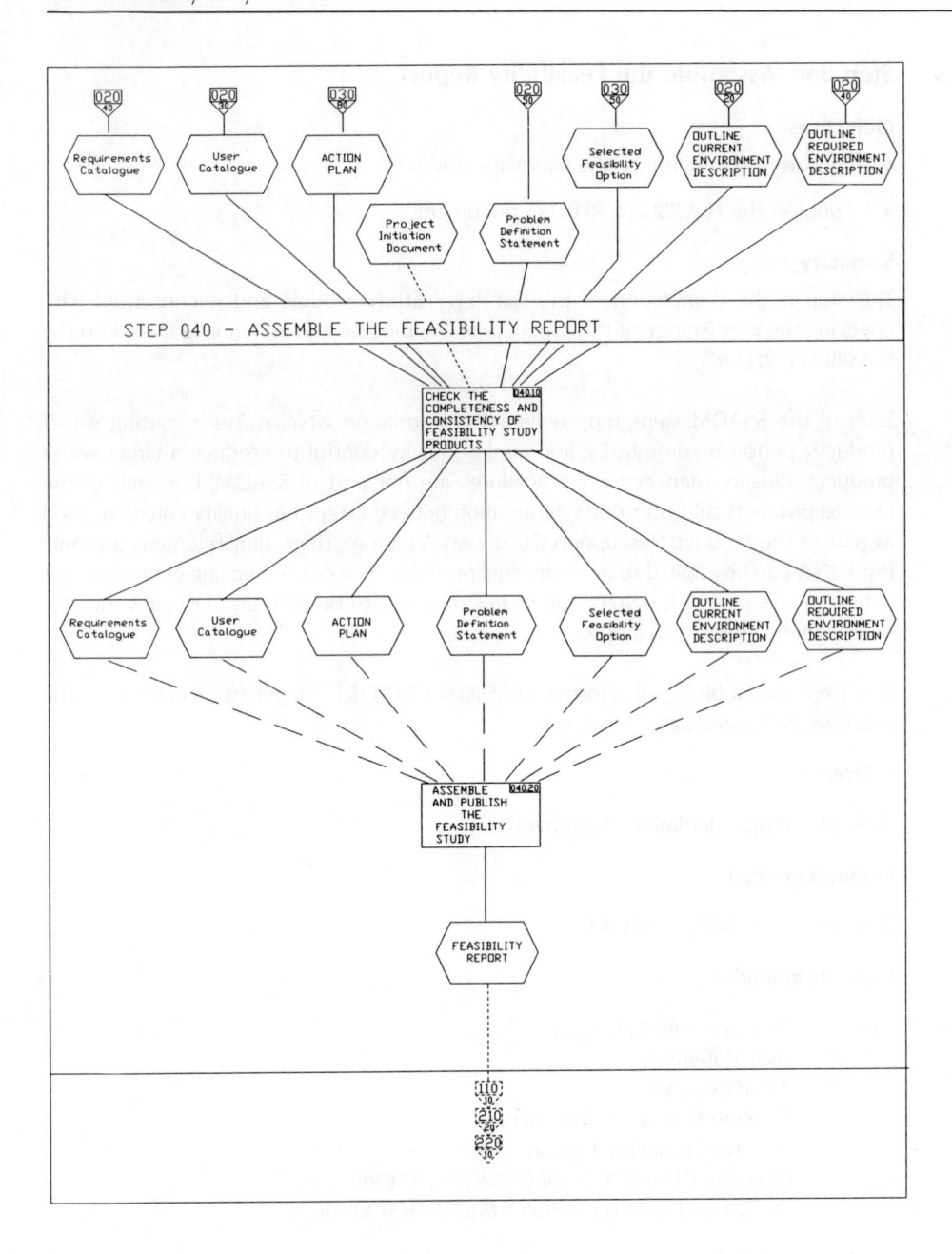

040.20 ASSEMBLE AND PUBLISH THE FEASIBILITY STUDY

Output: FEASIBILITY REPORT

Outputs to:
- 110/10
- 210/20
- 220/10

Activities

Task 10

10.1 Check the completeness and consistency of the Feasibility Study Module products by reviewing the

Requirements Catalogue
User Catalogue
ACTION PLAN
Problem Definition Statement
Selected Feasibility Option
OUTLINE CURRENT ENVIRONMENT DESCRIPTION
OUTLINE REQUIRED ENVIRONMENT DESCRIPTION

Amend the feasibility products if necessary, as a result of the reviews.

Task 20

20.1 Assemble and publish the FEASIBILITY REPORT documentation in accordance with organizational standards.

8 Requirements Analysis Module

This module consists of two stages, Stage 1 — Investigation of Current Environment, and Stage 2 — Business System Options, that together produce the ANALYSIS OF REQUIREMENTS.

Stage 1 produces the CURRENT SERVICES DESCRIPTION, Requirements Catalogue and User Catalogue. Note that the CURRENT SERVICES DESCRIPTION is a compound product that consists only of its constituent parts, and therefore is created implicitly rather than explicitly. In practice it is likely that an end-of-stage management report will be required to give an overview of the results of the investigation.

Stage 2 produces the SELECTED BUSINESS SYSTEM OPTION, and is the end of the module. As for the CURRENT SERVICES DESCRIPTION, the ANALYSIS OF REQUIREMENTS is a compound product that consists only of its constituent parts, and is therefore created implicitly. In practice an end-of-module management report will be required to give an overview of the investigations and the possible options.

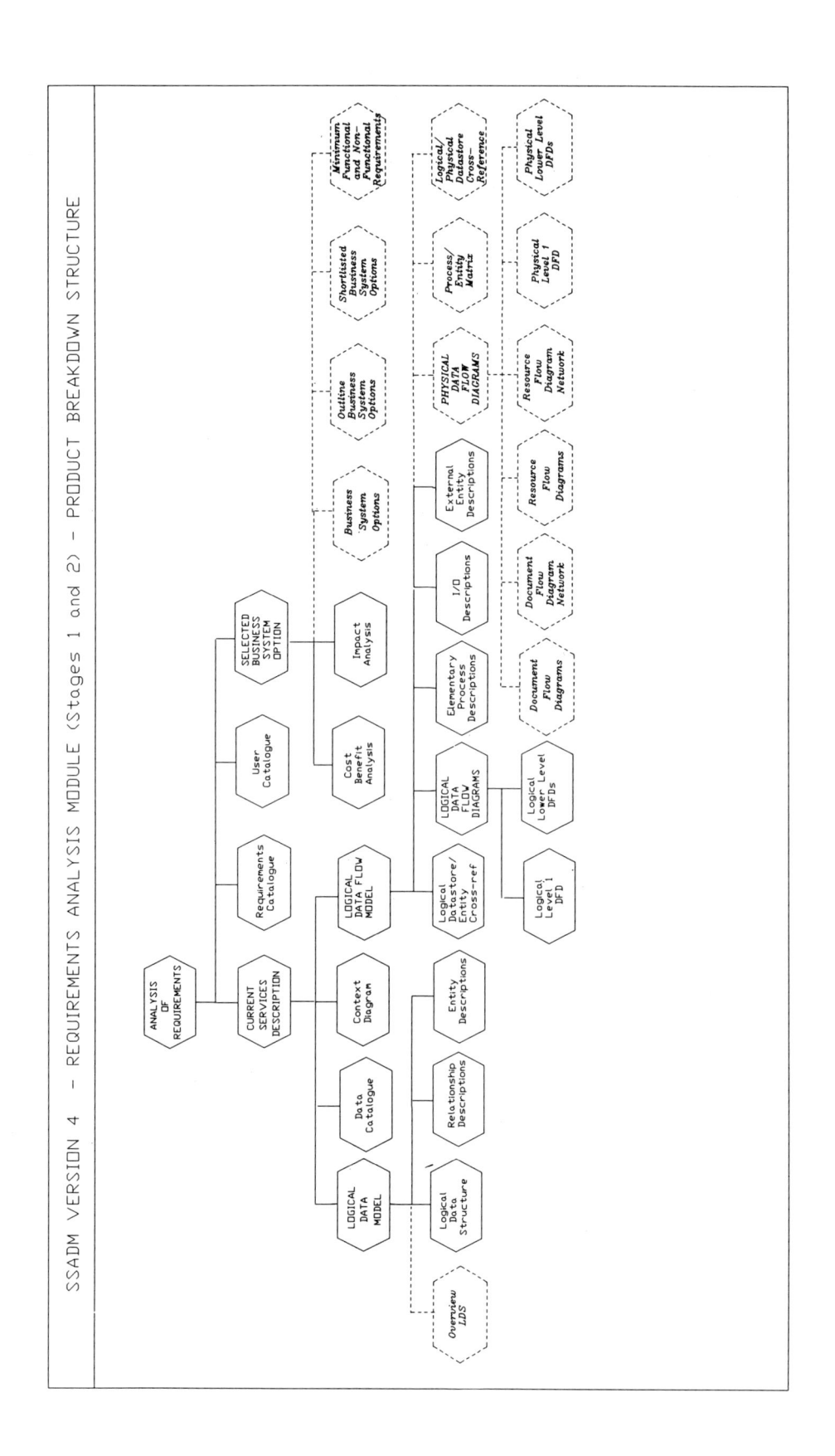

SSADM VERSION 4 – REQUIREMENTS ANALYSIS MODULE (Stages 1 and 2) – PRODUCT BREAKDOWN STRUCTURE

- ANALYSIS OF REQUIREMENTS
  - LOGICAL DATA MODEL
    - Logical Data Structure
      - *Overview LDS*
    - Data Catalogue
      - Relationship Descriptions
      - Entity Descriptions
  - CURRENT SERVICES DESCRIPTION
    - Context Diagram
    - LOGICAL DATA FLOW MODEL
      - Logical Datastore/Entity Cross-ref
      - LOGICAL DATA FLOW DIAGRAMS
        - Logical Level 1 DFD
        - Logical Lower Level DFDs
      - Elementary Process Descriptions
      - I/O Descriptions
      - External Entity Descriptions
      - *Document Flow Diagrams*
      - *Resource Flow Diagrams*
    - Requirements Catalogue
    - User Catalogue
    - Cost Benefit Analysis
    - Impact Analysis
  - SELECTED BUSINESS SYSTEM OPTION
    - *Business System Options*
      - *Outline Business System Options*
      - *Shortlisted Business System Options*
      - *Minimum Functional and Non-Functional Requirements*
    - PHYSICAL DATA FLOW DIAGRAMS
      - Process/Entity Matrix
      - *Logical/Physical Datastore Cross-Reference*
      - Resource Flow Diagram Network
      - Document Flow Diagram Network
      - Physical Level 1 DFD
      - *Physical Lower Level DFDs*

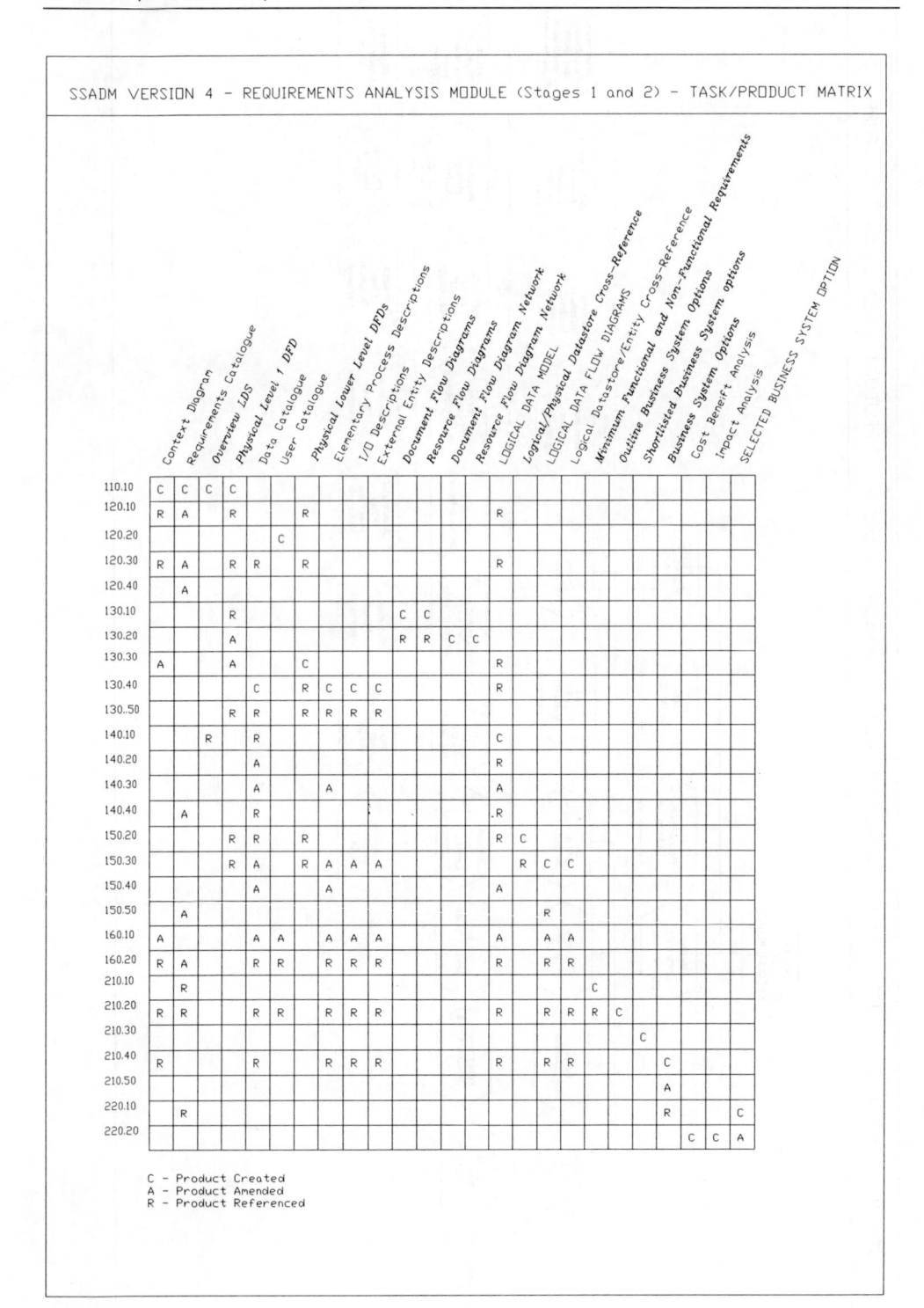

Requirements Analysis Module

SSADM VERSION 4 – REQUIREMENTS ANALYSIS MODULE (Stages 1 and 2) – TASK/PRODUCT MATRIX

Task	Context Diagram	Requirements Catalogue	Overview LDS	Physical Level 1 DFD	Data Catalogue	User Catalogue	Physical Lower Level DFDs	Elementary Process Descriptions	I/O Descriptions	External Entity Descriptions	Document Flow Diagrams	Resource Flow Diagrams	Document Flow Diagram Network	Resource Flow Diagram Network	LOGICAL DATA MODEL	Logical/Physical Datastore Cross-Reference	LOGICAL DATA FLOW DIAGRAMS	Logical Datastore/Entity Cross-Reference	Minimum Functional and Non-Functional Requirements	Outline Business System Options	Shortlisted Business System Options	Business System options	Cost Benefit Analysis	Impact Analysis	SELECTED BUSINESS SYSTEM OPTION
110.10	C	C	C	C																					
120.10	R	A		R			R								R										
120.20					C																				
120.30	R	A		R	R		R								R										
120.40		A																							
130.10			R					C	C																
130.20			A					R	R	C	C														
130.30	A		A		C										R										
130.40				C		R	C	C	C						R										
130.50			R	R		R	R	R	R																
140.10		R		R											C										
140.20				A											R										
140.30				A		A									A										
140.40	A			R											R										
150.20			R	R	R										R	C									
150.30			R	A	R	A	A	A								R	C	C							
150.40				A		A									A										
150.50		A													R										
160.10	A			A	A	A	A	A							A		A	A							
160.20	R	A		R	R	R	R	R							R		R	R							
210.10		R																	C						
210.20	R	R		R	R	R	R	R							R		R	R	R	C					
210.30																				C					
210.40	R			R			R	R	R						R		R	R			C				
210.50																					A				
220.10		R																		R			C		
220.20																						C	C	A	

C – Product Created
A – Product Amended
R – Product Referenced

Stage 1 — Investigation of Current Environment

This stage consists of the following steps:
- Step 110: Establish Analysis Framework
- Step 120: Investigate and Define Requirements
- Step 130: Investigate Current Processing
- Step 140: Investigate Current Data
- Step 150: Derive Logical View of Current Services
- Step 160: Assemble Investigation Results

STAGE 1 - ACTIVITY NETWORK

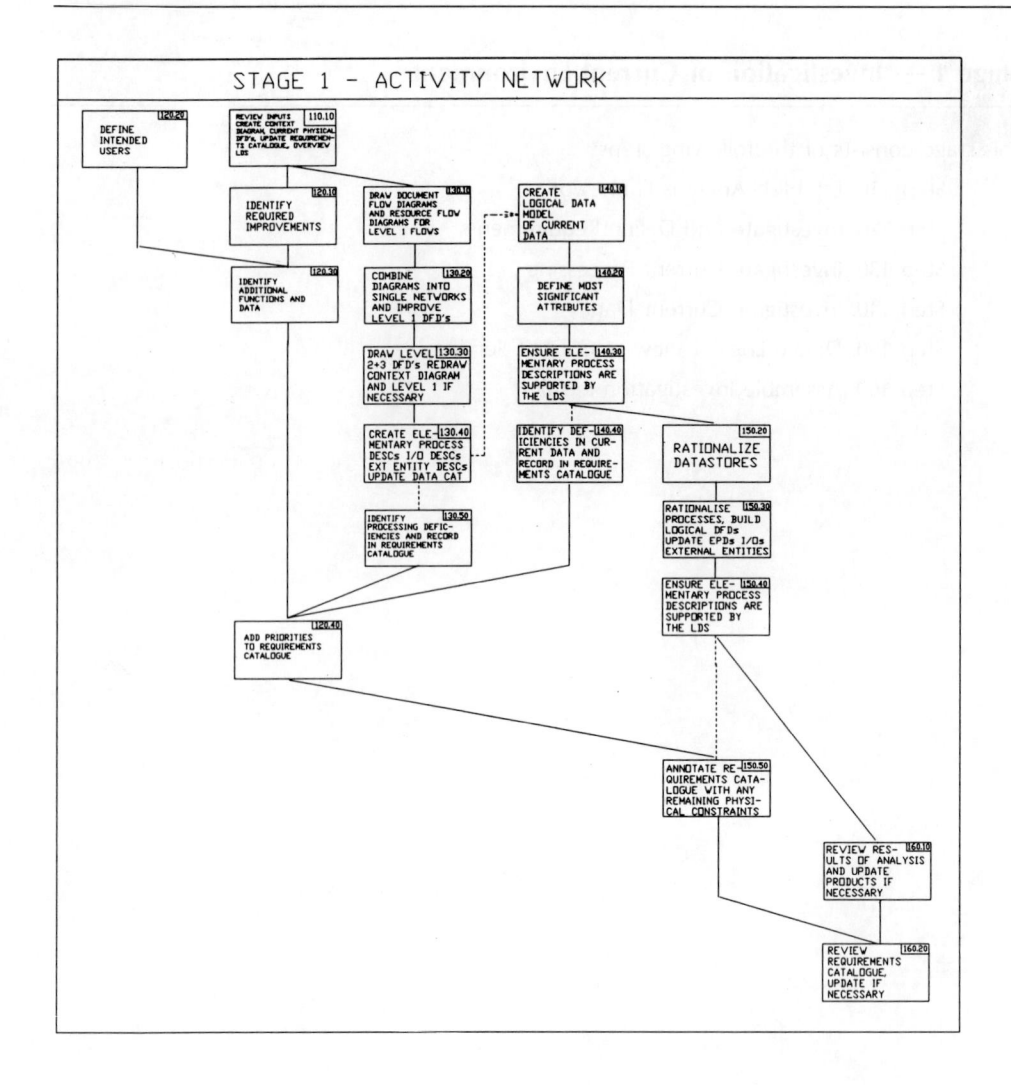

8.1 Step 110: Establish Analysis Framework

Objectives

- To review the results of previous studies and extract the identified system requirements.

- To confirm the system scope and boundaries defined in the Project Initiation Document.

Summary

This step is principally concerned with assimilating information from previous studies and preparing for more detailed analysis. The Project Initiation Document contains the terms of reference for the project, describes the scope of the investigations and identifies any relevant constraints. It is assumed that some form of preliminary study has been completed, although not necessarily as an SSADM Feasibility Study. If another study has been used it is this step that transforms the study products into overview SSADM products.

A review of the step inputs is conducted to ensure that previous conclusions are still relevant, and consistent with the project brief and the defined business objective. Any significant difficulties in carrying out the project as specified must be resolved with the Project Board before proceeding beyond this step. This may entail some additional investigative work, but this should be kept to a minimum in advance of Step 120: Investigate and Define Requirements.

References

Task 10:   Relevant background material, e.g. Business Objectives, Business Plans, IS/IT Strategy Statement, Data Administration Policies, Corporate Business Models,
Project Initiation Document
FEASIBILITY REPORT

Products created

Task 10:   Context Diagram
Requirements Catalogue
Overview LDS
Physical Level 1 DFD

Techniques

Data Flow Modelling — used in Task 10
Logical Data Modelling — used in Task 10
Requirements Definition — used in Task 10

Activities

Task 10

10.1 Review the contents of the Project Initiation Document (or the equivalent terms of reference for the project), any relevant background material and the outputs from the previous studies, including the FEASIBILITY REPORT if one has been produced.

80 Requirements Analysis Module

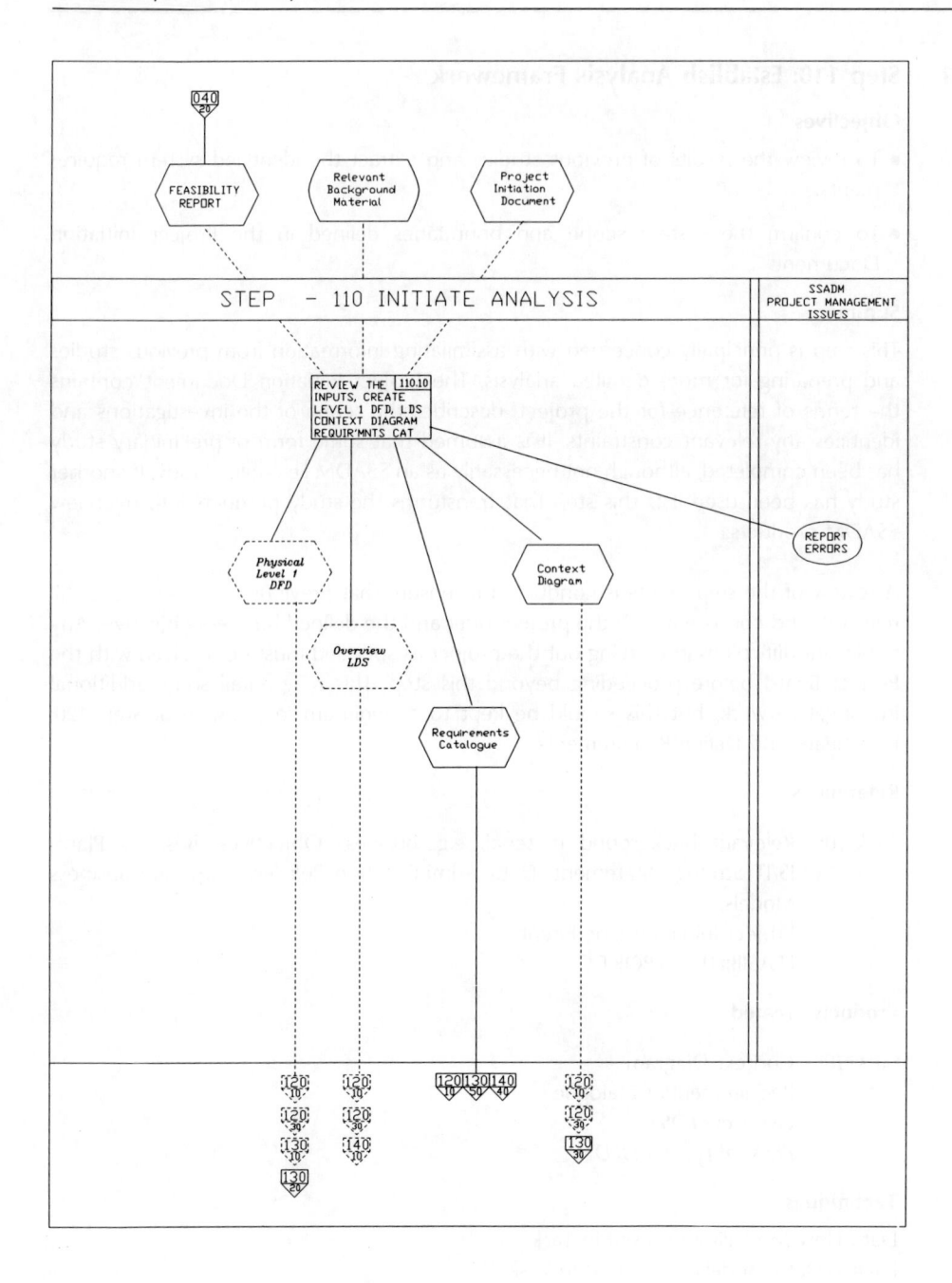

STEP – 110 INITIATE ANALYSIS

110.10 REVIEW THE INPUTS, CREATE LEVEL 1 DFD, LDS CONTEXT DIAGRAM REQUIR'MNTS CAT

Inputs:
- Feasibility Report (040/20)
- Relevant Background Material
- Project Initiation Document

Outputs:
- Physical Level 1 DFD
- Overview LDS
- Context Diagram
- Requirements Catalogue

SSADM PROJECT MANAGEMENT ISSUES: REPORT ERRORS

Exits to: 120/10, 120/30, 130/10, 130/20, 120/10, 120/30, 140/10, 120/30/140/40, 120/10, 120/30, 130/30

10.2 Create a Context Diagram (top-level DFD with one process box only) and *Physical Level 1 DFD*.

10.3 Create an *Overview LDS*.

10.4 Identify specific system requirements and record them in the Requirements Catalogue.

10.5 Report any errors and inconsistencies in the input products that prevent the analysis proceeding as planned.

8.2 Step 120: Investigate and Define Requirements

Objectives

- To identify the problems associated with the current environment that are to be resolved by the new system.
- To identify the additional services to be provided by the the new system.
- To define the users of the new system.

Summary

The Requirements Catalogue is initiated in Step 110, and in this step it is expanded as more detailed investigation is undertaken. Requirements are also identified in Step 130: Investigate Current Processing and Step 140: Investigate Current Data, which are carried out in parallel. There is a large degree of overlap between Tasks 120.10, 130.50 and 140.40.

Requirements are generally of two types: requirements for new facilities and requirements based on a problem in the current environment that is to be resolved. While requirements may only be described in broad terms initially, efforts should be made to ensure that, as far as possible, requirements are described in terms that can be quantified and measured. The aim is to produce a statement of requirements in sufficient detail for the definition of *Business System Options* in Step 210: Define Business Options.

Note that Task 120.40, the prioritization of the Requirements Catalogue, cannot be undertaken until Steps 130 and 140 are complete (see Stage 1 — Activity Network).

References

Task 10:   Context Diagram
            LOGICAL DATA MODEL
            PHYSICAL DATA FLOW DIAGRAMS

Task 20:   Project Initiation Document

Task 30:   Context Diagram
            Data Catalogue
            LOGICAL DATA MODEL
            PHYSICAL DATA FLOW DIAGRAMS

Products created

Task 20:   User Catalogue

Products amended

Task 10:   Requirements Catalogue

Task 30:   Requirements Catalogue

Task 40:   Requirements Catalogue

Techniques

Project Planning — used at the beginning of this step to create the Module and Stage Plans for the Requirements Analysis Module.

Requirements Analysis Module

STEP 120 – INVESTIGATE AND DEFINE REQUIREMENTS

Inputs:
- Requirements Catalogue (110/10)
- Context Diagram (110/10)
- Data Catalogue (130/40, 140/30)
- Logical Data Model (140/30)
- *Physical Data Flow Diagrams* (130/30)
- Requirements Catalogue (130/30, 140/40)
- Project Initiation Document

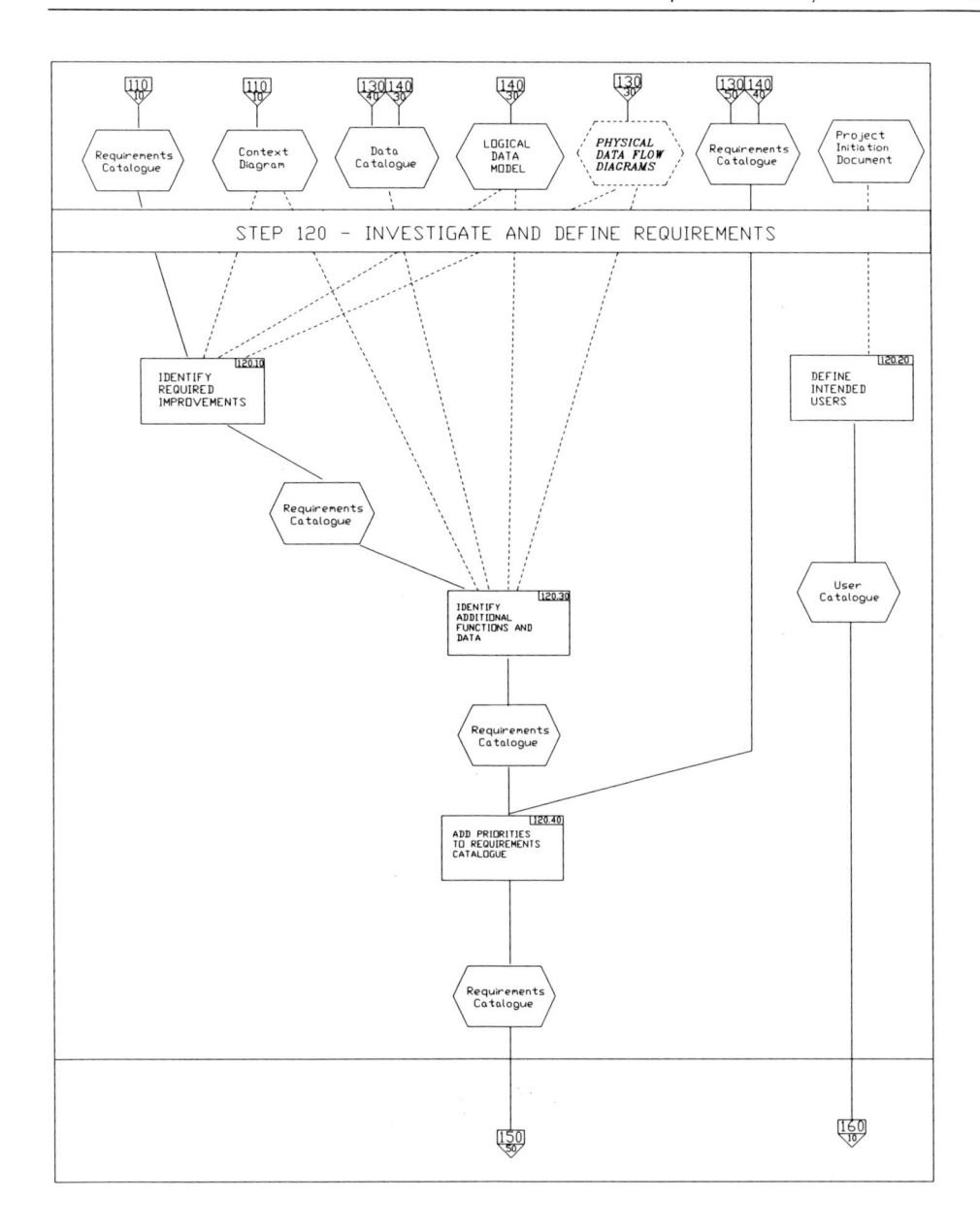

Tasks:
- 120.10 IDENTIFY REQUIRED IMPROVEMENTS → Requirements Catalogue
- 120.20 DEFINE INTENDED USERS → User Catalogue
- 120.30 IDENTIFY ADDITIONAL FUNCTIONS AND DATA → Requirements Catalogue
- 120.40 ADD PRIORITIES TO REQUIREMENTS CATALOGUE → Requirements Catalogue

Outputs: 150/50, 160/10

Dialogue Design — used in Task 20 to identify intended users. See pages F-DD-6, and F-DD-11 to 13 of the Technique Description in the reference manual.
Requirements Definition — used in Tasks 10, 30 and 40.

Activities

Task 10

10.1 Investigate the operation of the current system. Identify with the users the aspects of the current system where the service is unsatisfactory or needs improvement, and describe appropriate requirements in the Requirements Catalogue.

Task 20

20.1 Define the intended users of the new system in the User Catalogue.

Note that in both the Dialogue Design Technique Description and the User Catalogue Product Description there is an explicit assumption that users are job holders in the organization. This may not be the case. Wherever the word 'Job' is seen, it should be read as 'User/Job'.

Task 30

30.1 Identify with the users the additional functions and data required from the new system but not provided by the current system. This task should not be underestimated. If there is no current system, or it has little relevance to the required system, then this task will account for approximately 90 per cent of the effort required in Stage 1. See the Stage 1 Review on page 25.

Task 40

40.1 Add priorities to the Requirements Catalogue entries.

Note that this task is carried out after Steps 130 and 140 are complete, when all the entries in the Requirements Catalogue have been made.

8.3 Step 130: Investigate Current Processing

Objective

- To identify and describe the information flows of the current services.

Summary

This step investigates the information flow associated with the services currently provided, and describes them in the form of Data Flow Diagrams. The development of the *PHYSICAL DATA FLOW DIAGRAMS* uses information gathered in Step 110: Establish Analysis Framework and from interviews with user representatives. This step is carried out in parallel with Steps 120 and 140.

The *Physical Level 1 DFD* produced in Step 110: Establish Analysis Framework shows only the most significant information flows. A more detailed view is developed by taking each of these flows in turn and identifying the processes that transform the data. These individual views are then combined and used to refine the *Physical Lower Level DFDs*. At this point the Data Flow Diagrams represent the current services, with all their deficiencies. No attempt is made to incorporate required improvements or new facilities.

References

Task 10   *Physical Level 1 DFD*

Task 20: *Document Flow Diagrams*
          Resource Flow Diagrams

Task 30: LOGICAL DATA MODEL

Task 40: LOGICAL DATA MODEL
          Physical Lower Level DFDs

Task 50: *Physical Level 1 DFD*
          Physical Lower Level DFDs
          Elementary Process Descriptions
          I/O Descriptions
          External Entity Descriptions
          Data Catalogue

Products created

Task 30: *Physical Lower Level DFDs*

Task 40: Elementary Process Descriptions
          I/O Descriptions
          External Entity Descriptions
          Data Catalogue

Products optionally created

Task 10: *Document Flow Diagrams*
          Resource Flow Diagrams

86 Requirements Analysis Module

STEP 130 – INVESTIGATE CURRENT PROCESSING

Inputs:
- Context Diagram (110)
- Logical Data Model (140)
- Requirements Catalogue (110)
- Physical Level 1 DFD (110)

130.10 DRAW DOCUMENT FLOW DIAGRAMS AND RESOURCE FLOW DIAGRAMS FOR LEVEL 1 FLOWS
- produces: Document Flow Diagrams, Resource Flow Diagrams

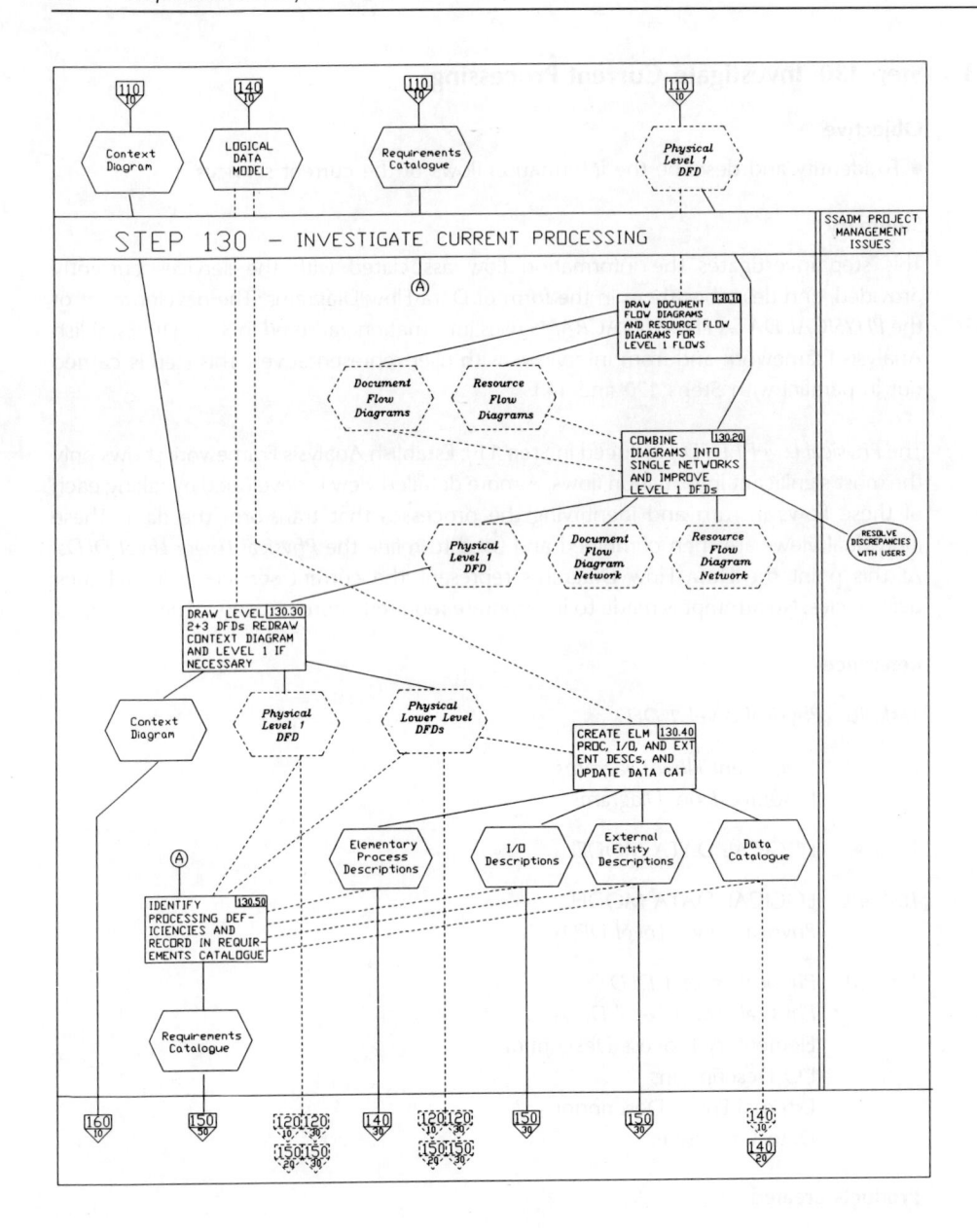

130.20 COMBINE DIAGRAMS INTO SINGLE NETWORKS AND IMPROVE LEVEL 1 DFDs
- inputs: Physical Level 1 DFD, Document Flow Diagram Network, Resource Flow Diagram Network
- RESOLVE DISCREPANCIES WITH USERS

130.30 DRAW LEVEL 2+3 DFDs REDRAW CONTEXT DIAGRAM AND LEVEL 1 IF NECESSARY
- produces: Context Diagram, Physical Level 1 DFD, Physical Lower Level DFDs

130.40 CREATE ELM PROC, I/O, AND EXT ENT DESCS, AND UPDATE DATA CAT
- produces: Elementary Process Descriptions, I/O Descriptions, External Entity Descriptions, Data Catalogue

130.50 IDENTIFY PROCESSING DEFICIENCIES AND RECORD IN REQUIREMENTS CATALOGUE
- produces: Requirements Catalogue

Outputs to: 160/10, 150/30, 120/10, 120/30, 150/20, 150/30, 140/30, 120/10, 120/30, 150/20, 150/30, 150/30, 150/30, 140/10, 140/20

SSADM PROJECT MANAGEMENT ISSUES

Task 20: Document Flow Diagram Network
Resource Flow Diagram Network

Products amended

Task 30: Context Diagram
Physical Level 1 DFD

Task 50: Requirements Catalogue

Products optionally amended

Task 20: Physical Level 1 DFD

Techniques

Data Flow Modelling — used in Tasks 10, 20, 30 and 40
Requirements Definition — used in Task 50

Activities

Task 10

10.1 Draw *Document Flow Diagrams* and *Resource Flow Diagrams* for each flow on the *Physical Level 1 DFD*.

Task 20

20.1 Combine the *Document Flow Diagrams* and *Resource Flow Diagrams* to produce a *Document Flow Diagram Network* and *Resource Flow Diagram Network*, and use these networks to improve the *Physical Level 1 DFD* already produced.

20.2 Resolve any discrepancies between the network diagrams and the *Physical Level 1 DFD* by discussion with the users.

Note that if the nature of the system being investigated is such that little would be learnt by investigating document and resource flows, Tasks 10 and 20 may be omitted.

Task 30

30.1 Develop the *PHYSICAL DATA FLOW DIAGRAMS* by decomposing the processes on the *Physical Level 1 DFD* to produce the *Physical Lower Level DFDs*, which may themselves be further decomposed until such a level is reached that the events the system responds to can be identified. This should normally only require up to two levels below Level 1. If it appears that further levels are still required, it may indicate that the project scope is too broad. (See the Data Flow Modelling technique review on page 14.

30.2 Redraw the Context Diagram and the *Physical Level 1 DFD* boundaries, if necessary.

Task 40

40.1 Create Elementary Process Descriptions for each process that responds to an event on the *PHYSICAL DATA FLOW DIAGRAMS*.

40.2 Create I/O Descriptions for each data flow crossing the system boundary at the event level.

40.3 Create External Entity Descriptions for each external entity on the Data Flow Diagrams.

40.5 Create the Data Catalogue incorporating Data Item Descriptions and Domain Descriptions identified on the I/O Descriptions.

Task 50

50.1 Identify with the users any deficiencies in the current processing and record these in the Requirements Catalogue.

8.4 Step 140: Investigate Current Data

Objective

- To identify and describe the structure of the system data, independently of the way the data is currently held and organized.

Summary

This step produces a model of the data that support the current services. The development of the model uses information gathered in Step 110 and in Step 130, where the Data Catalogue is created in Task 130.40.

The LOGICAL DATA MODEL represents only the data required to support the processing defined in the *PHYSICAL DATA FLOW DIAGRAMS*. No attempt is made to incorporate the additional data requirements of the new system identified in Task 120.30. The Elementary Process Descriptions supporting the *PHYSICAL DATA FLOW DIAGRAMS* are used to validate that the LOGICAL DATA MODEL does support the current processing. At this point, not necessarily all the attributes of all the entities will have been identified.

References

Task 10:   Overview LDS
             Data Catalogue

Task 20:   LOGICAL DATA MODEL

Task 40:   LOGICAL DATA MODEL
             Data Catalogue

Products created

Task 10:   LOGICAL DATA MODEL

Products amended

Task 20:   Data Catalogue

Task 30:   Data Catalogue
             LOGICAL DATA MODEL
             Elementary Process Descriptions

Task 40:   Requirements Catalogue

Techniques

Logical Data Modelling — used in Tasks 10, 20 and 30
Relational Data Analysis — used in Tasks 10 and 20 (see pages RS-RDA-4-to-6 of the Technique Description in the reference manual.)
Requirements Definition — used in Task 40

Activities

Task 10

10.1 Create a LOGICAL DATA MODEL from the *Overview LDS* and any new data items that have been added to the Data Catalogue.

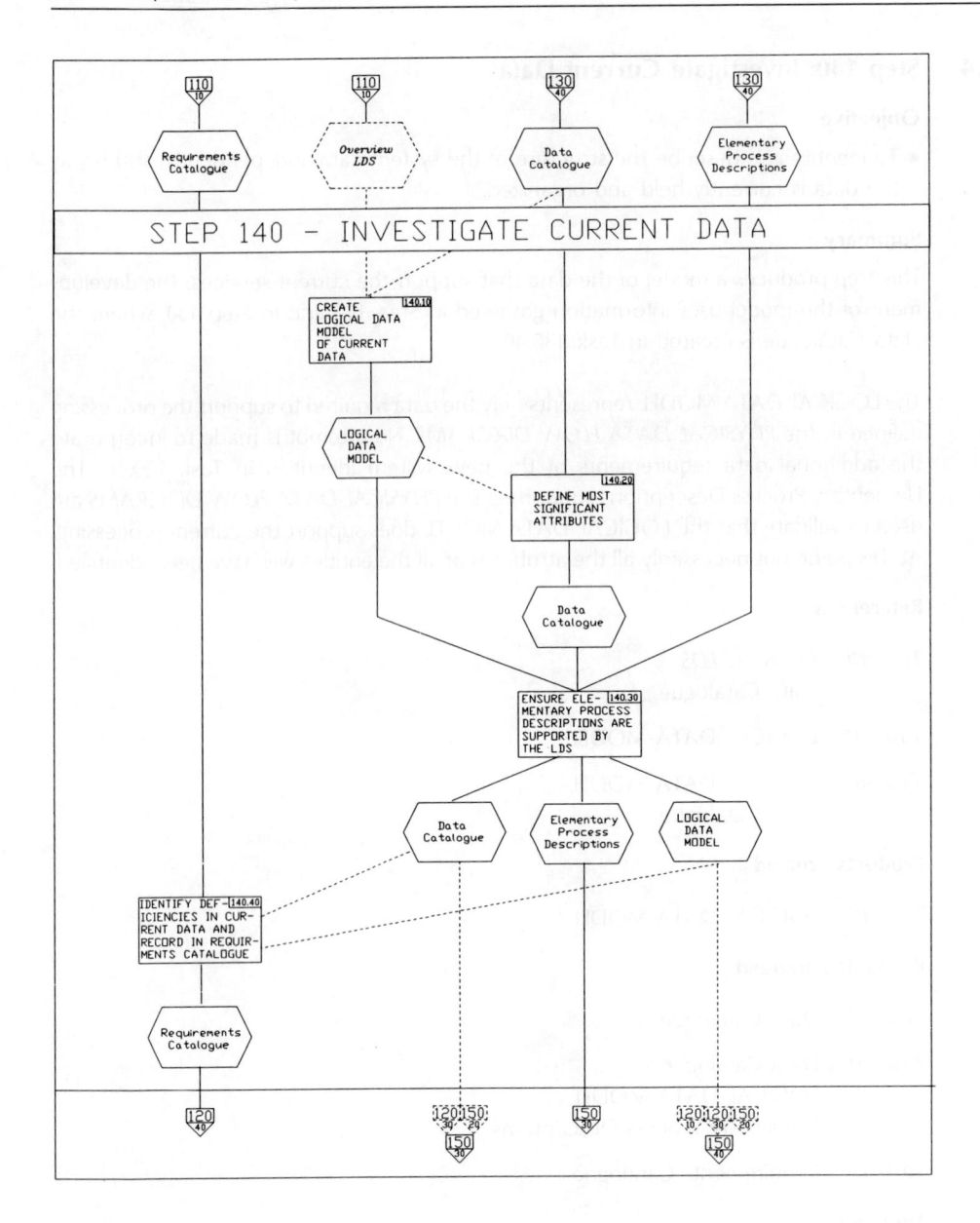

Requirements Analysis Module

STEP 140 – INVESTIGATE CURRENT DATA

Inputs:
- Requirements Catalogue (110/10)
- Overview LDS (110/10)
- Data Catalogue (130/40)
- Elementary Process Descriptions (130/40)

Tasks:
- 140.10 CREATE LOGICAL DATA MODEL OF CURRENT DATA → LOGICAL DATA MODEL
- 140.20 DEFINE MOST SIGNIFICANT ATTRIBUTES → Data Catalogue
- 140.30 ENSURE ELEMENTARY PROCESS DESCRIPTIONS ARE SUPPORTED BY THE LDS → Data Catalogue, Elementary Process Descriptions, LOGICAL DATA MODEL
- 140.40 IDENTIFY DEFICIENCIES IN CURRENT DATA AND RECORD IN REQUIREMENTS CATALOGUE → Requirements Catalogue

Outputs:
- 120/40
- 120/30, 150/20
- 150/30
- 150/30
- 120/10, 120/30, 150/20
- 150/40

Task 20

20.1 Update the Data Catalogue with the most significant attributes associated with each entity on the LOGICAL DATA MODEL.

Task 30

30.1 Ensure that the Elementary Process Descriptions can be supported by the LOGICAL DATA MODEL.

Note that access paths are not formally documented in this step, although it may be useful to create some as working documents to carry out this validation. See the Logical Data Modelling Technique Description, pages RA-LDM-33/34 and RA-LDM-38–45 in the reference manuals. The possible creation of access paths is not depicted in the structural model here.

30.2 Resolve any discrepancies and update the Elementary Process Descriptions, LOGICAL DATA MODEL and Data Catalogue as required.

Task 40

40.1 Identify with the users any deficiencies in the current data, and record these in the Requirements Catalogue.

8.5 Step 150: Derive Logical View of Current Services

Objective

- To describe the logical information system that supports only those essential processes and data in the current environment that are to be supported in the new system.

Summary

The *PHYSICAL DATA FLOW DIAGRAMS* are converted into a logical view by removing the physical aspects of the current implementation. The revised LOGICAL DATA FLOW DIAGRAMS represent the logical information system embedded in the current physical environment. They define part of the requirement for the system to be developed — the services to be carried forward.

Although the removal of physical constraints may resolve some of the current problems identified, the extension of the LOGICAL DATA FLOW DIAGRAMS to resolve outstanding problems and incorporate new requirements is not done formally until Step 310: Define Required System Processing. Note, however, that it may be carried out to some extent in the support of the Business System Options (see Step 210, Task 40).

The LOGICAL DATA MODEL and the Data Catalogue are verified to ensure that they still support the processing described in the Elementary Process Descriptions.

Note that Task 10 in the reference manuals has been omitted, because it is only an overview of the activities in Task 20 and the beginning of Task 30. The other tasks have not been renumbered, to aid cross-referral to the reference manuals (see the Stage 1 Review on page 25).

References

Task 20:   LOGICAL DATA MODEL
          Data Catalogue
          PHYSICAL DATA FLOW DIAGRAMS

Task 30:   PHYSICAL DATA FLOW DIAGRAMS
          Logical/Physical Datastore Cross-Reference

Task 50:   LOGICAL DATA FLOW DIAGRAMS

Products created

Task 20:   Logical/Physical Datastore Cross-Reference

Task 30:   LOGICAL DATA FLOW DIAGRAMS
          Logical Datastore/Entity Cross-Reference

Products optionally created

Task 30:   Process/Entity Matrix

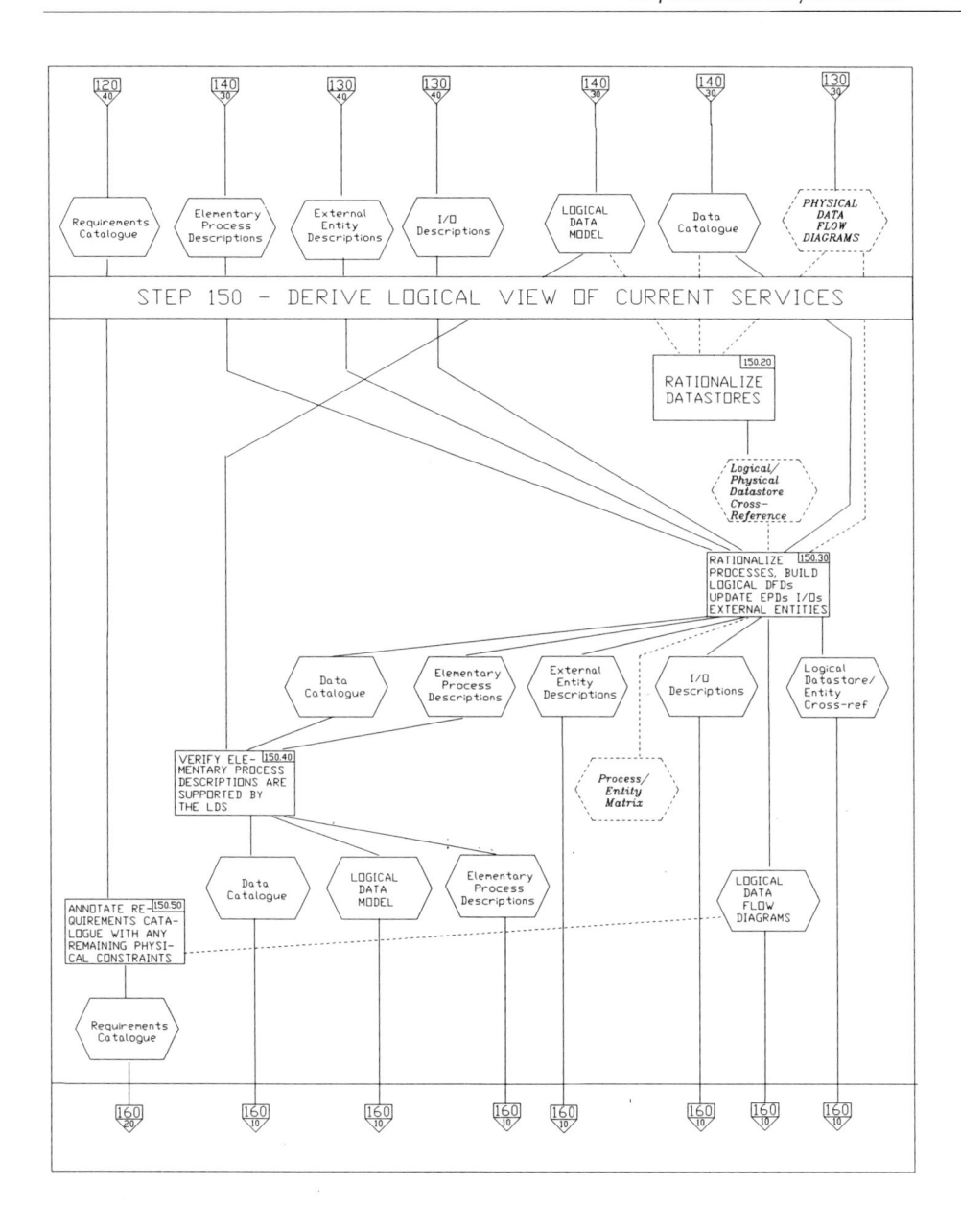

Requirements Analysis Module

STEP 150 – DERIVE LOGICAL VIEW OF CURRENT SERVICES

Products amended

Task 30: Elementary Process Descriptions
External Entity Descriptions
I/O Descriptions
Data Catalogue

Task 40: Data Catalogue
LOGICAL DATA MODEL
Elementary Process Descriptions

Task 50: Requirements Catalogue

Techniques
Data Flow Modelling — used in Tasks 20 and 30
Logical Data Modelling — used in Task 40
Requirements Definition — used in Task 50

Activities

Task 20

20.1 Rationalize the datastores so that each datastore consists of one or more related entity types on the Logical Data Model.

20.2 Create a *Logical/Physical Datastore Cross-Reference*.

Task 30

30.1 Rationalize the processes on the *Physical Lower Level DFDs*, and build LOGICAL DATA FLOW DIAGRAMS from the bottom up.

Note that it may help to produce a *Process/Entity Matrix* (see the reference manuals, pages RA-DFM-40–47 in general, and pages RA-DFM-43–45 in particular).

30.2 Amend the Elementary Process Descriptions, I/O Descriptions and External Entity Descriptions to reflect the new diagrams. Update the Data Catalogue as required.

30.3 Create a Logical Datastore/Entity Cross-Reference diagram.

Task 40

40.1 Verify that the Elementary Process Descriptions can be supported by the LOGICAL DATA MODEL and Data Catalogue.

Note that, as for Task 30 in Step 140, access paths are not formally documented in this step, although it may be useful to create some as working documents to carry out this verification. See the reference manuals' Logical Data Modelling Technique Description, pages RA-LDM-33/34 and RA-LDM-38–45. The possible creation of access paths is not depicted in the structural model in this handbook.

40.2 Resolve any discrepancies and update the Elementary Process Descriptions, LOGICAL DATA MODEL and Data Catalogue as required.

Task 50

50.1 Annotate the Requirements Catalogue to show any physical constraints that are still valid.

8.6 Step 160: Assemble Investigation Results

Objective

- To ensure the integrity of the products describing the current services.

Summary

This step is the completion of the investigation of the current environment, and is concerned with checking the consistency of the products of Stage 1 — Investigation of Current Environment.

Each of the SSADM steps represents a transformation which takes a starting set of products, performs some tasks, and applies quality control to produce a target set of products. Quality management procedures are not part of SSADM, but each of the SSADM products that transports information between steps has quality criteria defined as part of the Product Description (Dictionary Volume). These quality criteria are only those that can be applied to individual products. The cross-checking of products for consistency is part of this step. The review methods to be used are defined in the quality management procedures.

References

Task 10:   Project Initiation Document
           Feasibility Report

Task 20:   Context Diagram
           Data Catalogue
           Logical Datastore/Entity Cross-Reference
           Elementary Process Descriptions
           External Entity Descriptions
           LOGICAL DATA MODEL
           LOGICAL DATA FLOW DIAGRAMS
           I/O Descriptions
           User Catalogue

Products amended

Task 10:   Context Diagram
           Data Catalogue
           Logical Datastore/Entity Cross-Reference
           Elementary Process Descriptions
           External Entity Descriptions
           LOGICAL DATA MODEL
           LOGICAL DATA FLOW DIAGRAMS
           I/O Descriptions
           User Catalogue

Task 20:   Requirements Catalogue

Techniques

Requirements Definition — used in Task 20

Requirements Analysis Module

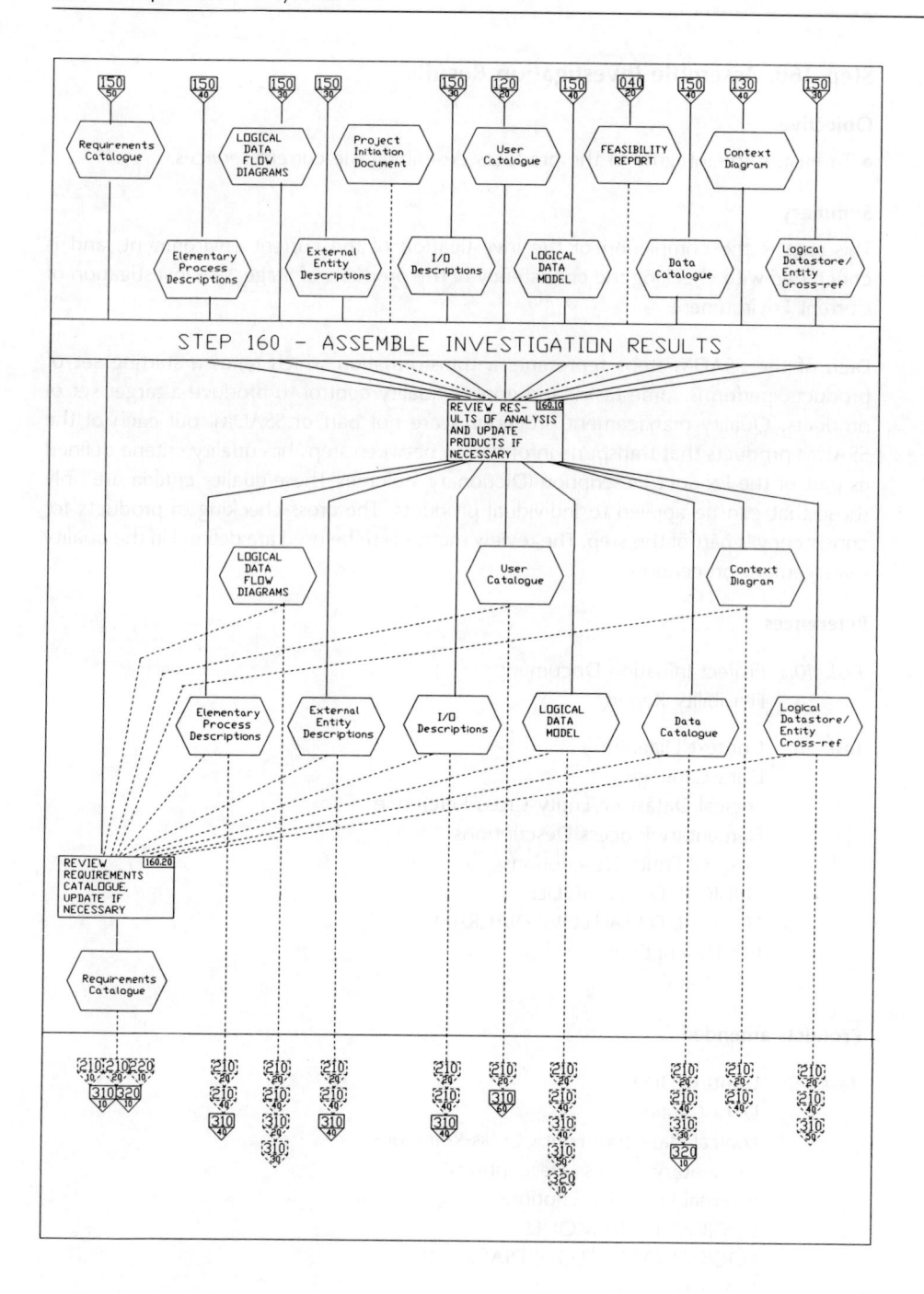

Activities

Task 10

10.1 All the Stage 1 products are reviewed, checking for completeness and consistency, and Stage 1 deliverables updated as necessary. Note that no particular technique is shown in the reference manuals as being used in this task, as it is largely a matter of common sense.

As a guide, diagrammatic products should be checked to ensure that they conform to the required notation. The Data Catalogue should be checked to ensure that each data item appears on an I/O Description, and each attribute on an Entity Description. Conversely, the I/O Descriptions and Entity Descriptions should be checked to ensure that each data item and attribute are described in the Data Catalogue. The Logical Lower Level DFDs (lowest level only) should be checked to ensure that each data flow that crosses the system boundary is described in an I/O Description; that each process is described in an Elementary Process Description; and that there is a description for each External Entity. The Logical Datastore/Entity Cross-Reference should be checked to ensure that all entities are represented and only appear in one datastore. The Context Diagram and Logical Level 1 DFD should be checked to ensure that the system boundaries are still correct. The User Catalogue should be checked to ensure that it includes an entry for all Users/Jobs.

Task 20

20.1 Review/consolidate the Requirements Catalogue entries with the relevant users; review priority levels, functional and non-functional requirements, benefits, suggested solutions and any related requirements, taking into account any changes made to the products in Task 10.

The Structural Model for Stage 2 — Business System Options

This stage consist of the following steps:
    Step 210: Define Business System Options (5 Tasks)
    Step 220: Select Business System Option (2 Tasks)

```
┌─────────────────────────────────────────────────────────────────┐
│           SSADM VERSION 4 - STAGE 2 ACTIVITY NETWORK            │
│                                                                 │
│                          ┌──────────────┐210.10                 │
│                          │COMPILE LIST OF│                      │
│                          │MINIMUM        │                      │
│                          │REQUIREMENTS   │                      │
│                          └───────┬───────┘                      │
│                                  │                              │
│                          ┌───────┴──────┐210.20                 │
│                          │DEFINE UP TO  │                       │
│                          │SIX BSOs      │                       │
│                          │SATISFYING    │                       │
│                          │THE MINIMUM   │                       │
│                          │REQUIREMENTS  │                       │
│                          └───────┬──────┘                       │
│                                  │                              │
│                          ┌───────┴──────┐210.30                 │
│                          │PRODUCE       │                       │
│                          │SHORTLIST     │                       │
│                          │OF OPTIONS    │                       │
│                          └───────┬──────┘                       │
│                                  │                              │
│                          ┌───────┴──────┐210.40                 │
│                          │DEVELOP       │                       │
│                          │BUSINESS      │                       │
│                          │SYSTEM        │                       │
│                          │OPTIONS       │                       │
│                          └───────┬──────┘                       │
│                                  │                              │
│                          ┌───────┴──────┐210.50                 │
│                          │ADD COST/     │                       │
│                          │BENEFIT ANALYSIS│                     │
│                          │AND IMPLICATIONS│                     │
│                          │TO BSOs       │                       │
│                          └───────┬──────┘                       │
│                                  │                              │
│                          ┌───────┴──────┐220.10                 │
│                          │SELECT        │                       │
│                          │BUSINESS SYSTEM│                      │
│                          │OPTION AND    │                       │
│                          │RECORD REASONS│                       │
│                          └───────┬──────┘                       │
│                                  │                              │
│                          ┌───────┴──────┐220.20                 │
│                          │DEVELOP THE   │                       │
│                          │SELECTED      │                       │
│                          │BUSINESS      │                       │
│                          │OPTION        │                       │
│                          └──────────────┘                       │
│                                                                 │
└─────────────────────────────────────────────────────────────────┘
```

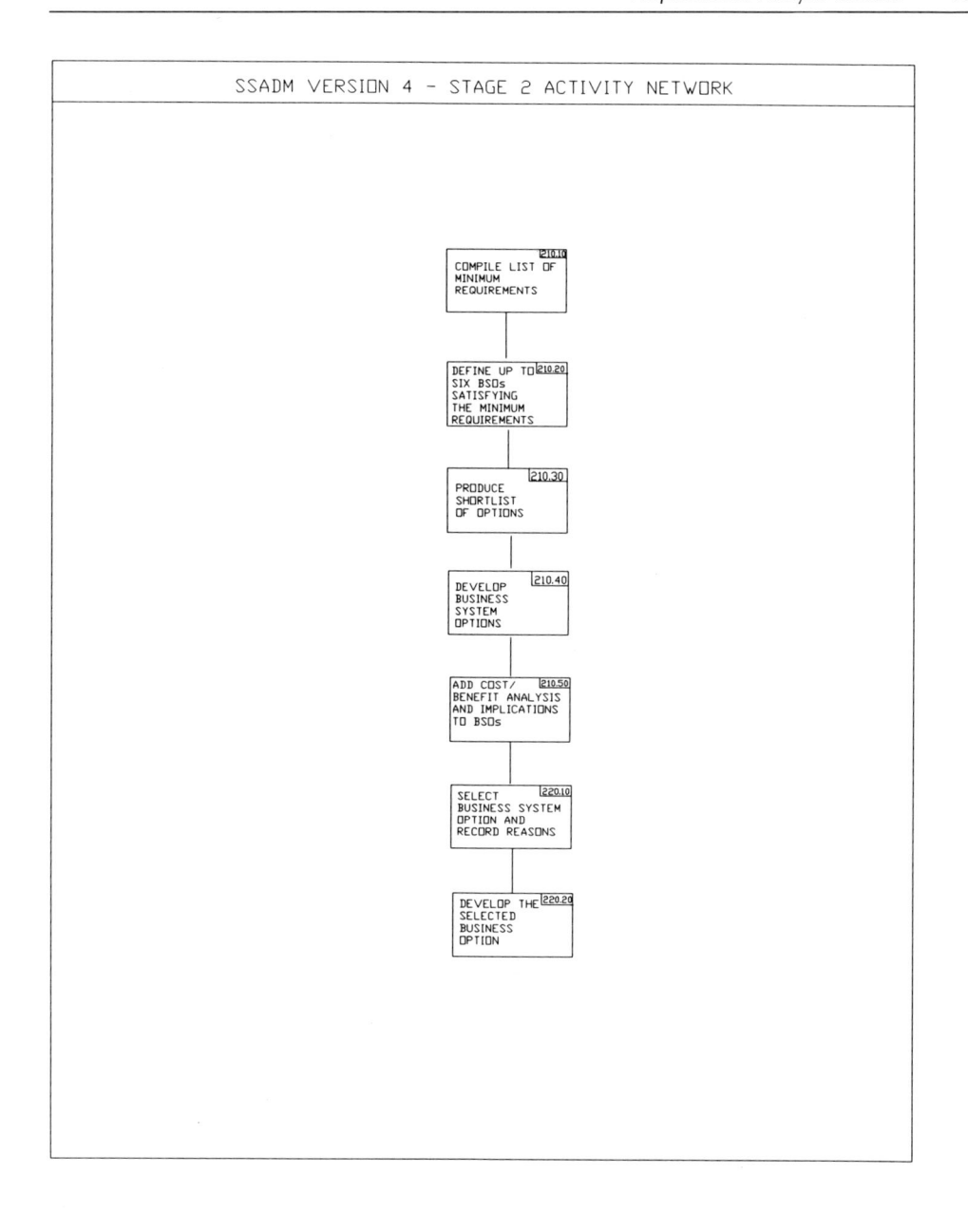

8.7 Step 210: Define Business System Options

Objective

- To develop a range of system options that meet the defined requirements, from which the users can select.

Summary

The *Business System Options* created in this step are possible logical solutions to the users' requirements. Each option includes a description of its boundary, inputs and outputs, and some description of what happens within it.

This step is concerned with identifying a number of possible solutions, and developing two or three of those for presentation to the Project Board. There is no single 'correct' solution — invariably there are many possible systems which could be developed, differing in terms of functionality and impact on the organization, and with different cost/benefit profiles. The Project Board must select the combination of elements that will best suit the requirements as perceived at the time. In some projects, the view of possible functional choices may be significantly different from that envisaged in the Project Initiation Document. Indeed, this step provides a vital opportunity to re-evaluate and to change the proposals made earlier, including the system boundary and the scope of the requirements.

References

Task 10: Requirements Catalogue

Task 20: Requirements Catalogue
Minimum Functional and Non-functional Requirements
User Catalogue
Project Initiation Document
FEASIBILITY REPORT
CURRENT SERVICES DESCRIPTION

Task 40: CURRENT SERVICES DESCRIPTION

Products created

Task 10: Minimum Functional and Non-functional Requirements

Task 20: Outline Business System Options

Task 30: Shortlisted Business System Options

Task 40: Business System Options

Products amended

Task 50: Business System Options

Techniques

Business System Option — used in Tasks 10, 20, 30, 40 and 50
Data Flow Modelling — used in Task 40
Logical Data Modelling — used in Task 40

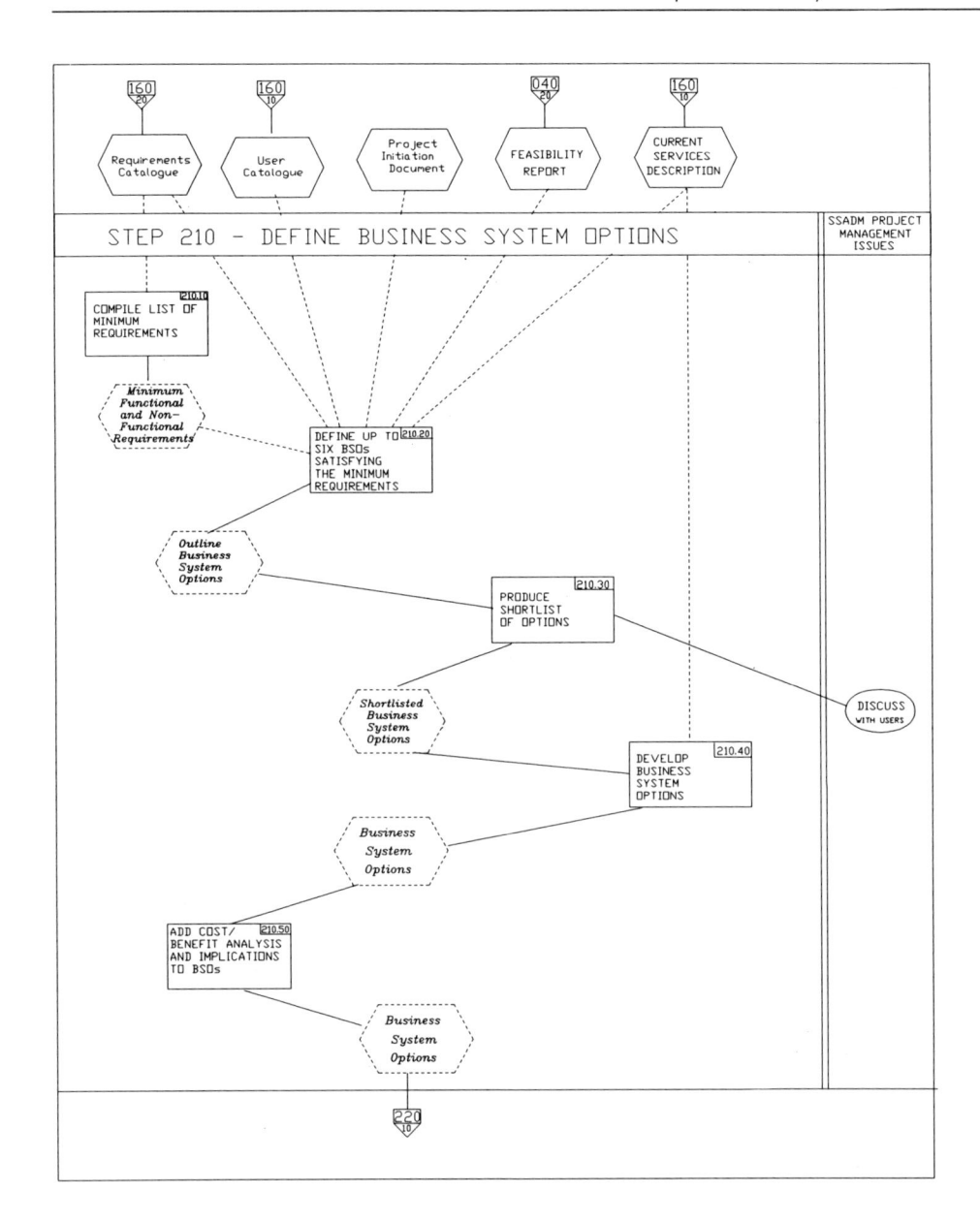

Requirements Analysis Module

STEP 210 – DEFINE BUSINESS SYSTEM OPTIONS

Inputs:
- Requirements Catalogue (160/20)
- User Catalogue (160/10)
- Project Initiation Document
- Feasibility Report (040/20)
- Current Services Description (160/10)

SSADM PROJECT MANAGEMENT ISSUES

210.10 COMPILE LIST OF MINIMUM REQUIREMENTS
→ *Minimum Functional and Non-Functional Requirements*

210.20 DEFINE UP TO SIX BSOs SATISFYING THE MINIMUM REQUIREMENTS
→ *Outline Business System Options*

210.30 PRODUCE SHORTLIST OF OPTIONS — DISCUSS WITH USERS
→ *Shortlisted Business System Options*

210.40 DEVELOP BUSINESS SYSTEM OPTIONS
→ *Business System Options*

210.50 ADD COST/BENEFIT ANALYSIS AND IMPLICATIONS TO BSOs
→ *Business System Options*

Output to 220/10

Activities

Task 10

10.1 Compile a list of *Minimum Functional and Non-functional Requirements*. All the options must satisfy these.

Task 20

20.1 Define up to six *Outline Business System Options*, representing a range of possible functional solutions to the requirements, but satisfying the minimum requirements.

Task 30

30.1 Discuss the options with the users and produce a shortlist of two or three *Shortlisted Business System Options*.

Task 40

40.1 Develop a description of each *Business System Option*. The description must be expressed textually but may be supported by logical data models and data flow diagrams illustrating the differences.

Note that the degree to which logical data models and data flow diagrams are developed is dependent upon the relevance of the current system in Stage 1. In the extreme case, if there is no current system these models must be produced as they depict the first view of the required system.

Task 50

50.1 Develop a cost/benefit analysis and outline the organizational implications (impact analysis) for each Business System Option.

Note that these form an initial view, are only produced in outline, and are incorporated as part of each *Business System Option*. They are fully developed in the next step, and become deliverable products in their own right as part of the SELECTED BUSINESS SYSTEM OPTION.

8.8 Step 220: Select Business System Option

Objective

- To ensure user ownership of the technical direction of the project by presenting the *Business System Options* to the Project Board and assisting in the selection of the preferred option.

Summary

This step completes the Requirements Analysis Module and is concerned with the presentation of the *Business System Options* to the project Board and the Selection of the preferred option. The SELECTED BUSINESS SYSTEM OPTION defines the boundary of the system to be developed in the Requirements Specification Module.

It may be necessary to make presentations to a wider audience than the Project Board, to canvass opinions and promote acceptance and commitment. The selected option is often a hybrid of more than one option, including suggestions made during the presentation and selection process. The base option definition is therefore amended to describe the requirement in sufficient detail to define the scope of the required system.

References

Task 10:   Requirements Catalogue
           Project Initiation Document
           FEASIBILITY REPORT
           Business System Options

Products created

Task 10:   Selected Business System Option

Task 20:   Cost/Benefit Analysis
           Impact Analysis

Products amended

Task 20:   SELECTED BUSINESS SYSTEM OPTION

Techniques

Business System Option — used in Tasks 10 and 20
Project Planning — used at the end of this step to create the Module/Stage Plans for the Requirements Specification Module.

Activities

Task 10

10.1 Present the *Business System Options* to the Project Board and other selected audiences.

10.2 Assist the decision-making process by further explanation and discussion of the implications of the options if required, and record the reasons for particular decisions. The selected option may well be an amalgamation of those presented.

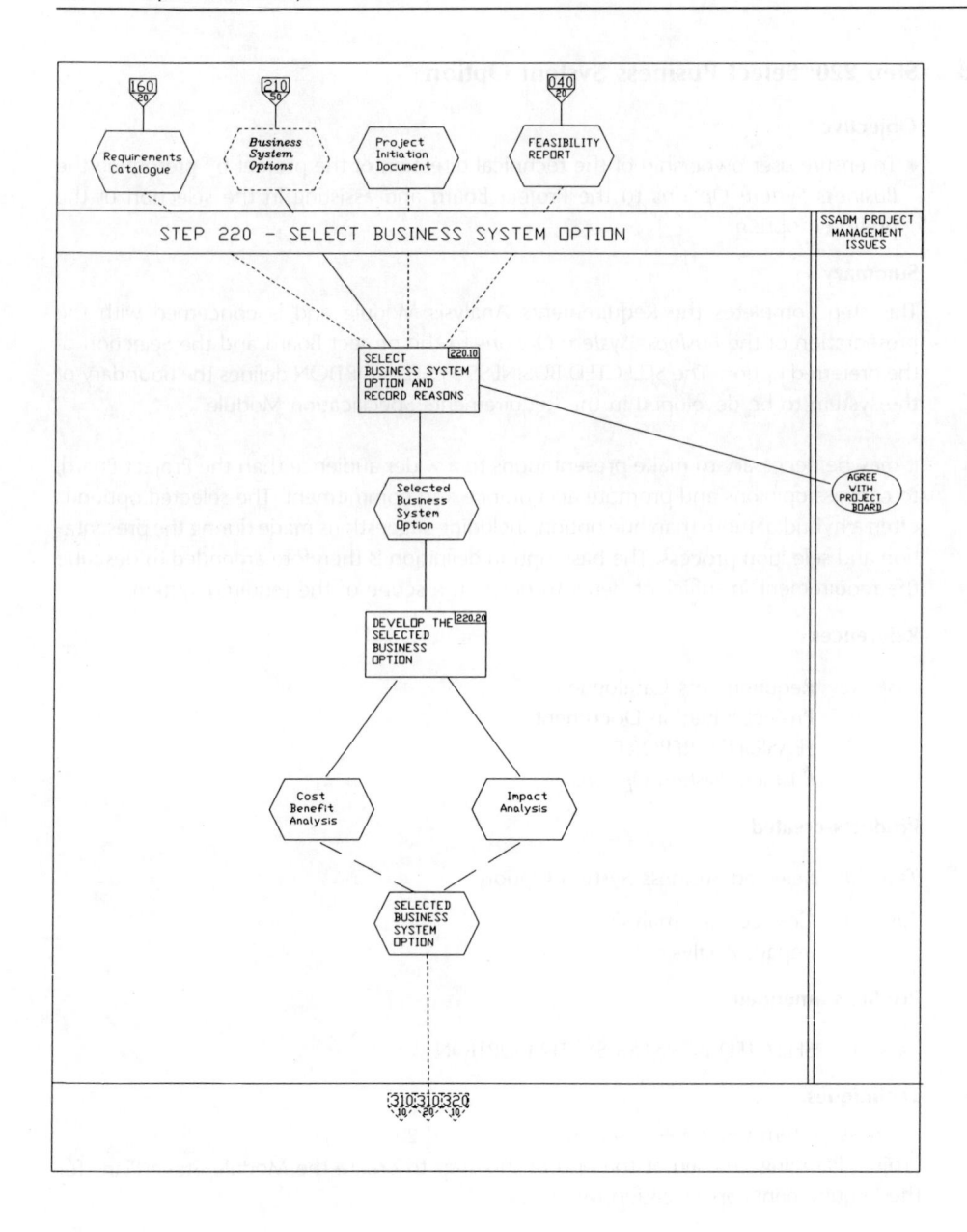

Requirements Analysis Module

STEP 220 – SELECT BUSINESS SYSTEM OPTION

Inputs:
- Requirements Catalogue (160/20)
- Business System Options (210/50)
- Project Initiation Document
- FEASIBILITY REPORT (040/20)

220.10 SELECT BUSINESS SYSTEM OPTION AND RECORD REASONS

→ Selected Business System Option

220.20 DEVELOP THE SELECTED BUSINESS OPTION

- Cost Benefit Analysis
- Impact Analysis

→ SELECTED BUSINESS SYSTEM OPTION

Outputs to: 310/10, 310/20, 320/10

SSADM PROJECT MANAGEMENT ISSUES: AGREE WITH PROJECT BOARD

Note that, on the diagram for this step the Selected Business System Option, as created in this task, is depicted as an Elementary Deliverable Product (standard typeface, lower case). It is in the next task that all of its constituent products are fully developed, and thus it becomes a compound deliverable product.

Task 20

20.1 Develop a description of the SELECTED BUSINESS SYSTEM OPTION. This will fix the system boundary and form the basis for the specification of the required system in Stage 3. If the selected option is one of those presented, then most of the description will already be available. However, if the selected option is an amalgam of those presented, a new description is produced. In either case the SELECTED BUSINESS SYSTEM OPTION document must contain the reasons for the selection of that option, and for the rejection of others.

20.2 Develop a Cost/Benefit Analysis for the selected option.

20.3 Develop an Impact Analysis for the selected option.

9 Requirements Specification Module

This module consists of one stage, Stage 3 — Definition of Requirements, that produces the REQUIREMENTS SPECIFICATION.

SSADM VERSION 4 - REQUIREMENTS SPECIFICATION MODULE (Stage 3) - PRODUCT BREAKDOWN STRUCTURE

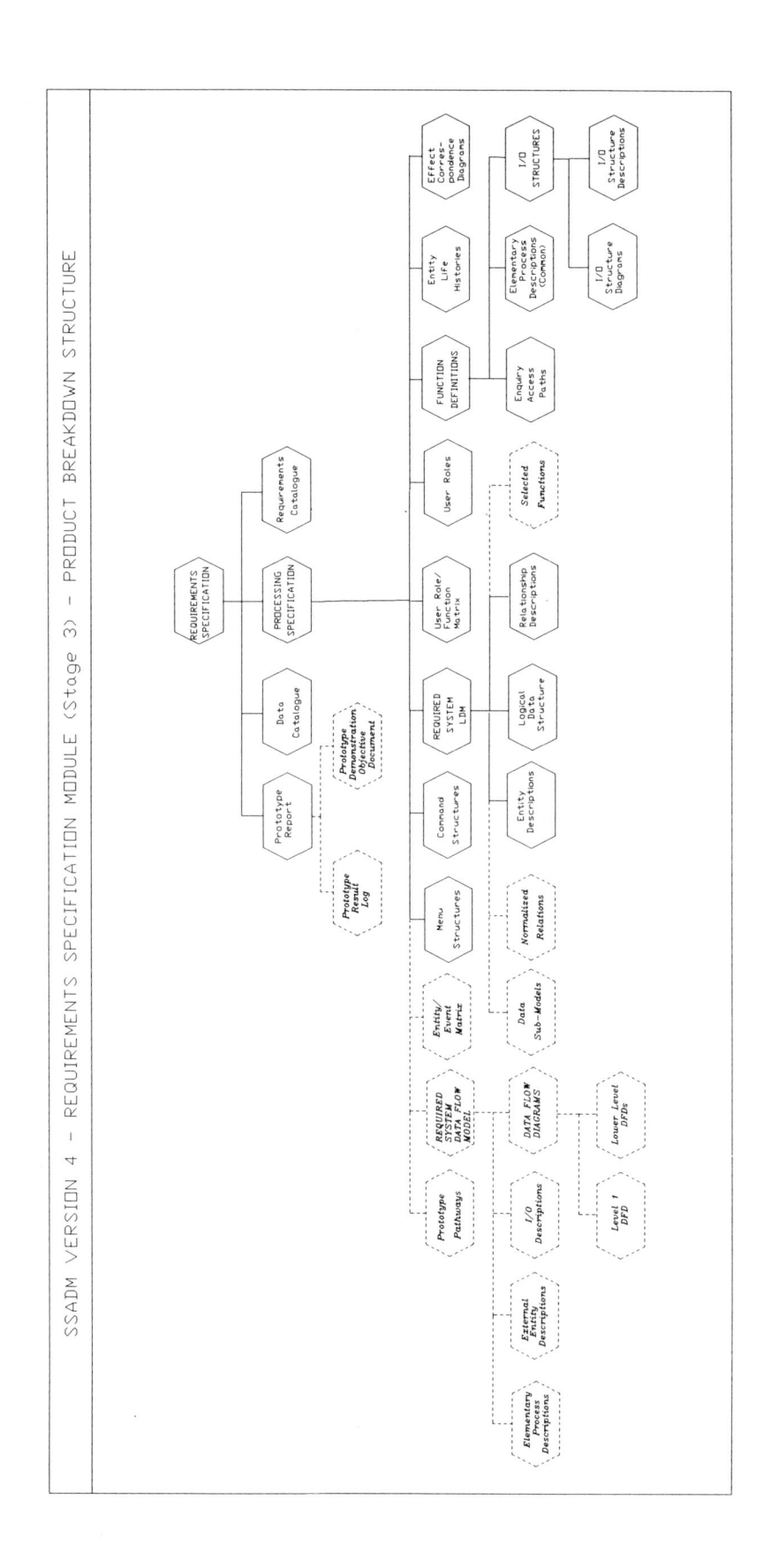

SSADM VERSION 4 - REQUIREMENTS SPECIFICATION MODULE (Stage 3) - TASK/PRODUCT MATRIX

Task	Requirements Catalogue	Data Catalogue	FUNCTION DEFINITIONS	DATA FLOW DIAGRAMS	Elementary Process Descriptions	I/O Descriptions	External Entity Descriptions	User Roles	REQUIRED SYSTEM LDM	I/O STRUCTURES	User Role/Function Matrix	Selected Functions	Normalised Relations	Data Submodels	Selected Dialogues and Reports	Menu Structures	Compound Structures	Logical Grouping of Dialogue Elements	Prototype Pathways	Prototype Demonstration Objective Document	Prototype Result Log	Prototype Report	Entity/Event Matrix	Entity Life Histories	Effect Correspondence Diagrams	Enquiry Access Paths	REQUIREMENTS SPECIFICATION
310.10	A																										
310.20				A																							
310.30	A	R		A					R																		
310.40		A		R	A	A	A		R																		
310.50		A			A				R																		
310.60						R	C																				
320.10	A	A							C																		
320.20		A			A				A																		
320.30	R	A							A																		
330.10	R		C	R	R																						
330.20	R		C	R	R																						
330.30		A		R	R							C															
330.40		A				R						C															
330.50		A																									
340.10		R			R						C																
340.20					R						R	C															
340.30											R	C															
340.40		A			R			A					R														
350.10		R	R					R		R					C												
350.20															R	C	C										
350.30		R				R	R								R	R	R	C	C								
350.40																		R	R								
350.50																				C							
350.60																					R						
350.70								·				·				·						C					
350.80	A																				R	C					
360.10		R				R																	C				
360.20			R	R	A																		C				
360.30			R			R	R																R	C			
360.40	A	A			A																		R	R			
360.50		R	A		R																				C		
360.60		A			A																						
370.10	A		A		R		R																				
370.20	A		A		A																						
370.30			A																								
370.40					A																						
380.10	A	A	A	A		A	A	A				A	A					R				A	A	A			
380.20	I	I	I	I		I	I	I				I	I					I			I	I	I	I	C		

C - Product Created
A - Product Amended
R - Product Referenced
I- -Product Included as part of a compound product

Stage 3 — Definition of Requirements

This stage consists of the following steps:

Step 310: Define Required System Processing
Step 320: Develop Required Data Model
Step 330: Derive System Functions
Step 340: Enhance Required Data Model
Step 350: Develop Specification Prototypes
Step 360: Derive Processing Specification
Step 370: Confirm System Objectives
Step 380: Assemble Requirements Specification

STAGE 3 - ACTIVITY NETWORK

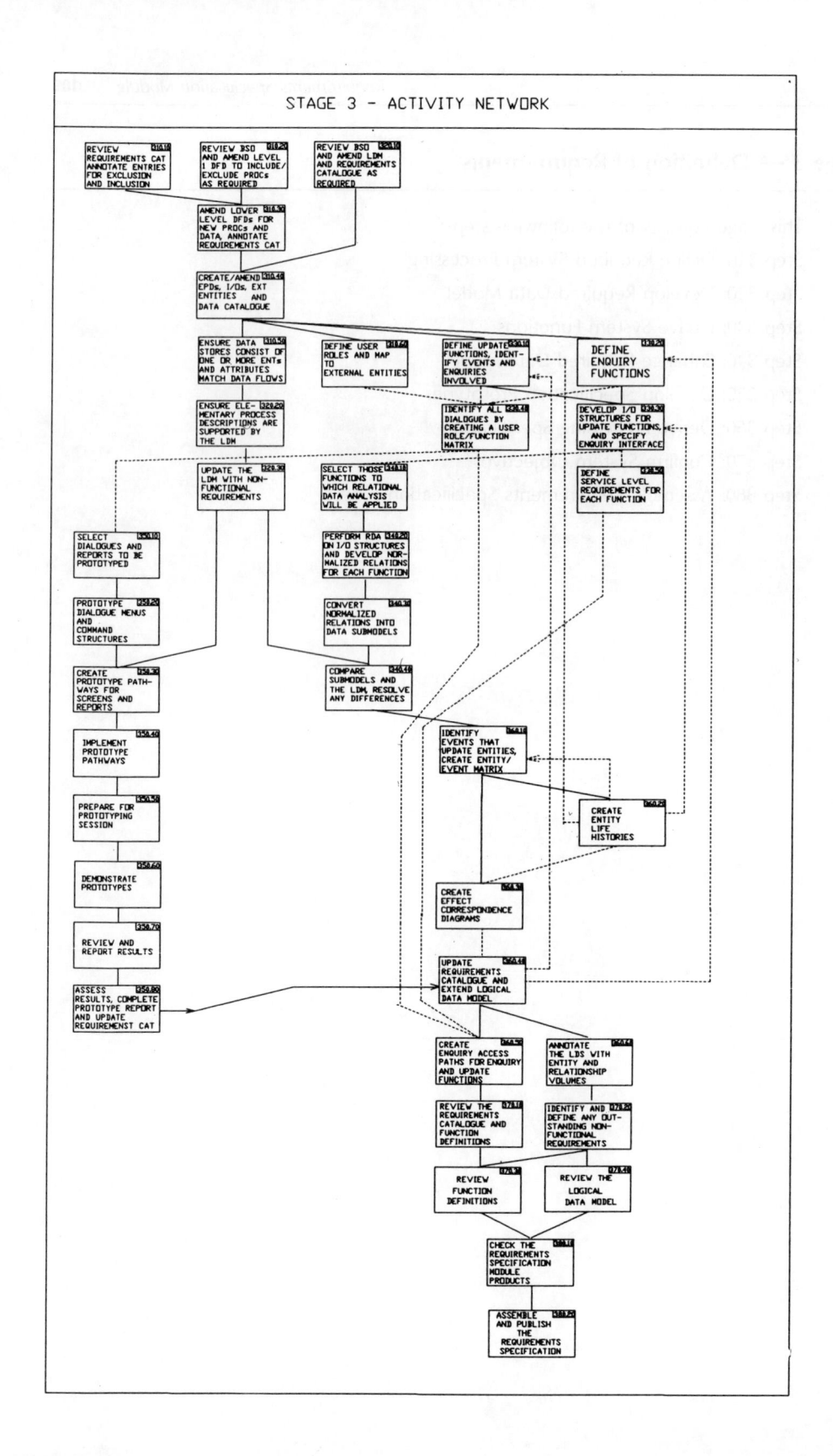

9.1 Step 310: Define Required System Processing

Objectives

- To amend the requirements to reflect the SELECTED BUSINESS SYSTEM OPTION.
- To develop an outline description of the required system in terms of system data flows.
- To define the User Roles within the new system.

Summary

This step is undertaken in parallel with Step 320: Develop Required Data Model. The LOGICAL DATA FLOW DIAGRAMS and the Requirements Catalogue are adjusted to reflect the SELECTED BUSINESS SYSTEM OPTION. The LOGICAL DATA FLOW DIAGRAMS are extended to include the additional requirements of the new system that have so far been defined in the Requirements Catalogue. Although the contents of data flows crossing the system boundary may have been documented previously, it is at this point that they must be fully defined.

References

Task 10: SELECTED BUSINESS SYSTEM OPTION

Task 20: SELECTED BUSINESS SYSTEM OPTION

Task 30: Level 1 DFD
Data Catalogue
REQUIRED SYSTEM LDM

Task 40: Lower Level DFDs
REQUIRED SYSTEM LDM

Task 50: REQUIRED SYSTEM LDM
Logical Datastore/Entity Cross-Reference

Task 60: External Entity Descriptions
User Catalogue

Products created

Task 60: User Roles

Products amended

Task 10: Requirements Catalogue

Task 20: Level 1 DFD

Task 30: Requirements Catalogue
Lower Level DFDs

Requirements Specification Module

STEP 310 – DEFINE REQUIRED SYSTEM PROCESSING

Inputs:
- Requirements Catalogue (160/20)
- Level 1 DFD (220/20)
- Lower Level DFDs (160/10)
- Selected Business System Option (160/10, 320/10)
- Data Catalogue (160/10)
- I/O Descriptions (160/10)
- Elementary Process Descriptions (160/10)
- External Entity Descriptions (160/10)
- Required System LDM (320/10)
- Logical Datastore/Entity Cross-ref (160/10)
- User Catalogue (160/10)

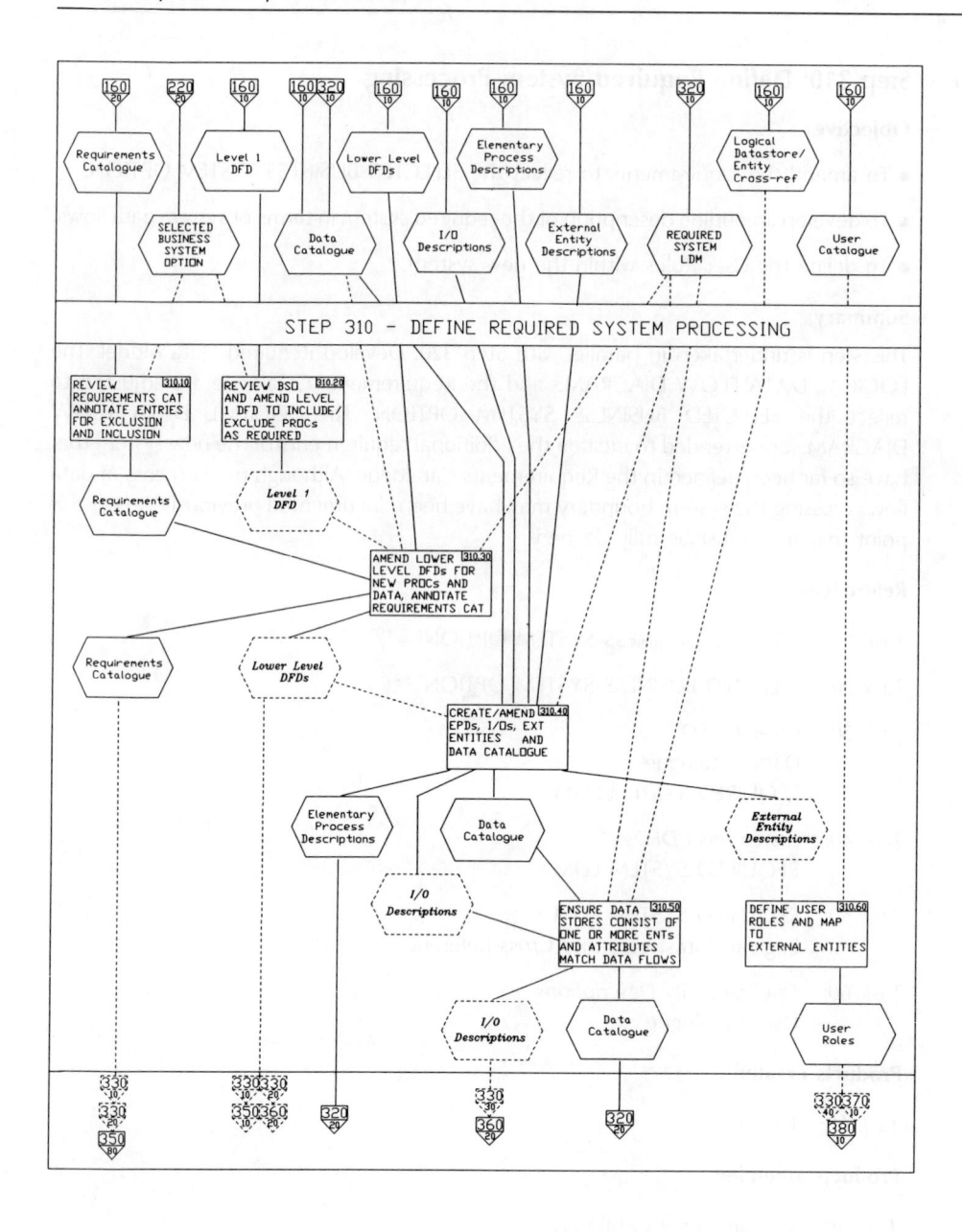

Tasks:
- 310.10 REVIEW REQUIREMENTS CAT ANNOTATE ENTRIES FOR EXCLUSION AND INCLUSION → Requirements Catalogue
- 310.20 REVIEW BSO AND AMEND LEVEL 1 DFD TO INCLUDE/EXCLUDE PROCs AS REQUIRED → Level 1 DFD
- 310.30 AMEND LOWER LEVEL DFDs FOR NEW PROCs AND DATA, ANNOTATE REQUIREMENTS CAT → Requirements Catalogue, Lower Level DFDs
- 310.40 CREATE/AMEND EPDs, I/Os, EXT ENTITIES AND DATA CATALOGUE → Elementary Process Descriptions, Data Catalogue, I/O Descriptions, External Entity Descriptions
- 310.50 ENSURE DATA STORES CONSIST OF ONE OR MORE ENts AND ATTRIBUTES MATCH DATA FLOWS → I/O Descriptions, Data Catalogue
- 310.60 DEFINE USER ROLES AND MAP TO EXTERNAL ENTITIES → User Roles

Outputs:
- 330/10, 330/10, 330/20, 330/10, 350/10, 360/20, 320/20, 330/30, 360/20, 320/20, 330/40, 370/10, 380/10

Task 40: Data Catalogue
Elementary Process Descriptions
External Entity Descriptions
I/O Descriptions

Task 50: Data Catalogue
I/O Descriptions

Techniques

Data Flow Modelling — used in Tasks 20, 30 and 40
Dialogue Design — used in Task 60
Requirements Definition — used in Task 10

Activities

Task 10

10.1 Review the Requirements Catalogue, to identify any requirements that are not part of the SELECTED BUSINESS SYSTEM OPTION. Annotate entries with reasons for their exclusion.

Task 20

20.1 Review the SELECTED BUSINESS SYSTEM OPTION and amend the *Level 1 DFD* to include any additional business processes identified in the SELECTED BUSINESS SYSTEM OPTION, and excluding processes no longer within that option.

Task 30

30.1 Amend the *Lower Level DFDs* to support new processing requirements. These may be a more detailed expression of new level 1 processes, or processes necessary to support requirements previously described in the Requirements Catalogue.

30.2 Annotate the Requirements Catalogue to describe the inclusion of new requirements in the *DATA FLOW DIAGRAMS*.

30.3 Amend the *Lower Level DFDS* to include processes to maintain new data in the REQUIRED SYSTEM LDM.

Note that this task is carried out in two phases: the first two activities use the Lower Level DFDs produced in the Requirements Analysis Module as input; the third activity uses the *Lower Level DFDs* developed in the first two activities plus the REQUIRED SYSTEM LDM developed in Step 320, Task 10.

Task 40

40.1 Create new Elementary Process Descriptions from existing Elementary Process Descriptions, amended where necessary, and for new lowest level processes on the *Lower Level DFDs*.

40.2 Create an *I/O Description* for each lowest-level data flow crossing the system boundary, using existing descriptions where appropriate, and amended if necessary.

40.4 Create *External Entity Descriptions* from existing ones where appropriate, amended as necessary, and for new external entities on the *Lower Level DFDs*.

Task 50

50.1 Ensure that each datastore consists of one or more related entity types on the REQUIRED SYSTEM LDM, and that the attributes of the entities that make up a datastore are consistent with the content of the data flows to and from that datastore. Update the Data Catalogue as required.

Task 60

60.1 Define the User Roles in the required system, and ensure that User Roles can be mapped to *External Entities* on the *REQUIRED SYSTEM DATA FLOW MODEL*.

9.2 Step 320: Develop Required Data Model

Objectives

- To develop a logical data model capable of supporting the processing in the required system.

- To define the non-functional requirements associated with the logical data model.

Summary

This step is undertaken in parallel with Step 310. The LOGICAL DATA MODEL of the current environment is extended to support the new requirements defined in the Requirements Catalogue. Only the most significant data items for each entity will have been defined in Stage 1, and it is at this step that entities and relationships are fully defined. Relevant non-functional requirements contained in the Requirements Catalogue are documented in the REQUIRED SYSTEM LDM.

References

Task 10   SELECTED BUSINESS SYSTEM OPTION
            LOGICAL DATA MODEL

Task 30: Requirements Catalogue

Products created

Task 10: REQUIRED SYSTEM LDM

Products amended

Task 10: Requirements Catalogue
            Data Catalogue

Task 20: REQUIRED SYSTEM LDM
            Data Catalogue
            Elementary Process Descriptions

Task 30: REQUIRED SYSTEM LDM
            Data Catalogue

Techniques

Logical Data Modelling — used in Tasks 10 and 30
Requirements Definition — used in Task 10

Activities

Task 10

10.1 Create the REQUIRED SYSTEM LDM by reviewing the SELECTED BUSINESS SYSTEM OPTION and prune the LOGICAL DATA MODEL to support only those aspects that are part of the SELECTED BUSINESS SYSTEM OPTION.

STEP 320 - DEVELOP REQUIRED DATA MODEL

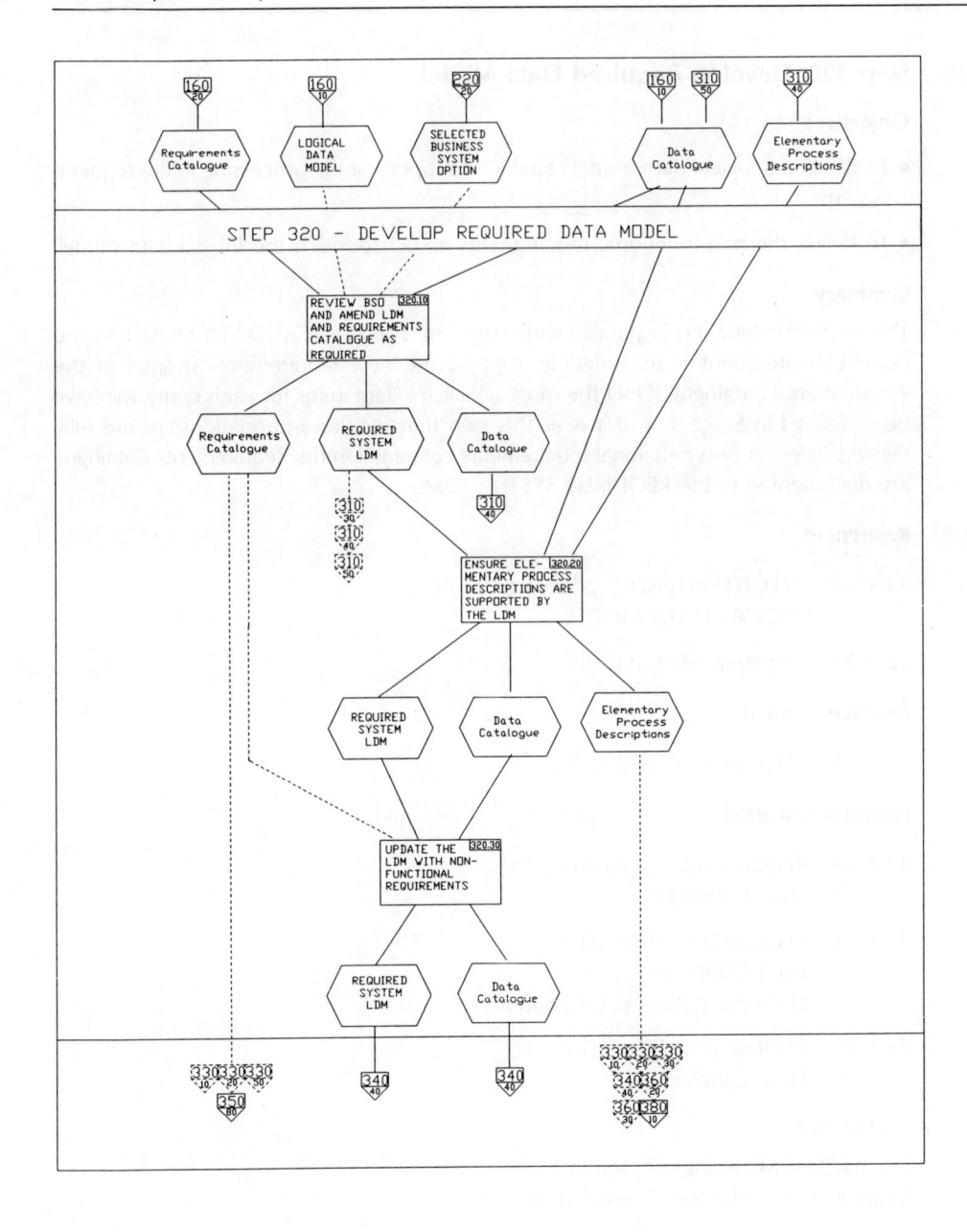

320.10 REVIEW BSO AND AMEND LDM AND REQUIREMENTS CATALOGUE AS REQUIRED

320.20 ENSURE ELEMENTARY PROCESS DESCRIPTIONS ARE SUPPORTED BY THE LDM

320.30 UPDATE THE LDM WITH NON-FUNCTIONAL REQUIREMENTS

Inputs: Requirements Catalogue (160/20), Logical Data Model (160/10), Selected Business System Option (220/20), Data Catalogue (160/10, 310/50), Elementary Process Descriptions (310/40)

Outputs: Requirements Catalogue, Required System LDM, Data Catalogue, Elementary Process Descriptions → 330/10, 330/20, 330/30, 340/40, 350/80, 340/40, 330/10, 330/20, 330/30, 340/40, 340/20, 360/30, 380/10

10.2 Extend the REQUIRED SYSTEM LDM to support the additional requirements of the new system. It is at this point that the remaining attributes associated with each entity are defined.

10.3 Update the Data Catalogue as required.

10.4 Annotate the Requirements Catalogue to reference the incorporation of new requirements.

Task 20

20.1 Verify that the Elementary Process Descriptions can be supported by the REQUIRED SYSTEM LDM. Do not document access paths formally at this step.

Task 30

30.1 Update the REQUIRED SYSTEM LDM with the non-functional requirements (including access restrictions, security requirements, archiving requirements, etc.) identified in the Requirements Catalogue.

9.3 Step 330: Derive System Functions

Objectives

- To define the FUNCTIONS of the required system, and specify the inputs to and outputs from the FUNCTIONS.
- To identify the component events and enquiries of the FUNCTIONS.
- To identify the required online dialogues.
- To define the service-level requirements for each FUNCTION.

Summary

This step initially uses the *Lower Level DFDs* and the Requirements Catalogue to identify update and enquiry FUNCTIONS. An initial list of events and the entities they affect will be identified and input to Entity Life History Analysis. Service-level requirements are defined for each function.

During the parallel definition of data and processing, additional events are identified which cause existing FUNCTIONS to be updated and new FUNCTIONS to be defined. Function Definition is not, therefore, regarded as complete until the end of Step 360: Develop Processing Specification. FUNCTIONS may be regarded as containers for information collected using other techniques throughout Stage 3 — Definition of Requirements.

Dialogue identification is carried out in this step in preparation for dialogue design in the Logical Design Stage. The Dialogues required by the user are defined and those that are critical to the success of the system are identified.

References

Task 10:   Requirements Catalogue
          Lower Level DFDs
          Elementary Process Descriptions

Task 20:   Requirements Catalogue
          Lower Level DFDs
          Elementary Process Descriptions

Task 30:   I/O Descriptions
          Elementary Process Descriptions

Task 40:   User Roles

Products created

Task 10:   Function Definitions

Task 20:   Function Definitions

Task 30:   I/O STRUCTURES

Task 40:   User Role/Function Matrix

Products amended

Task 30:   FUNCTION DEFINITIONS

Task 40:   FUNCTION DEFINITIONS

Task 50:   FUNCTION DEFINITIONS

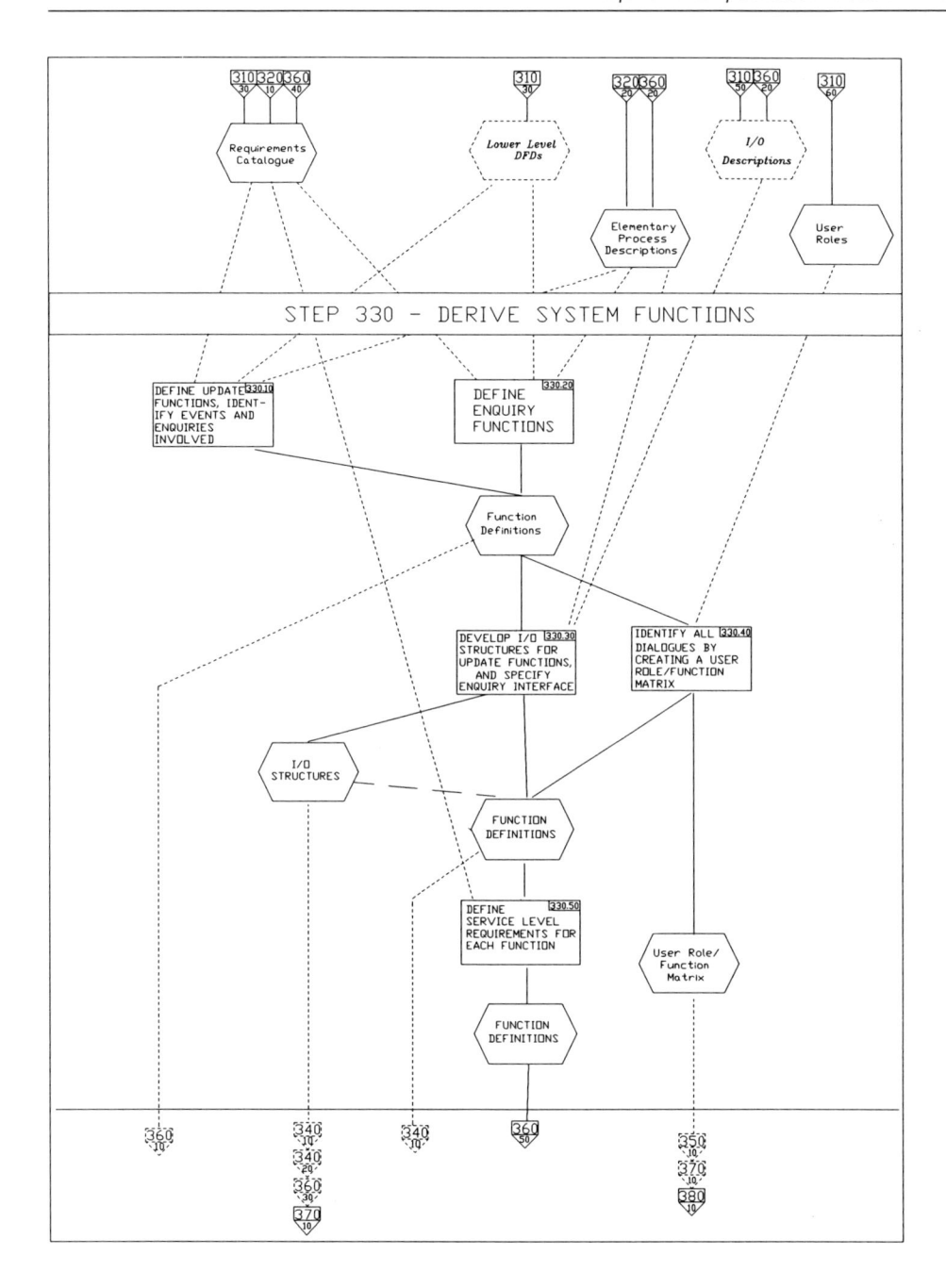

Requirements Specification Module

Techniques

Dialogue Design — used in Task 40

Function Definition — used in Tasks 10, 20, 30 and 50

Activities

Task 10

10.1 Define update functions. Initially these are identified from the *Lower Level DFDs* in consultation with the users, but additional Functions are subsequently defined as new events are identified during Entity Life History Analysis.

10.2 Ensure that all the bottom-level data flow diagram processes have been allocated to at least one Function. This activity may reveal the need for amendments to the REQUIRED SYSTEM DATA FLOW MODEL in Step 310: Define Required System Processing.

10.3 Identify the Events and enquiries contained within each update Function.

Task 20

20.1 Define enquiry Functions. These are identified from the Requirements Catalogue, from the *Lower Level DFDs* or directly from users.

Task 30

30.1 Specify the user interface for each FUNCTION, as I/O STRUCTURES. *I/O Descriptions* supporting the *DATA FLOW DIAGRAMS* are the basis for the interface specification for update FUNCTIONS. The enquiry interface is specified in consultation with the users for those enquiries that have not been included on the *DATA FLOW DIAGRAMS*.

Note that, if the FUNCTION consists of the processing to respond to more than one event, then an I/O STRUCTURE is created for the processing for each event. Further, separate I/O STRUCTURES are created for enquiries that are not part of an update FUNCTION.

Note also that, in Tasks 10 and 20, functions are depicted as elementary products. It is not until this task that they are fully developed by the creation and inclusion of I/O STRUCTURES, and thereby become compound products.

Task 40

40.1 Identify the required system Dialogues by cross-referencing the User Roles and the FUNCTIONS on the User Role/Function Matrix.

40.2 Identify those Dialogues that are critical to the success of the required system.

Task 50

50.1 Define the service-level requirements for each FUNCTION.

9.4 Step 340: Enhance Required Data Model

Objective

- To improve the quality of the REQUIRED SYSTEM LDM by the application of Relational Data Analysis.

Summary

This step uses the Relational Data Analysis technique to validate the REQUIRED SYSTEM LDM produced in Step 320.

The input and output data items are specified for each FUNCTION in Step 330, and these specifications are used as the sources for Relational Data Analysis. Only a selection of the system's FUNCTIONS are used, as it is unnecessary and impractical to normalize all inputs and outputs. The *Normalized Relations* are used to build individual *Data Submodels* which are then compared to the existing REQUIRED SYSTEM LDM. The resolution of structural differences is a matter of judgement, based on a knowledge of the present and likely future processing requirements. In many cases, the optimum structure may not be achieved until after Entity Life History Analysis.

References

Task 10: FUNCTION DEFINITIONS
         I/O STRUCTURES

Task 20: Selected Functions
         I/O STRUCTURES

Task 30: Normalized Relations

Task 40: Data Submodels
         Elementary Process Descriptions

Products created

Task 10: Selected Functions

Task 20: Normalized Relations

Task 30: Data Submodels

Products amended

Task 40: REQUIRED SYSTEM LDM
         Data Catalogue

Techniques

Logical Data Modelling — used in Tasks 30 and 40
Relational Data Analysis — used in Task 20

Activities

Task 10

10.1 Compile a list of the *Selected Functions* whose I/O STRUCTURES are to have relational data analysis applied.

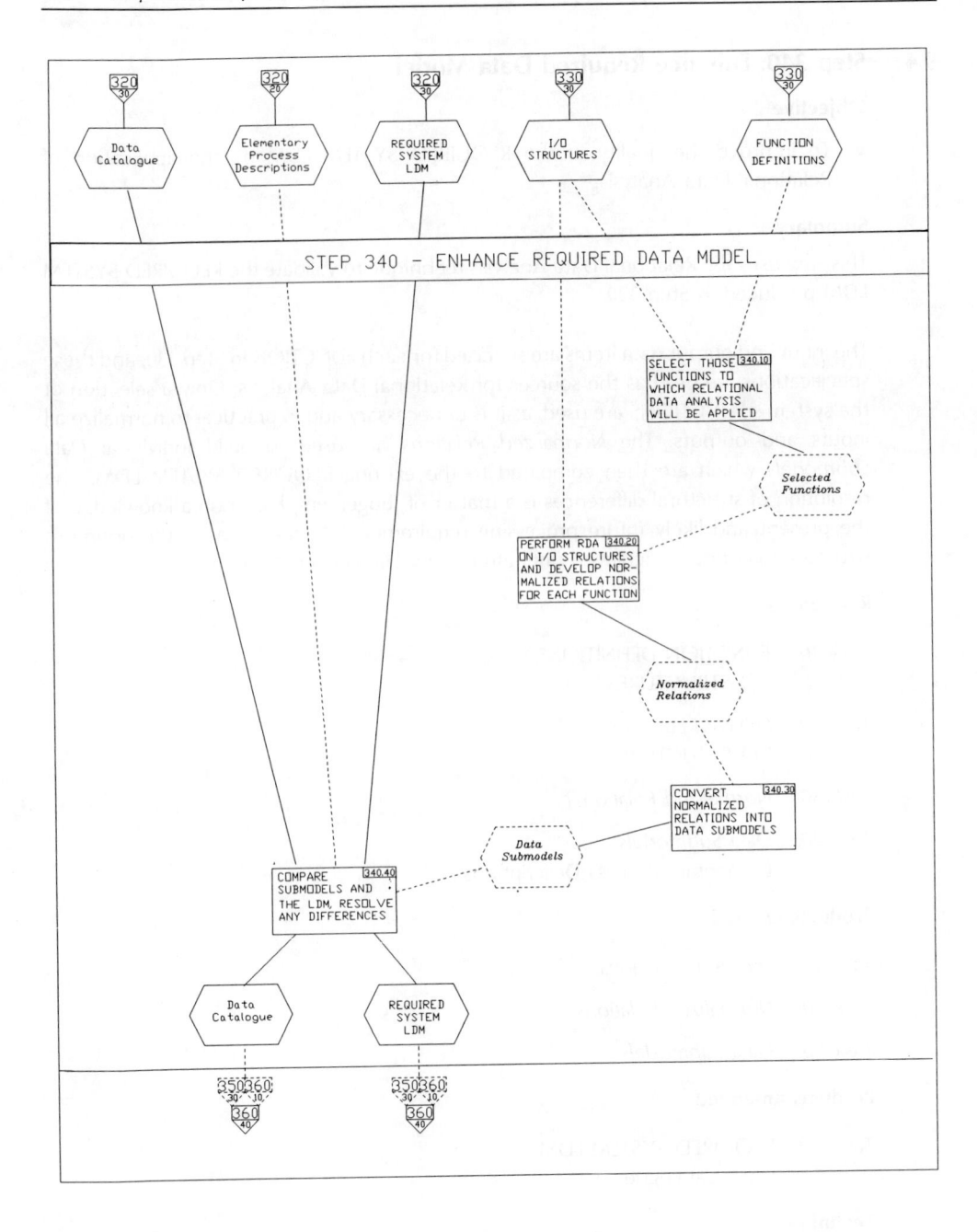

122 *Requirements Specification Module*

Task 20

20.1 Perform relational data analysis on the I/O STRUCTURES and develop a set of *Normalized Relations* for each *Selected Function*.

Task 30

30.1 Convert the *Normalized Relations* for each *Selected Function* into a logical data model-style *Data Submodel*.

Task 40

40.1 Compare the *Data Submodels* with the appropriate part of the REQUIRED SYSTEM LDM. If features of the submodel are not present on the REQUIRED SYSTEM LDM, resolve the differences by reference to the Elementary Process Descriptions and the users, and selectively update the REQUIRED SYSTEM LDM with new entities and relationships.

9.5 Step 350: Develop Specification Prototypes

Objectives

- To identify errors in the REQUIREMENTS SPECIFICATION, so that they may be eliminated in advance of detailed design.
- To establish additional presentational requirements for the user interface.

Summary

Specification prototyping is used to describe selected parts of the REQUIREMENTS SPECIFICATION in an animated form, for demonstration to the users. The purpose of the prototyping is not to incrementally develop a working version of the system, but to demonstrate that the requirements have been properly understood and to establish additional requirements concerning the style of the I/O interface.

The scope of the prototyping exercise, the detailed objectives, and how it is to be controlled, are specified by the Project Management in the Prototyping Scope document. Menus and Command Structures are developed for selected User Roles, the remainder being completed during Step 510: Define Dialogues. The prototypes of the individual dialogues (*Prototype Pathways*) are regarded as disposable, with the results of the activity being included in the Requirements Catalogue and an improved REQUIREMENTS SPECIFICATION. There is a strong interaction between this step and Step 330: Derive System Functions.

References

Task 10:   FUNCTION DEFINITIONS
Prototyping Scope
User Role/Function Matrix
REQUIRED SYSTEM LDM
Data Catalogue

Task 20:   Installation Style Guide
Selected Dialogues and Reports

Task 30:   Data Catalogue
REQUIRED SYSTEM LDM
Menu Structures
Command Structures
I/O STRUCTURES
Installation Style Guide
Selected Dialogues and Reports

Task 40:   Prototype Pathways
Logical Grouping of Dialogue Elements

Task 60:   Prototype Demonstration Objective Document

Task 80:   Prototype Result Log

Products created

Task 10:   Selected Dialogues and Reports

Requirements Specification Module

STEP 350 – DEVELOP SPECIFICATION PROTOTYPES

Inputs:
- I/O Structures (330)
- Installation Style Guide (340)
- Required System LDM (340)
- Data Catalogue (340)
- Prototyping Scope (330)
- Function Definitions (330)
- User Role/Function Matrix (330)
- Requirements Catalogue (320)

Tasks:
- 350.10 SELECT DIALOGUES AND REPORTS TO BE PROTOTYPED
  - → Selected Dialogues and Reports
- 350.20 PROTOTYPE DIALOGUE MENUS AND COMMAND STRUCTURES
  - → Menu Structures
  - → Command Structures
- 350.30 CREATE PROTOTYPE PATHWAYS FOR SCREENS AND REPORTS
  - → Prototype Pathways
  - → Logical Grouping of Dialogue Elements
- 350.40 IMPLEMENT PROTOTYPE PATHWAYS
- 350.50 PREPARE FOR PROTOTYPING SESSION
  - → Prototype Demonstration Objective Document
- 350.60 DEMONSTRATE PROTOTYPES
- 350.70 REVIEW AND REPORT RESULTS
  - → Prototype Result Log
- 350.80 ASSESS RESULTS, COMPLETE PROTOTYPE REPORT AND UPDATE REQUIREMENTS CAT
  - → Requirements Catalogue
  - → Prototype Report

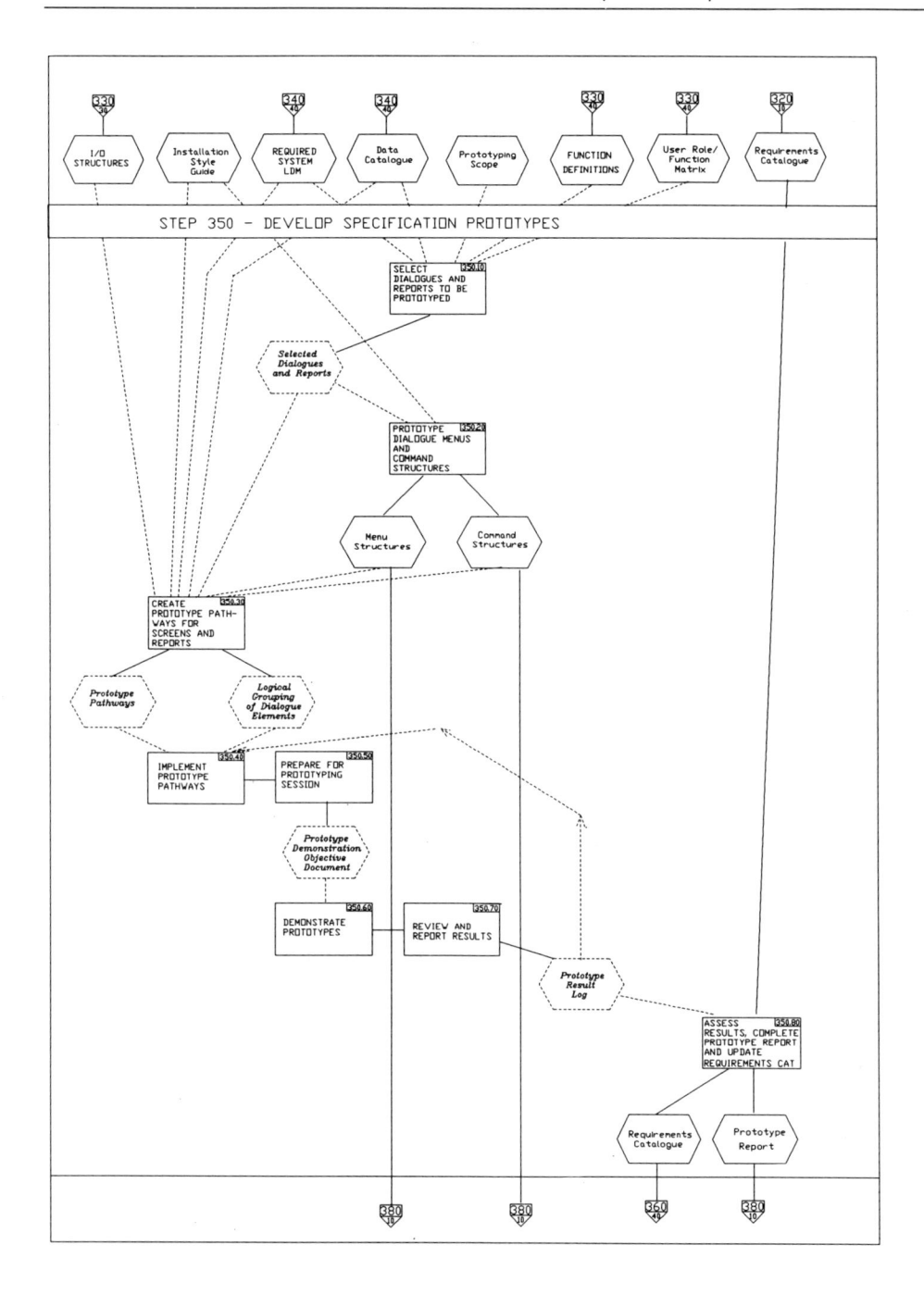

Outputs to: 380, 380, 360, 380

Task 20: Menu Structures
Command Structures

Task 30: Logical Grouping of Dialogue Elements
Prototype Pathways

Task 50: Prototype Demonstration Objective Document

Task 70: Prototype Result Log

Task 80: Prototype Report

Products amended

Task 80: Requirements Catalogue

Techniques

Dialogue Design — used in Task 30
Specification Prototyping — used in Tasks 20, 40, 50, 60, 70 and 80
Requirements Definition — used in Task 80

Activities

Task 10

10.1 Create a list of *Selected Dialogues and Reports* to be prototyped by reviewing the User Role/Function Matrix, FUNCTION DEFINITIONS, REQUIRED SYSTEM LDM and Data Catalogue, based on the criteria in the Prototyping Scope.

Task 20

20.1 Prototype Menu Structures and Command Structures for the User Roles specified in the Prototyping Scope. These will include as a minimum the *Selected Dialogues and Reports* identified in Task 10, but may well have to include others to make the Menu and Command Structures appear realistic.

20.2 Demonstrate the prototypes to the nominated users for the appropriate User Role.

20.3 Modify the prototypes and demonstrate as necessary.

Task 30

30.1 Identify the *Logical Grouping of Dialogue Elements* on the I/O STRUCTURES for the dialogues to be prototyped.

30.2 Identify the report components to be prototyped.

30.3 Create *Prototype Pathways* by combining the *Logical Grouping of Dialogue Elements* and report components with the menu structures.

Tasks 40–70 are performed at least once for each *Prototype Pathway*, but may be repeated depending on the results of the demonstration sessions.

Task 40

40.1 Implement the *Prototype Pathway* using the selected prototyping tool.

Task 50

50.1 Prepare for the prototyping session with users by creating a *Prototype Demonstration Objective Document*.

Task 60

60.1 Demonstrate the prototypes to the nominated users for the appropriate User Role.

Task 70

70.1 Review the prototyping session and write up the results in a *Prototype Result Log*.

70.2 Report on the results of the session and decide whether it is necessary to make any amendments to the *Prototype Pathways* and redemonstrate them.

Task 80

80.1 Assess the results of prototyping and highlight identified errors in, or required changes to, any of the products of the REQUIREMENTS SPECIFICATION. Define the user interface requirements established during the prototyping in the Requirements Catalogue.

80.2 Complete the Prototype Report on the results of the prototyping sessions.

9.6 Step 360: Develop Processing Specification

Objectives

- To develop a more detailed view of how the required system will work.
- To define the database update processes.
- To define the database access requirements of enquiry functions.

Summary

This step is principally concerned with defining the detailed update and enquiry processing for the required system, previously only described in outline by the data flow diagrams. Logical Data Modelling and Entity–Event Modelling are the major analysis and design tools in SSADM, leading the analyst to a thorough and more detailed understanding of the system. Entity–Event Modelling as an analysis tool raises detailed questions about how the system is to work, and in doing so completes the Logical Data Model. As a design tool it produces, via the Effect Correspondence Technique, a specification of the database update processing, which is completed in the Logical Design Stage.

An initial set of events is identified during Step 330: Derive System Functions. Since further events are identified during this step, these may result in the creation of new functions or the modification of existing functions. The database access requirements for each enquiry function, and the data volumes, are also specified in this step.

References

Task 10: Function Definitions
REQUIRED SYSTEM LDM

Task 20: Lower Level DFDs
Entity/Event Matrix
Elementary Process Descriptions

Task 30: I/O STRUCTURES
Entity/Event Matrix
Entity Life Histories
REQUIRED SYSTEM LDM
Elementary Process Descriptions

Task 40: Entity Life Histories
Effect Correspondence Diagrams

Task 50: REQUIRED SYSTEM LDM
Data Catalogue

Products created

Task 10: Entity/Event Matrix

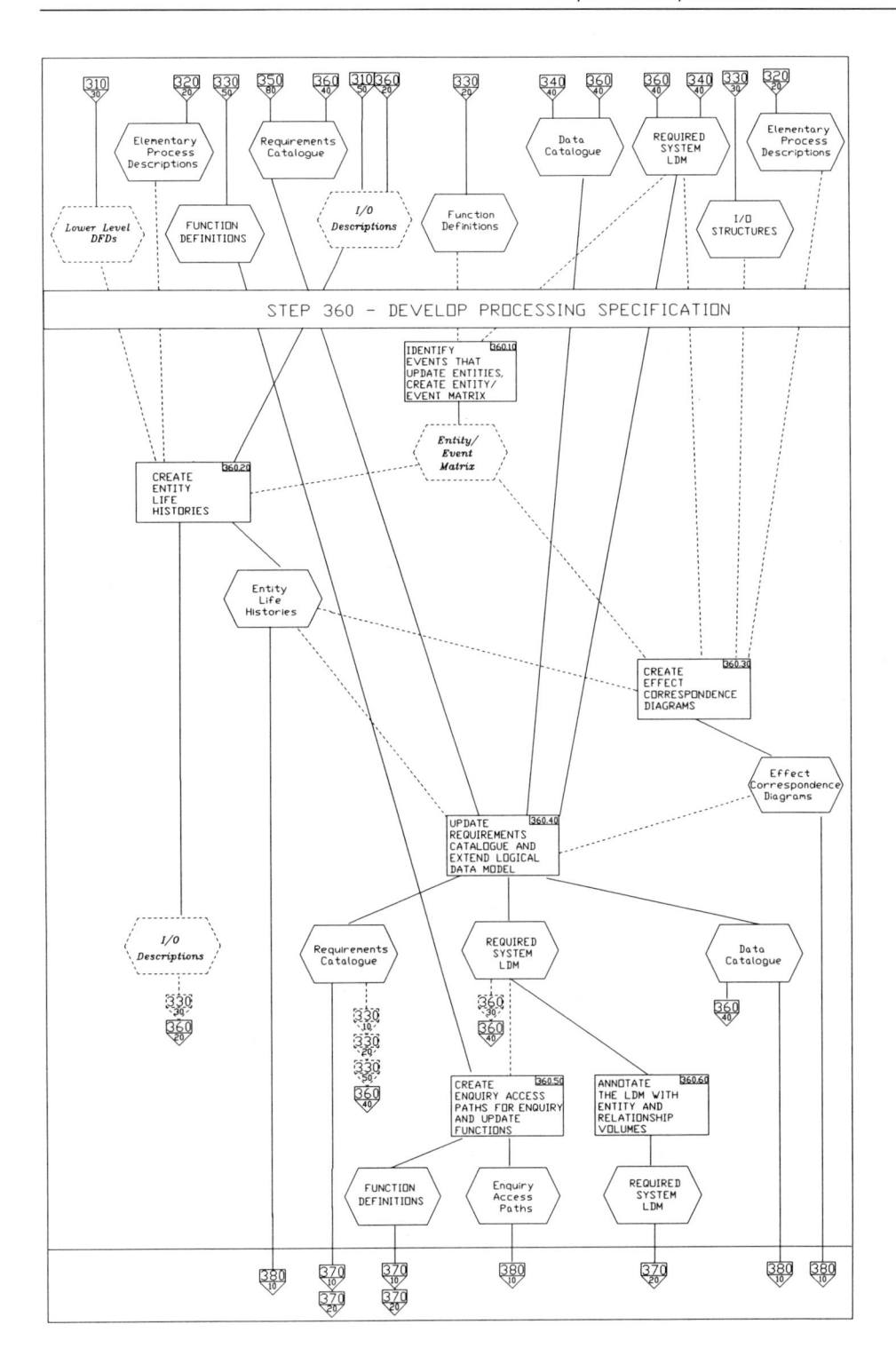

Requirements Specification Module

STEP 360 – DEVELOP PROCESSING SPECIFICATION

Task 20: Entity Life Histories

Task 30: Effect Correspondence Diagrams

Task 50: Enquiry Access Paths

Products amended

Task 20: *I/O Descriptions*

Task 40: Requirements Catalogue
Data Catalogue
REQUIRED SYSTEM LDM

Task 50: FUNCTION DEFINITIONS

Task 60: REQUIRED SYSTEM LDM
Data Catalogue

Techniques

Entity–Event Modelling — used in Tasks 20 and 30
Logical Data Modelling — used in Tasks 40 and 50

Activities

Task 10

10.1 Working from the bottom of the REQUIRED SYSTEM LDM to the top, for each entity identify the events that have an updating effect upon that entity. Function Definition will have identified a startup set of events.

Tasks 20 to 40 are concurrent activities.

Task 20

20.1 Working from the bottom of the REQUIRED SYSTEM LDM to the top, create 'simple' Entity Life Histories.

20.2 Modify the Entity Life Histories to resolve parallelism.

20.3 Working from the top of the REQUIRED SYSTEM LDM to the bottom, extend the Entity Life Histories to include abnormal death events, reversion events, and events which affect relationships to related entities. Add and maintain operations on the Entity Life Histories as they are developed.

20.4 Document each new event identified as an *I/O Description*.

Task 30

30.1 Create an Effect Correspondence Diagram for each event.

30.2 Ensure that the input data items required by the event are included in the *I/O Description* for that event.

Task 40

40.1 Update the Requirements Catalogue with the new requirements identified during the Entity Life History Analysis, and with references to other specification products for those requirements that have been integrated.

40.2 Extend the REQUIRED SYSTEM LDM to include the new or redefined entities, and update the Data Catalogue as required.

Functions are defined or redefined in Step 330: Derive System Functions, for additional events identified in this step.

Task 50

50.1 Create an Enquiry Access Path for each enquiry function (either standalone or as part of an update function), and update the FUNCTION DEFINITION to refer to it.

Task 60

60.1 Annotate the REQUIRED SYSTEM LDM with entity and relationship volumes.

9.7 Step 370: Confirm System Objectives

Objectives

- To confirm that requirements are fully addressed in the REQUIREMENTS SPECIFICATION.
- To ensure that the functional requirements are associated with objective measures of how well that facility should be provided.
- To confirm that non-functional requirements have been identified and are fully described.

Summary

During Stages 1 and 3 the requirements will have been recorded, as they are identified, in the Requirements Catalogue. This step represents the final review of the requirements before the completion of the REQUIREMENTS SPECIFICATION that will be the basis for the development of *Technical System Options*.

Referring to the User Roles and User Role/Function Matrix, the Requirements Catalogue, FUNCTION DEFINITIONS and the REQUIRED SYSTEM LDM are checked to ensure that they provide a fully documented expression of requirements, and that the functional requirements have been incorporated in appropriate REQUIREMENTS SPECIFICATION products. Non-functional requirements are defined in Step 320 and Step 330. This step confirms that all the non-functional requirements have been defined and properly addressed.

References

Task 10:   User Roles and User Role/Function Matrix

Products amended

Task 10:   FUNCTION DEFINITIONS
             Requirements Catalogue

Task 20:   FUNCTION DEFINITIONS
             Requirements Catalogue
             REQUIRED SYSTEM LDM

Task 30:   FUNCTION DEFINITIONS

Task 40:   REQUIRED SYSTEM LDM

Techniques

Function Definition — used in Tasks 10, 20 and 30
Logical Data Modelling — used in Task 40
Requirements Definition — used in Tasks 10 and 20

Activities

Task 10

10.1 Referring to the User Roles and User Role/Function Matrix, review the Requirements Catalogue and ensure that each functional and non-functional requirement is fully defined.

Requirements Specification Module

STEP 370 – CONFIRM SYSTEM OBJECTIVES

Inputs:
- 330/40 User Role/Function Matrix
- 310/60 User Roles
- 360/50 FUNCTION DEFINITIONS
- 360/40 Requirements Catalogue
- 360/60 REQUIRED SYSTEM LDM

Tasks:
- 370.10 REVIEW THE REQUIREMENTS CATALOGUE AND FUNCTION DEFINITIONS
- 370.20 IDENTIFY AND DEFINE ANY OUTSTANDING NON-FUNCTIONAL REQUIREMENTS
- 370.30 REVIEW FUNCTION DEFINITIONS
- 370.40 REVIEW THE LOGICAL DATA MODEL

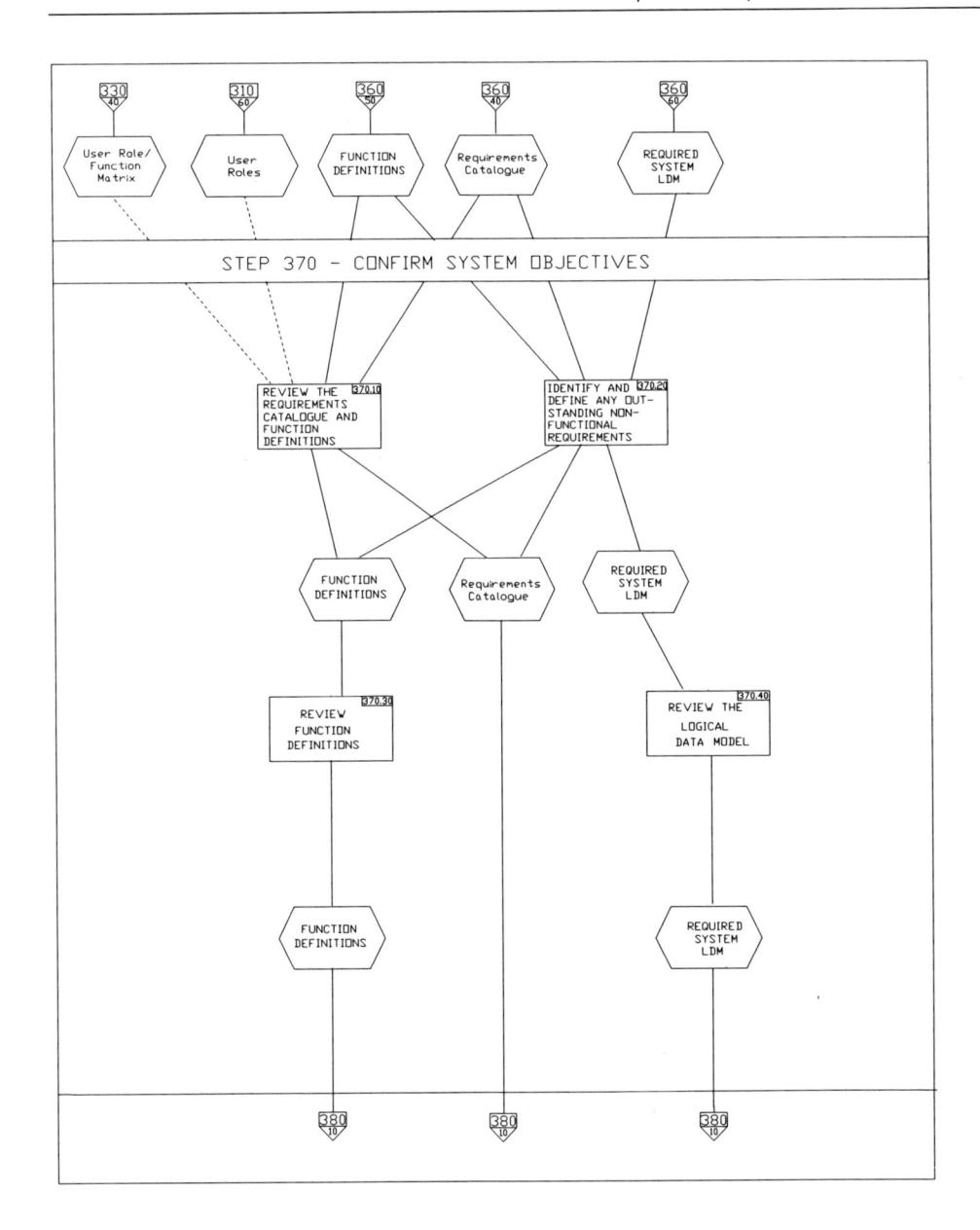

Intermediate products:
- FUNCTION DEFINITIONS
- Requirements Catalogue
- REQUIRED SYSTEM LDM

Outputs:
- FUNCTION DEFINITIONS → 380/10
- Requirements Catalogue → 380/10
- REQUIRED SYSTEM LDM → 380/10

10.2 Check that each functional requirement is satisfied in the REQUIREMENTS SPECIFICATION, and that the requirement is referenced to the appropriate specification element.

Task 20

20.1 Identify any outstanding non-functional requirements and define them in the Requirements Catalogue, FUNCTION DEFINITIONS and/or REQUIRED SYSTEM LDM.

Task 30

30.1 Review the FUNCTION DEFINITIONS to ensure that each function is fully defined, including objective measures and service-level requirements.

Task 40

40.1 Review the REQUIRED SYSTEM LDM and ensure that all relevant non-functional requirements are included, with appropriate objective measures.

9.8 Step 380: Assemble Requirements Specification

Objectives

- To ensure the integrity of the products describing the REQUIREMENTS SPECIFICATION.
- To assemble and publish the REQUIREMENTS SPECIFICATION.

Summary

This step is the completion of the Requirements Specification Module and is concerned with checking the consistency of the products of the module and assembling them into the REQUIREMENTS SPECIFICATION.

Each of the SSADM steps represents a transformation which takes a starting set of products, performs some tasks, and applies quality control to produce a target set of products. Quality management procedures are not part of SSADM, but each of the SSADM products that transports information between steps has quality criteria defined as part of the Product Description (Dictionary Volume). These quality criteria are only those that can be applied to the individual products. The cross-checking of products for consistency is part of this step. The review methods to be used are defined within the quality management procedures.

This step also publishes the formal REQUIREMENTS SPECIFICATION document.

References

Task 10:   SELECTED BUSINESS SYSTEM OPTION
           Prototype Report

Products created

Task 20:   REQUIREMENTS SPECIFICATION

Products amended

Task 10:   Data Catalogue
           Menu Structures
           Command Structures
           Effect Correspondence Diagrams
           Entity Life Histories
           Enquiry Access Paths
           FUNCTION DEFINITIONS
           I/O STRUCTURES
           REQUIRED SYSTEM LDM
           Elementary Process Descriptions
           Requirements Catalogue
           User Roles
           User Role/Function Matrix

Products included

Task 20:   Prototype Report
           Data Catalogue

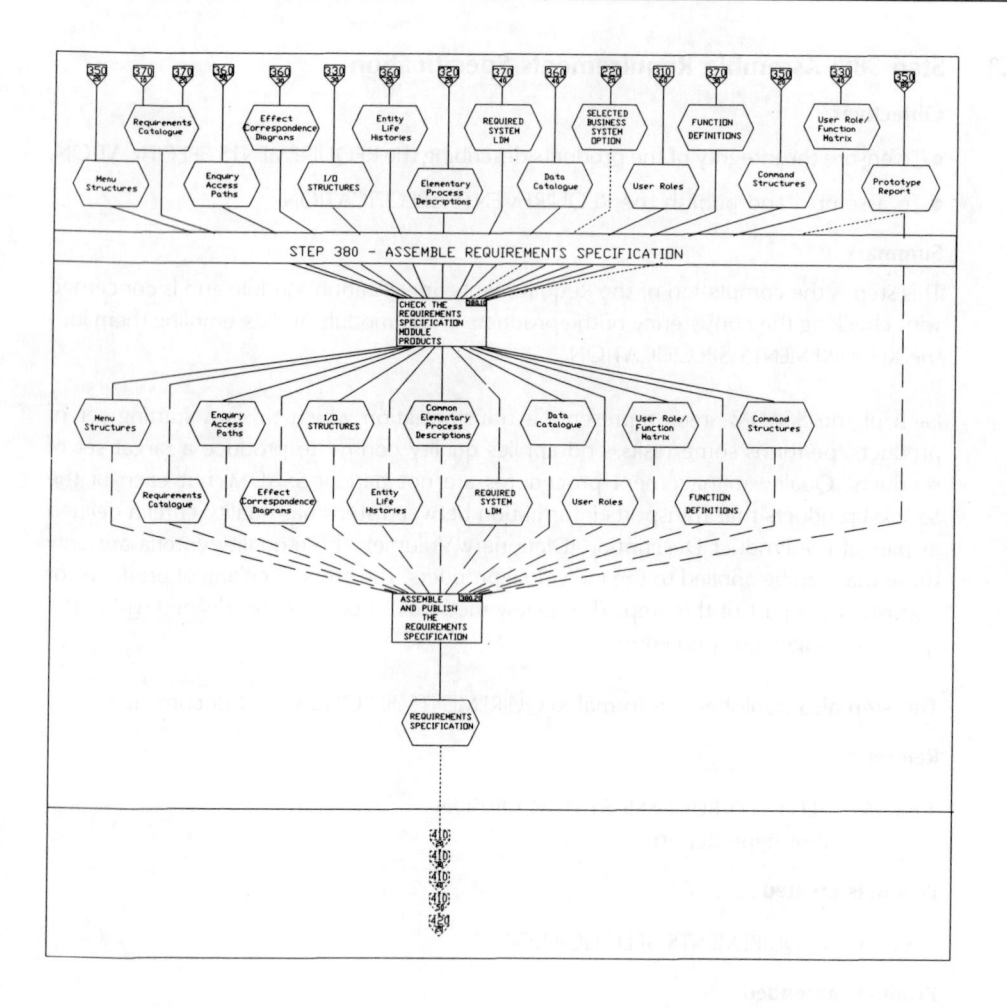

136 *Requirements Specification Module*

STEP 380 – ASSEMBLE REQUIREMENTS SPECIFICATION

>Command Structures
>Menu Structures
>Effect Correspondence Diagrams
>Entity Life Histories
>Enquiry Access Paths
>FUNCTION DEFINITIONS
>I/O STRUCTURES
>REQUIRED SYSTEM LDM
>Requirements Catalogue
>Elementary Process Descriptions
>(for common processes only)
>User Roles
>User Role/Function Matrix

Techniques

None

Activities

Task 10

10.1 Referring to the SELECTED BUSINESS SYSTEM OPTION and the Prototype Report, review the completeness and consistency of the components of the REQUIREMENTS SPECIFICATION, viz:
>Data Catalogue
>Menu Structures
>Command Structures
>Effect Correspondence Diagrams
>Entity Life Histories
>Enquiry Access Paths
>FUNCTION DEFINITIONS
>I/O STRUCTURES
>REQUIRED SYSTEM LDM
>Elementary Process Descriptions
>Requirements Catalogue
>User Roles
>User Role/Function Matrix

Taking each functional requirement in turn from the Requirements Catalogue, check that its entry is complete and consistent. In particular, check that the Resolution element refers to at least one FUNCTION DEFINITION. Check that the FUNCTION DEFINITIONS referred to are complete, and that the elements of the REQUIREMENTS SPECIFICATION referred to are complete, consistent, and fully supported by the REQUIRED SYSTEM LDM.

10.2 Check each FUNCTION DEFINITION to ensure that it refers to a functional requirement in the Requirements Catalogue.

10.3 Taking each non-functional requirement in turn from the Requirements Catalogue, check that its entry is complete and consistent. In particular, check that the Related

Requirements entry refers to one or more functional requirements, or if not, ensure that the requirement clearly describes what aspect of the system it refers to.

10.4 Amend the REQUIREMENTS SPECIFICATION products, if necessary, as a result of the reviews.

Task 20

20.1 Assemble and publish the REQUIREMENTS SPECIFICATION in accordance with the organization's standards, including the following products:
   Prototype Report
   Data Catalogue
   Menu Structures
   Command Structures
   Effect Correspondence Diagrams
   Entity Life Histories
   Enquiry Access Paths
   FUNCTION DEFINITIONS
   I/O STRUCTURES
   REQUIRED SYSTEM LDM
   Elementary Process Descriptions
   (for common processes only)
   Requirements Catalogue
   User Roles
   User Role/Function Matrix

Note that, although throughout this stage reference has been made to the Elementary Process Descriptions, theoretically it is only the Common Elementary Process Descriptions that are deliverable products from the module.

10 Logical System Specification Module

This module consists of two stages: Stage 4 — Technical System Options and Stage 5 — Logical Design, that together produce the LOGICAL SYSTEM SPECIFICATION.

Stage 4 produces the TECHNICAL ENVIRONMENT DESCRIPTION, the SELECTED TECHNICAL SYSTEM OPTION and the Application Style Guide.

Stage 5 produces the LOGICAL DESIGN.

Note that the LOGICAL SYSTEM SPECIFICATION is a compound product that consists only of its constituent parts. In practice, an end-of-module management report will be required that provides an overview of the LOGICAL SYSTEM SPECIFICATION.

SSADM VERSION 4 - LOGICAL SYSTEM SPECIFICATION MODULE (Stages 4 and 5) - PRODUCT BREAKDOWN STRUCTURE

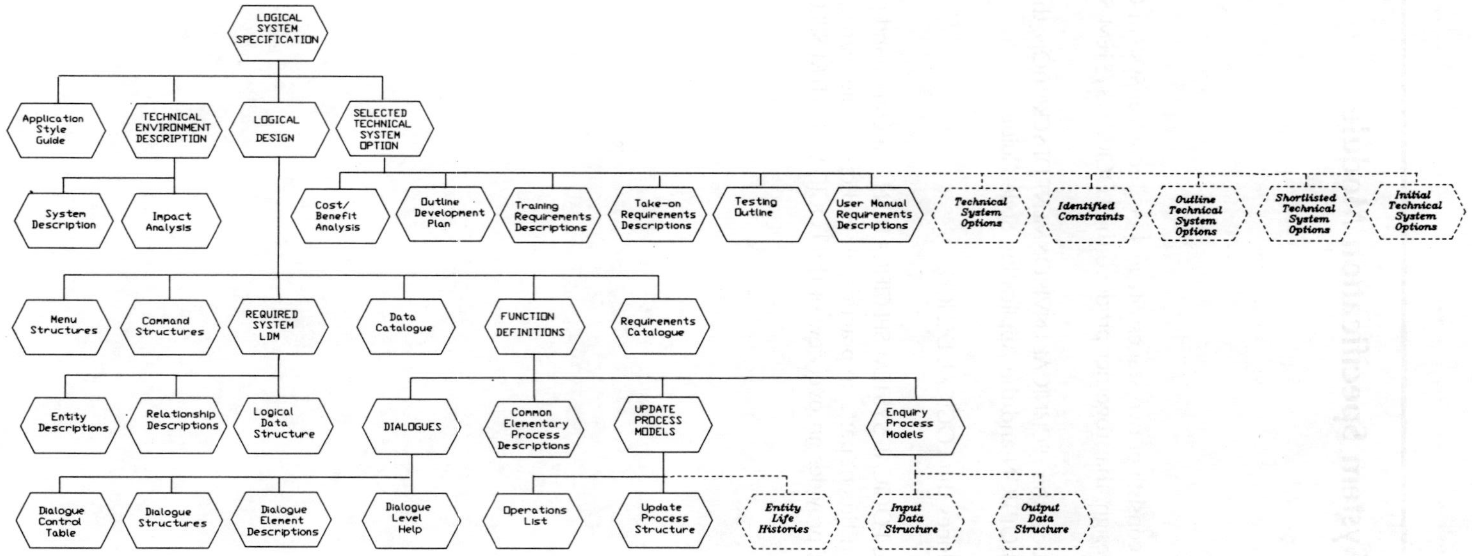

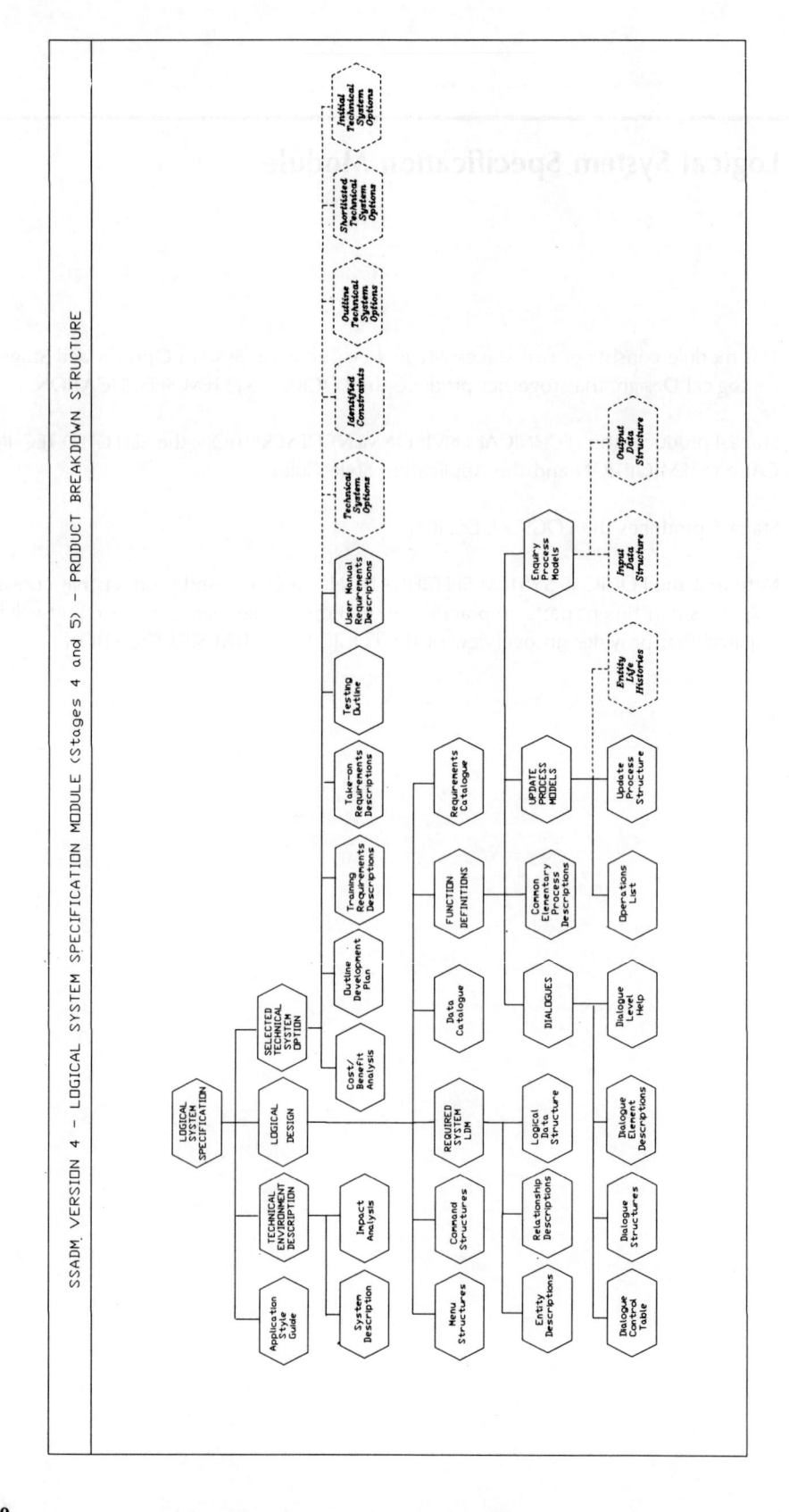

Logical System Specification Module

SSADM VERSION 4 – LOGICAL SYSTEM SPECIFICATION MODULE (Stages 4 and 5) – TASK/PRODUCT MATRIX

Task	Identified Constraints	Outline Technical System Options	Shortlisted Technical System Options	Initial Technical System Options	Technical System Options	SELECTED TECHNICAL SYSTEM OPTION	TECHNICAL ENVIRONMENT DESCRIPTION	Application Style Guide	Dialogue Element Descriptions	Dialogue Structures	Menu Structures	Command Structures	Dialogue Control Table	Dialogue Level Help	Requirements Catalogue	Data Catalogue	Entity Life Histories	Update Process Structure	Operations List	UPDATE PROCESS MODELS	Input Data Structure	Output Data Structure	Enquiry Process Models	FUNCTION DEFINITIONS	REQUIRED SYSTEM LDM	Common Elementary Process Descriptions	LOGICAL DESIGN	LOGICAL SYSTEM SPECIFICATION
410.10	C													R														
410.20	R	C																										
410.30		R	C																									
410.40			R	C																								
410.50			A																									
410.60			A	C																								
420.10				R	C																							
420.20				A	C																							
420.30				R	R																							
420.40					R	C																						
510.10						C	C													R		R						
510.20						R		C																				
510.30						R	C/A	C/A																				
510.40								R	R	C	R																	
520.10																A												
520.20																C						R						
520.30																R	C					R						
520.40																A	A											
520.50																A	C											
530.10																		C				R						
530.20																			C									
530.30																		R	R	C								
530.40																				A								
530.50																				A								
540.10					A	A	A	A	A	A	A					A			A	A	A	A	C					
540.20				I	I	I	I	I	I	I	I	I				I			I	I	I	I		C				

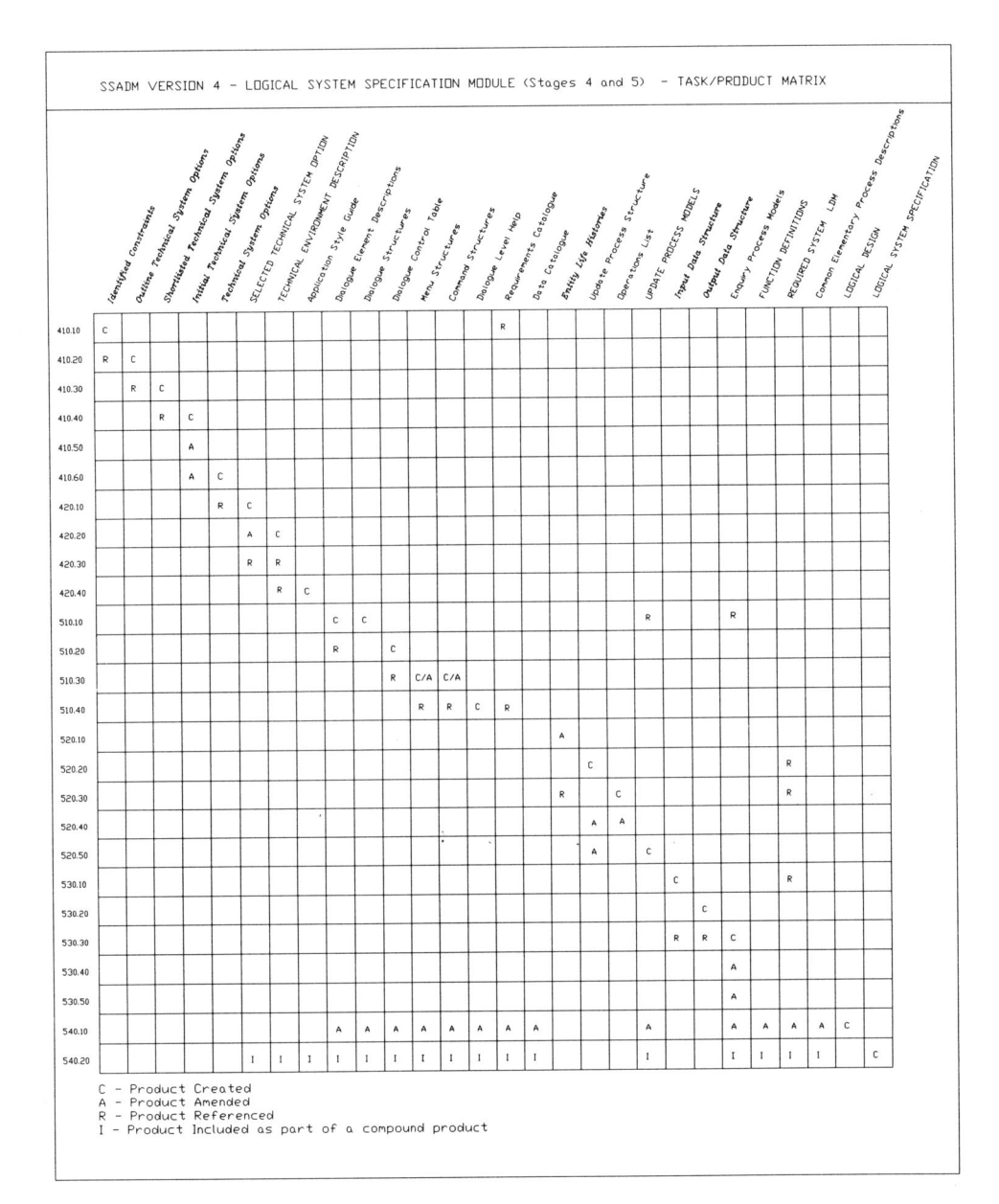

C – Product Created
A – Product Amended
R – Product Referenced
I – Product Included as part of a compound product

Stage 4 — Technical System Options

This stage consists of the following steps:
> Step 410: Define Technical System Options
> Step 420: Select Technical System Option

Logical System Specification Module

```
┌─────────────────────────────────────────────────────────────┐
│           SSADM VERSION 4 - STAGE 4 ACTIVITY NETWORK        │
│                                                             │
│                    ┌─────────────┐ 410.10                   │
│                    │ IDENTIFY ALL│                          │
│                    │ THE CONSTRA-│                          │
│                    │ INTS THAT   │                          │
│                    │ THE TSOs    │                          │
│                    │ MUST SATISFY│                          │
│                    └──────┬──────┘                          │
│                           │                                 │
│                    ┌──────┴──────┐ 410.20                   │
│                    │ DEFINE UP TO│                          │
│                    │ SIX OUTLINE │                          │
│                    │ TECHNICAL   │                          │
│                    │ SYSTEM      │                          │
│                    │ OPTIONS     │                          │
│                    └──────┬──────┘                          │
│                           │                                 │
│                    ┌──────┴──────┐ 410.30                   │
│                    │ DISCUSS WITH│                          │
│                    │ USERS AND   │                          │
│                    │ PRODUCE A   │                          │
│                    │ SHORT-LIST  │                          │
│                    │ OF TWO TO   │                          │
│                    │ THREE OPTS. │                          │
│                    └──────┬──────┘                          │
│                           │                                 │
│                    ┌──────┴──────┐ 410.40                   │
│                    │ DEVELOP     │                          │
│                    │ INITIAL     │                          │
│                    │ TECHNICAL   │                          │
│                    │ SYSTEM      │                          │
│                    │ OPTIONS     │                          │
│                    └──────┬──────┘                          │
│                           │                                 │
│                    ┌──────┴──────┐ 410.50                   │
│                    │ ASSESS      │                          │
│                    │ CAPACITY    │                          │
│                    │ PLANNING    │                          │
│                    │ INFORMATION │                          │
│                    └──────┬──────┘                          │
│                           │                                 │
│                    ┌──────┴──────┐ 410.60                   │
│                    │ COMPLETE    │                          │
│                    │ TECHNICAL   │                          │
│                    │ SYSTEM      │                          │
│                    │ OPTIONS     │                          │
│                    └──────┬──────┘                          │
│                           │                                 │
│                    ┌──────┴──────┐ 420.10                   │
│                    │ PRESENT TSOs│                          │
│                    │ TO PROJECT  │                          │
│                    │ BOARD,      │                          │
│                    │ RECORD      │                          │
│                    │ REASONS FOR │                          │
│                    │ DECISION    │                          │
│                    └──┬────────┬─┘                          │
│                       │        │                            │
│          ┌────────────┴┐  ┌────┴────────┐ 420.30            │
│          │ UPDATE TSO  │  │ ENSURE      │                   │
│          │ TO REFLECT  │  │ SERVICE     │                   │
│          │ DECISION,   │  │ LEVEL       │                   │
│          │ DEVELOP     │  │ REQUIREMENTS│                   │
│          │ TECHNICAL   │  │ CAN BE MET  │                   │
│          │ ENVIRONMENT │  │ BY SELECTED │                   │
│          │ DESC. 420.20│  │ OPTION      │                   │
│          └──────┬──────┘  └─────────────┘                   │
│                 │                                           │
│          ┌──────┴──────┐ 420.40                             │
│          │ DEVELOP     │                                    │
│          │ APPLICATION │                                    │
│          │ STYLE GUIDE │                                    │
│          └─────────────┘                                    │
└─────────────────────────────────────────────────────────────┘
```

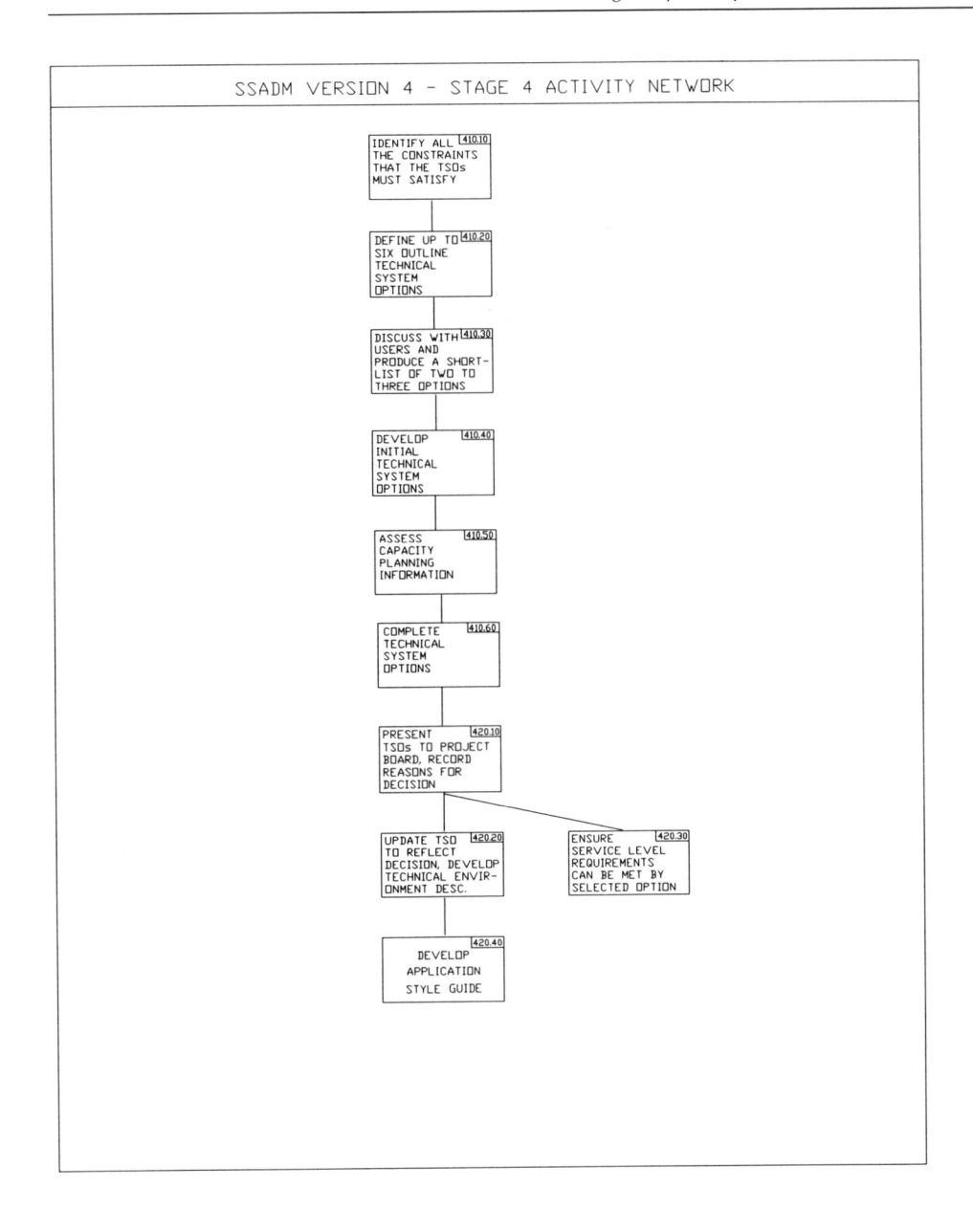

10.1 Step 410: Define Technical System Options

Objectives

- To identify and define the possible approaches to the physical implementation of the REQUIREMENTS SPECIFICATION.

- To validate the service-level requirements for the proposed system in the light of the technical environment. These service-level requirements will form the basis of performance targets for the physical design, and for the negotiation of the service-level agreement following system implementation.

Summary

The options created in this step describe possible physical implementations to meet the REQUIREMENTS SPECIFICATION.

The Feasibility Study will have identified any major decisions already made in respect of hardware and software as a result of an IS Strategy (e.g. mainframe, minicomputer or microcomputer; DBMS or conventional files). These will be reflected in the Requirements Catalogue, constrain the generic technical aspects of the SELECTED BUSINESS SYSTEM OPTION, and hence further constrain the *Technical System Options*. If they are not already in place, major hardware and software policies will need to be agreed with the Project Board in advance of this step.

In some circumstances, particularly turnkey procurements, it may only be possible to nominate, and not define, the shape of the hardware/software environment. The TECHNICAL ENVIRONMENT DESCRIPTION would then be restricted to identifying the major constraints on the potential system, such as location of peripherals, performance requirements and volumetrics.

The *Technical System Options* may also include possible variations on the system functionality, specified in the SELECTED BUSINESS SYSTEM OPTION as a result of more detailed analysis, cost/benefit information or technical investigation.

In some cases, the individual options may be provided by competing contracted organizations, working with client users on behalf of the Project Manager, who can each deliver options where a turnkey route is required. This approach is sometimes called the Technical Design Study.

References

Task 10:   Project Initiation Document
            Selected Business System Option
            Strategy Documents
            Requirements Catalogue

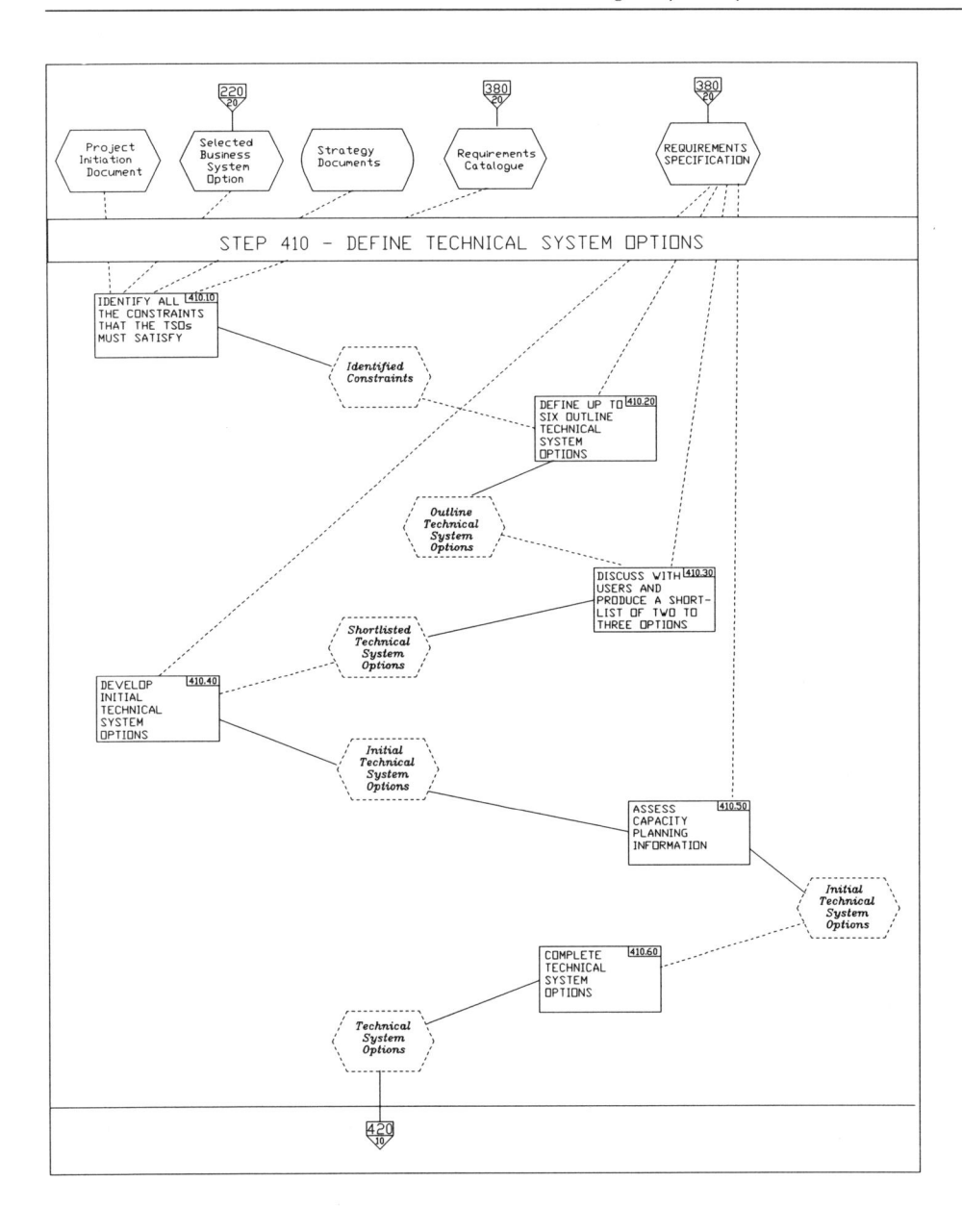

Logical System Specification Module **145**

STEP 410 – DEFINE TECHNICAL SYSTEM OPTIONS

- 410.10 IDENTIFY ALL THE CONSTRAINTS THAT THE TSOs MUST SATISFY
  - *Identified Constraints*
- 410.20 DEFINE UP TO SIX OUTLINE TECHNICAL SYSTEM OPTIONS
  - *Outline Technical System Options*
- 410.30 DISCUSS WITH USERS AND PRODUCE A SHORTLIST OF TWO TO THREE OPTIONS
  - *Shortlisted Technical System Options*
- 410.40 DEVELOP INITIAL TECHNICAL SYSTEM OPTIONS
  - *Initial Technical System Options*
- 410.50 ASSESS CAPACITY PLANNING INFORMATION
  - *Initial Technical System Options*
- 410.60 COMPLETE TECHNICAL SYSTEM OPTIONS
  - *Technical System Options*

Inputs:
- Project Initiation Document
- Selected Business System Option (220/20)
- Strategy Documents
- Requirements Catalogue (380/20)
- REQUIREMENTS SPECIFICATION (380/20)

Output to: 420/10

Logical System Specification Module

Task 20: REQUIREMENTS SPECIFICATION
Identified Constraints

Task 30: REQUIREMENTS SPECIFICATION
Outline Technical System Options

Task 40: REQUIREMENTS SPECIFICATION
Shortlisted Technical System Options

Task 50: REQUIREMENTS SPECIFICATION

Products created

Task 10: *Identified Constraints*

Task 20: *Outline Technical System Options*

Task 30: *Shortlisted Technical System Options*

Task 40: *Initial Technical System Options*

Task 60: *Technical System Options*

Products amended

Task 50: *Initial Technical System Options*

Task 60: *Initial Technical System Options*
(developed into *Technical System Options*)

Techniques

Technical System Option — used in Tasks 10, 20, 30, 40, 50 and 60

Activities

Task 10

10.1 Create a list of *Identified Constraints* from the Requirements Catalogue, the Project Initiation Document, the SELECTED BUSINESS SYSTEM OPTION and any strategy documents. All the options must satisfy these.

Task 20

20.1 Define up to six *Outline Technical System Options*, representing a range of technical solutions, but all satisfying the *Identified Constraints*.

Task 30

30.1 Discuss these high-level options with the users, and produce two or three *Shortlisted Technical System Options*.

Task 40

40.1 Develop a description of each *Initial Technical System Option*, including:
Technical Environment Description: at this stage it is only necessary to describe the type, quantity and distribution of the hardware/software. Necessary volumetric information is taken from the Requirements Specification. In some cases, in order to obtain a quantifiable view of the hardware/software requirement it may be necessary to produce an overview physical design.

System Description: identifying how the system will meet the requirement and specifying the requirements not being satisfied as anticipated in the SELECTED BUSINESS SYSTEM OPTION.

Note that the technical environment description and system description are only produced in outline in this task, and are included as part of each *Initial Technical System Option*. The TECHNICAL ENVIRONMENT DESCRIPTION is developed fully in the next step (Step 420) for the selected option. It becomes a deliverable compound product in its own right and includes the System Description and an Impact Analysis.

Task 50

50.1 Assess the capacity planning information for each option. Ensure that the service levels contained in the REQUIREMENTS SPECIFICATION can be met, or that variances are highlighted in the technical environment description.

Note that, although Capacity Planning Input is described as a separate product in the Dictionary Volume, it is not in fact created as one. In practice it consists of the volumetric information contained within the REQUIRED SYSTEM LDM, FUNCTION DEFINITIONS and Requirements Catalogue. The results of applying capacity planning to this information should be included in the technical environment description.

Task 60

60.1 Complete the specification of each *Technical System Option* by adding:
Impact Analysis: describing the effects of the option on the environment, in terms of organizational and operating changes, and assessing the advantages and disadvantages.
Outline Development Plan: including any necessary changes to the Structural Model, Activity Networks, Step Descriptions, Product Breakdown Structures and Product Descriptions; and resource estimates for the remainder of the development.
Cost/Benefit Analysis: providing an objective yardstick for comparing options.

10.2 Step 420: Select Technical System Options

Objectives

- To present the Technical System Options to the Project Board, enabling the selection of a technical solution to the system requirement.
- To develop the description of the selected option and the Technical Environment Description (TED), incorporating and documenting the option decisions, to define the context for the Physical Design Module.

Summary

This step is concerned with the presentation of the *Technical System Options* to the Project Board and the selection of the preferred option. The TED of the SELECTED TECHNICAL SYSTEM OPTION (STSO) sets the context for the Physical Design Module.

The selected option is often a hybrid, based on one option but containing features from others. A description of the selected option is documented in the TED, which is carried forward to Physical Design.

References

Task 10:   Technical System Options

Task 20:   REQUIREMENTS SPECIFICATION

Task 30:   TECHNICAL ENVIRONMENT DESCRIPTION
           SELECTED TECHNICAL SYSTEM OPTION

Task 40:   Installation Style Guide
           TECHNICAL ENVIRONMENT DESCRIPTION

Products created

Task 10:   Selected Technical System Option

Task 20:   TECHNICAL ENVIRONMENT DESCRIPTION

Task 40:   Application Style Guide

Products amended

Task 20:   SELECTED TECHNICAL SYSTEM OPTION

Techniques

Technical System Option — used in Tasks 10, 20, 30 and 40
Project Planning — used at the end of this step to create the Stage Plans for the Logical Systems Specification Stage.

Activities

Task 10

10.1 Present the *Technical System Options* to the Project Board and other selected audiences.

10.2 Assist the decision-making process by further explanation and discussion of the

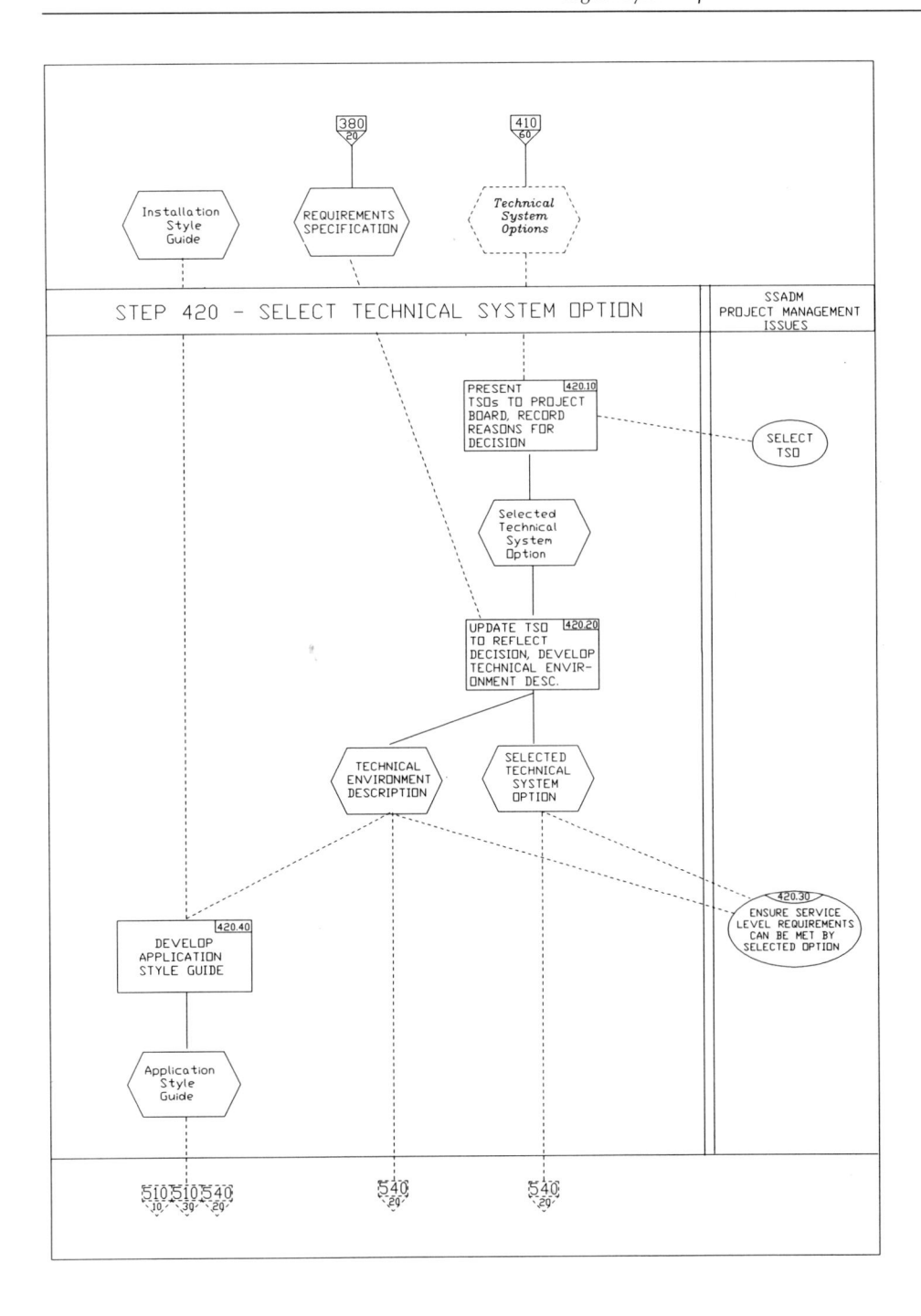

Logical System Specification Module **149**

STEP 420 – SELECT TECHNICAL SYSTEM OPTION

Inputs:
- 380/20 Installation Style Guide
- REQUIREMENTS SPECIFICATION
- 410/60 Technical System Options

420.10 PRESENT TSOs TO PROJECT BOARD, RECORD REASONS FOR DECISION
→ Selected Technical System Option

420.20 UPDATE TSO TO REFLECT DECISION, DEVELOP TECHNICAL ENVIRONMENT DESC.
→ TECHNICAL ENVIRONMENT DESCRIPTION
→ SELECTED TECHNICAL SYSTEM OPTION

420.40 DEVELOP APPLICATION STYLE GUIDE
→ Application Style Guide

420.30 ENSURE SERVICE LEVEL REQUIREMENTS CAN BE MET BY SELECTED OPTION

SSADM PROJECT MANAGEMENT ISSUES:
- SELECT TSO

Outputs: 510/10, 510/30, 540/20, 540/20, 540/20

implications of the options if required, and record the reasons for particular decisions.

10.3 Create the STSO by incorporating all the features decided upon from those presented and discussed.

Note that, on the diagram for this step, the STSO as created in this task is depicted as an Elementary Deliverable Product (standard typeface, lower case). It is in the next task that all of its constituent products are fully developed, and the STSO thus becomes a compound deliverable product.

Task 20

20.1 Develop the description of the STSO to reflect the decisions taken.

20.3 The outline Cost/Benefit Analysis should be completed and included as part of the STSO.

20.4 Create an Outline Development Plan for the STSO.

20.5 Produce a description of the training requirements implied by the STSO. This should encompass the needs of users, technicians, implementors and management.

20.6 Produce a Testing Outline, including functional and environmental test criteria, and a test plan covering all levels of testing.

20.7 Produce a description of the requirements for a user manual, covering all the user issues relating to the smooth running of the system.

20.8 Develop the TED for the STSO. The TED should include the fully developed System Description for the STSO.

20.9 Develop the Impact Analysis for the STSO and include it in the TED.

Task 30

30.1 Ensure that the service-level requirements can still be met by the selected option, by applying capacity planning to the volumetric information contained in Requirements Specification products. See the note on Task 50 in Step 410.

If there is any likelihood that any of the service-level requirements cannot be met, the matter should be brought to the attention of Project Management.

Task 40

40.1 Develop an Application Style Guide that is specific to the application, based on the installation standard style guide.

Stage 5 — Logical System Specification

This stage consists of the following steps:

    Step 510: Define User Dialogues (4 Tasks)

    Step 520: Define Update Processes (5 Tasks)

    Step 530: Define Enquiry Processes (5 Tasks)

    Step 540: Assemble Logical System Specification

152 *Logical System Specification Module*

SSADM VERSION 4 - STAGE 5 ACTIVITY NETWORK

```
┌─────────────┐  ┌─────────────┐  ┌─────────────┐  ┌─────────────┐
│ ALLOCATE    │  │ CONVERT     │  │ CONVERT     │  │ CREATE      │
│ STATE       │520.10│ ECDs FOR │520.20│ ENQUIRY  │530.10│ OUTPUT  │530.20
│ INDICATOR   │  │ EACH        │  │ ACCESS      │  │ DATA        │
│ VALUES TO   │  │ EVENT INTO  │  │ PATH INTO A │  │ STRUCTURE   │
│ ELHs, AND   │  │ PROCESSING  │  │ PROCESSING  │  │ FROM        │
│ UPDATE      │  │ STRUCTURES  │  │ STRUCTURE   │  │ I/O         │
│ ENTITY      │  │             │  │             │  │ STRUCTURE   │
│ DESCRIPTIONS│  │             │  │             │  │             │
└─────────────┘  └─────────────┘  └─────────────┘  └─────────────┘
```

- **520.10** ALLOCATE STATE INDICATOR VALUES TO ELHs, AND UPDATE ENTITY DESCRIPTIONS
- **520.20** CONVERT ECDs FOR EACH EVENT INTO PROCESSING STRUCTURES
- **520.30** LIST THE OPERATIONS FOR EACH ENTITY ON THE PROCESSING STRUCTURE
- **520.40** ALLOCATE THE OPERATIONS TO ELEMENTS ON THE PROCESSING STRUCTURE
- **520.50** SPECIFY ERROR OUTPUTS
- **530.10** CONVERT ENQUIRY ACCESS PATH INTO A PROCESSING STRUCTURE
- **530.20** CREATE OUTPUT DATA STRUCTURE FROM I/O STRUCTURE
- **530.30** MERGE THE STRUCTURES TO FORM A SINGLE PROCESSING STRUCUTRE
- **530.40** LIST THE OPERATIONS AND ALLOCATE THEM TO THE PROCESSING STRUCTURE
- **530.50** SPECIFY ERROR OUTPUTS
- **510.10** IDENTIFY LGDEs ON THE DIALOGUE STRUCTURES
- **510.20** IDENTIFY NAVIGATION PATHS AND COMPLETE DIALOGUE CONTROL TABLE
- **510.30** CREATE THE MENU HIERARCHY AND DEFINE VALID CONTROL PATHS
- **510.40** DEFINE REQUIREMENTS FOR DIALOGUE LEVEL HELP FACILITIES
- **540.10** REVIEW THE PRODUCTS OF LOGICAL DESIGN
- **540.20** ASSEMBLE AND PUBLISH THE LOGICAL SYSTEM SPECIFICATION

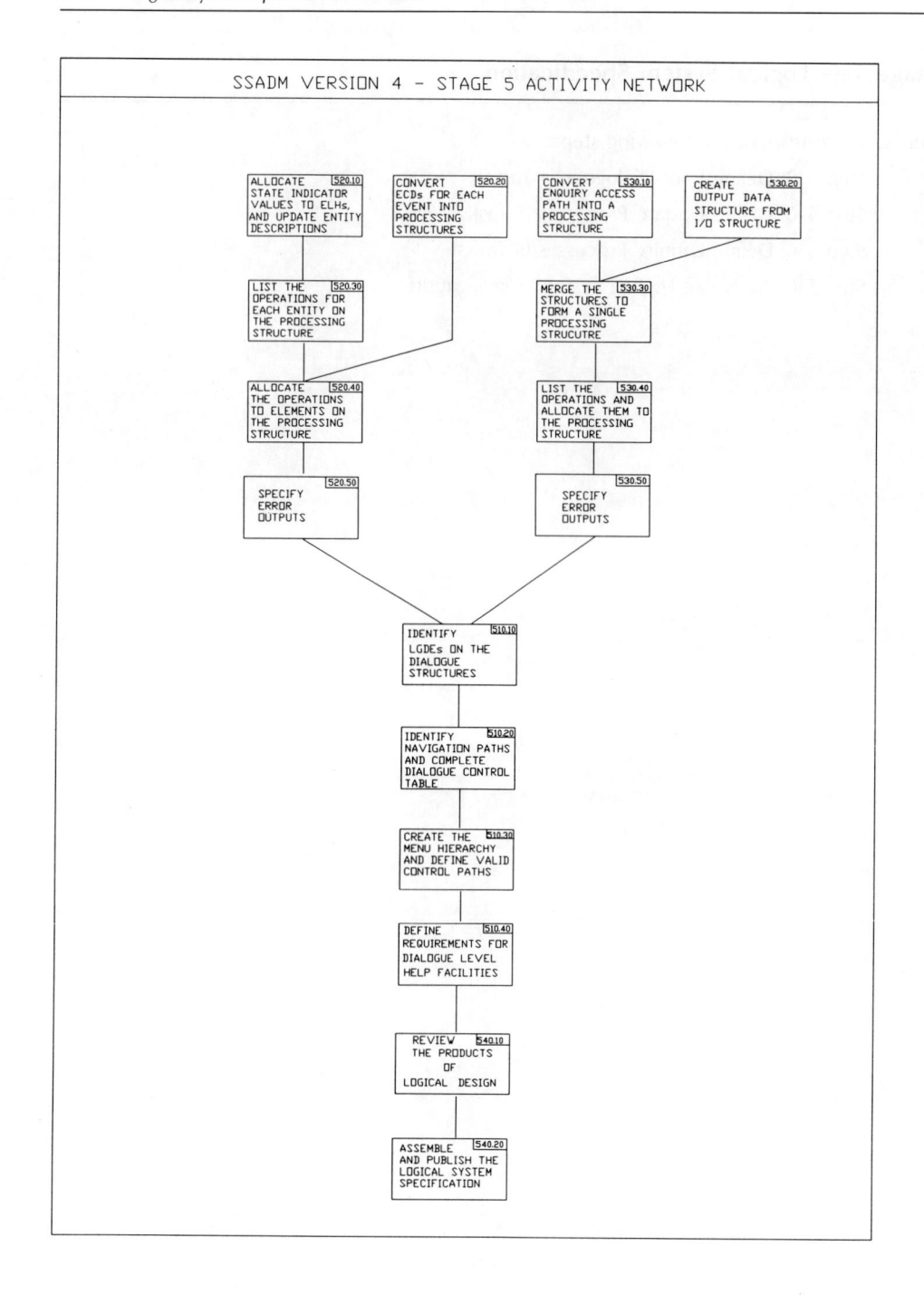

10.3 Step 510: Define User Dialogues

Objectives

- To define the structure and processing of each DIALOGUE.
- To define the Menu and Command Structures.

Summary

The DIALOGUES required to support the outline function will have been identified in Step 330. This step defines the structure and processing (in terms of operations) of each DIALOGUE and identifies the navigation requirements, both within the DIALOGUE and between DIALOGUES.

At this point DIALOGUES are defined in terms of Dialogue Structures and Dialogue Element Descriptions, without detailed consideration of the physical constraints, although certain style issues will be taken into account. Screen formats are not designed until Stage 6.

References

Task 10:   Application Style Guide
            I/O STRUCTURES
            UPDATE PROCESS MODELS
            Enquiry Process Models

Task 20:   User Roles
            User Role/Function Matrix

Task 30:   Application Style Guide
            Dialogue Control Table
            User Roles
            User Role/Function Matrix

Task 40:   Menu Structures
            Command Structures
            Requirements Catalogue

Products created

Task 10:   Dialogue Element Descriptions
            Dialogue Structures

Task 20:   Dialogue Control Table

Task 40:   Dialogue Level Help

Products amended

Task 20:   Dialogue Element Descriptions

Task 30:   Menu Structures
            Command Structures

Techniques

Dialogue Design — used in Tasks 10, 20, 30 and 40

Logical System Specification Module

STEP 510 – DEFINE USER DIALOGUES

510.10 CREATE DIALOGUE ELEMENT DESCRIPTIONS AND STRUCTURES

510.20 IDENTIFY NAVIGATION PATHS AND COMPLETE DIALOGUE CONTROL TABLE

510.30 CREATE THE MENU HIERARCHY AND DEFINE VALID CONTROL PATHS

510.40 DEFINE REQUIREMENTS FOR DIALOGUE LEVEL HELP FACILITIES

Inputs: Requirements Catalogue, Application Style Guide, Menu Structures, User Roles, User Role/Function Matrix, Command Structures, Update Process Model, Enquiry Process Model, I/O Structures

Outputs: Dialogue Element Descriptions, Dialogue Structures, Dialogue Control Table, Menu Structures, Command Structures, Dialogue Level Help

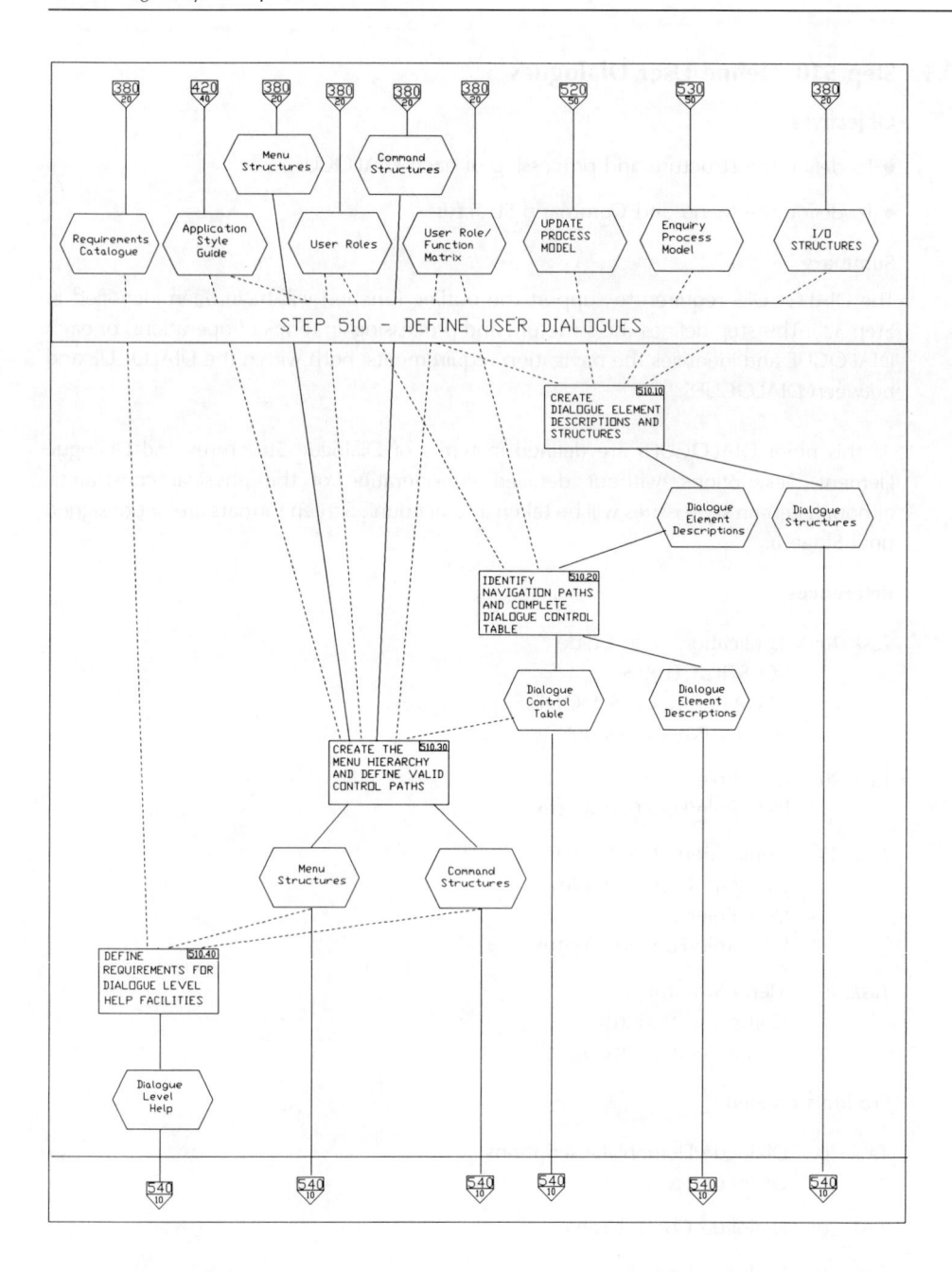

Activities

Task 10

10.1 Create the Dialogue Element Descriptions by listing the dialogue elements and associated data items on the Dialogue Element Description form. This information is copied from the I/O Structure Descriptions.

10.2 In consultation with the users, and referring to the Application Style Guide, identify the logical groupings of dialogue elements on the I/O STRUCTURES, and in so doing develop the Dialogue Structures from the I/O Structure Diagrams.

10.3 Update the Dialogue Element Description by appending the appropriate logical grouping of the dialogue element's identifier to each dialogue element. It may be necessary to reorder the dialogue elements on the form so that all of the elements for each logical grouping are grouped together.

The following activities within Task 10 are in addition to those described in the reference manuals. They have been included to complete the specification of the Dialogue Structures as described in the dictionary (Volume 4).

The specifications of Dialogue Structures and the generic SSADM Structure Diagram clearly indicate that operations should be included on the diagrams. At the beginning of Stage 5, update operations were defined on the Entity Life Histories. Steps 520 and 530 create the UPDATE PROCESS MODELS and Enquiry Process Models, which include the operations. Step 510 is therefore shown on the Activity Network as being dependent upon the completion of Steps 520 and 530, rather than being done in parallel as depicted in the reference manual.

10.4 The operations from the UPDATE PROCESS MODELS, for update processes that are to be implemented as DIALOGUES, should be added to the Dialogue Structure for that process.

It should be borne in mind that the concept of 'sequence' on the UPDATE PROCESS MODELS is supported solely by the sequence numbers of the operations, not by the diagram. The sequence numbers were derived by reference to the I/O STRUCTURES, which were the basis for the Dialogue Structures created in activity 10.1. This transposition of operations should therefore be a simple mechanistic activity.

Each operation is transferred in turn, in the order of the sequence numbers, to the appropriate box on the Dialogue Structure. The Dialogue Element Description should be checked to ensure that the operation is supported by the required data items.

If there is any difficulty, in that the operations do not appear to be supported by the required data items, the UPDATE PROCESS MODEL, Entity Life History, Effect Correspondence Diagram, I/O STRUCTURE, Dialogue Structure and Dialogue Element Description should be reviewed to establish the cause of the inconsistency. The appropriate products should then be reworked to make them consistent, so that the Dialogue Structures can be satisfactorily completed.

10.5 The operations from the Enquiry Process Models, for enquiry processes that are to be implemented as DIALOGUES, should be added to the Dialogue Structure for those processes.

Both the Dialogue Structure and Enquiry Process Model for the process will have been developed using the I/O STRUCTURE as a starting point. Both are based on the generic SSADM Structure Diagram and support the concepts of sequence, selection and iteration. At this point the Dialogue Structure is the users' view of the inputs and outputs required for the processing, whereas the Enquiry Process Model is the system's view of the required processing, including additional process boxes to support navigation that would be transparent to the user, plus all the required operations. However, the basic structure of both diagrams, in terms of sequence, selection and iteration, should be the same.

Each operation is transferred in turn, in the order of the sequence numbers, to the appropriate box on the Dialogue Structure. The Dialogue Element Description should be checked to ensure that the operation is supported by the required data items.

If there is any difficulty, in that the operations do not appear to be supported by the required data items or the basic structures do not match in terms of sequence selection and iteration, the Enquiry Process Model, Enquiry Access Path, I/O Structure, Dialogue Structure and Dialogue Element Description should be reviewed to establish the cause of the inconsistency. The appropriate products should then be reworked to make them consistent, so that the Dialogue Structures can be satisfactorily completed.

Task 20

20.1 Identify the possible navigation paths within each dialogue, and create a Dialogue Control Table.

20.2 Classify each logical grouping of dialogue elements as either mandatory or optional, and update the Dialogue Element Description form.

Task 30

30.1 Create/amend a Menu Structure for each User Role by referring to the User Role/Function Matrix, taking into account any style issues by referring to the Application Style Guide.

30.2 Establish the valid control paths on completion of each DIALOGUE, and create/amend Command Structures.

Task 40

40.1 In discussion with the users, and referring to the Requirements Catalogue, define the requirements for Dialogue Level Help.

10.4 Step 520: Define Update Processes

Objectives

- To complete the specification of the database processing required for each event.
- To define the semantic-error handling for each event.

Summary

This step completes the logical specification of update functions. In Stage 3 the required database updates for each event are defined for each entity. At this point the defined entity reads and updates are consolidated into an UPDATE PROCESS MODEL for each event.

Initially the Entity Life Histories have state indicator values added, to enable the semantic validation to be defined. Taking each event in turn, the Effect Correspondence Diagram developed in Step 360 is used as a basis to develop a processing structure for the event, to which operations (including semantic validation) and conditions are allocated, forming the UPDATE PROCESS MODEL for the event.

References

Task 20: Effect Correspondence Diagrams
REQUIRED SYSTEM LDM

Task 30: REQUIRED SYSTEM LDM
Entity Life Histories
Effect Correspondence Diagrams

Products created

Task 20: Update Process Structures

Task 30: Operations List

Task 50: UPDATE PROCESS MODEL

Products amended

Task 10: REQUIRED SYSTEM LDM
Entity Life Histories

Task 40: Update Process Structure
Operations List

Task 50: Update Process Structure

Techniques

Entity–Event Modelling — used in Task 10
Logical Database Process Design — used in Tasks 20, 30, 40 and 50

Activities

Task 10

10.1 Allocate state indicator values to the *Entity Life Histories* and document the meaning of the values for each entity on the Entity Description.
Tasks 20–50 are performed for each event.

158 *Logical System Specification Module*

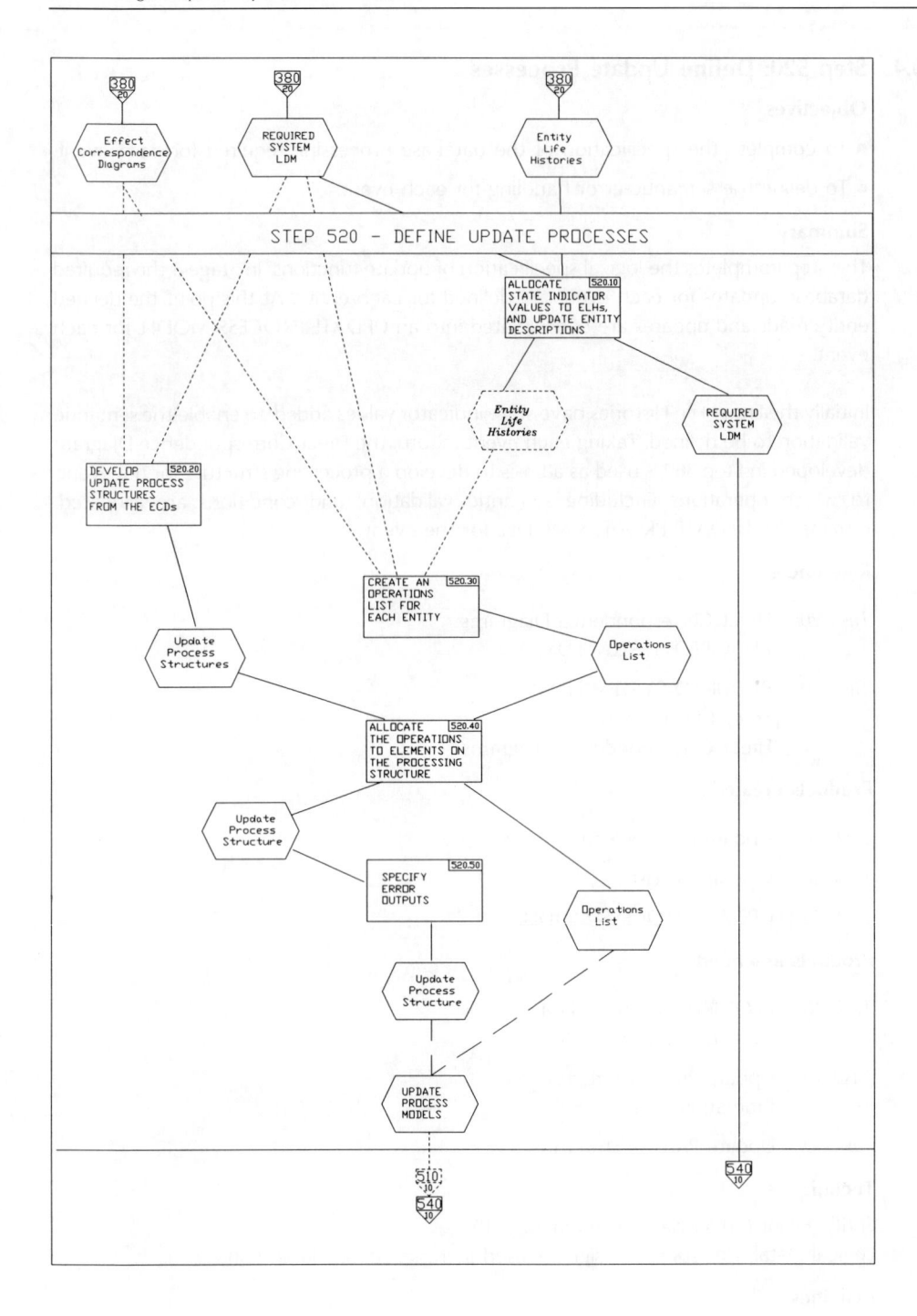

Task 20

20.1 Referring to the REQUIRED SYSTEM LDM, develop an Update Process Structure for each event based on the Effect Correspondence Diagram for that event.

Task 30

30.1 Referring to the REQUIRED SYSTEM LDM and the *Entity Life Histories*, create an Operations List for each entity affected by the event.

30.2 Referring to the Effect Correspondence Diagram for the event, add read operations to the Operations List for each enquiry-only entity that was included on the Effect Correspondence Diagram.

Task 40

40.1 Specify integrity error conditions by adding fail conditions to the Operations List.

40.2 Allocate the operations from the Operations List to the Update Process Structure.

40.3 Allocate conditions to the Update Process Structure to govern each selection and iteration.

Task 50

50.2 Specify and add error outputs to the Update Process Structure for the integrity errors, thereby completing the UPDATE PROCESS MODEL.

10.5 Step 530: Define Enquiry Processes

Objectives

- To complete the specification of the database enquiry processing.
- To define the semantic-error handling for each enquiry.

Summary

This step completes the logical specification of enquiry functions. Enquiries will have been defined at Stage 3 in terms of the data items input and output (I/O STRUCTURES), and a data access path (Enquiry Access Path). At this point a single processing structure for the enquiry is developed. The Enquiry Access Path is used to develop an *Input Data Structure*, and an *Output Data Structure* is derived from the I/O STRUCTURE. The two data structures are merged to form an Enquiry Process Model for the enquiry, to which operations (including semantic validation) and conditions are allocated.

References

Task 10:   Enquiry Access Path
           REQUIRED SYSTEM LDM

Task 20:   I/O STRUCTURES

Task 30:   Input Data Structure
           Output Data Structure

Products created

Task 10:   Input Data Structure

Task 20:   Output Data Structure

Task 30:   Enquiry Process Model

Products amended

Task 40:   Enquiry Process Model

Task 50:   Enquiry Process Model

Techniques

Logical Database Process Design — used in Tasks 10, 20, 30, 40 and 50

Activities

Task 10

10.1 Develop an *Input Data Structure* from the Enquiry Access Path for the enquiry.

Task 20

20.1 Create an *Output Data Structure*, based on the output data identified in the I/O STRUCTURE.

Task 30

30.1 Identify the correspondences between the *Input Data Structure* and *Output Data Structure*, and merge the two structures to form a single Enquiry Process Model.

Logical System Specification Module

STEP 530 – DEFINE ENQUIRY PROCESSES

Inputs:
- Enquiry Access Path (380/20)
- Required System LDM (380/20)
- I/O Structures (380/20)

530.10 DEVELOP INPUT DATA STRUCTURE FROM ENQUIRY ACCESS PATH → *Input Data Structure*

530.20 CREATE OUTPUT DATA STRUCTURE FROM I/O STRUCTURE → *Output Data Structure*

530.30 MERGE THE STRUCTURES TO FORM A SINGLE PROCESSING STRUCUTRE → Enquiry Process Models

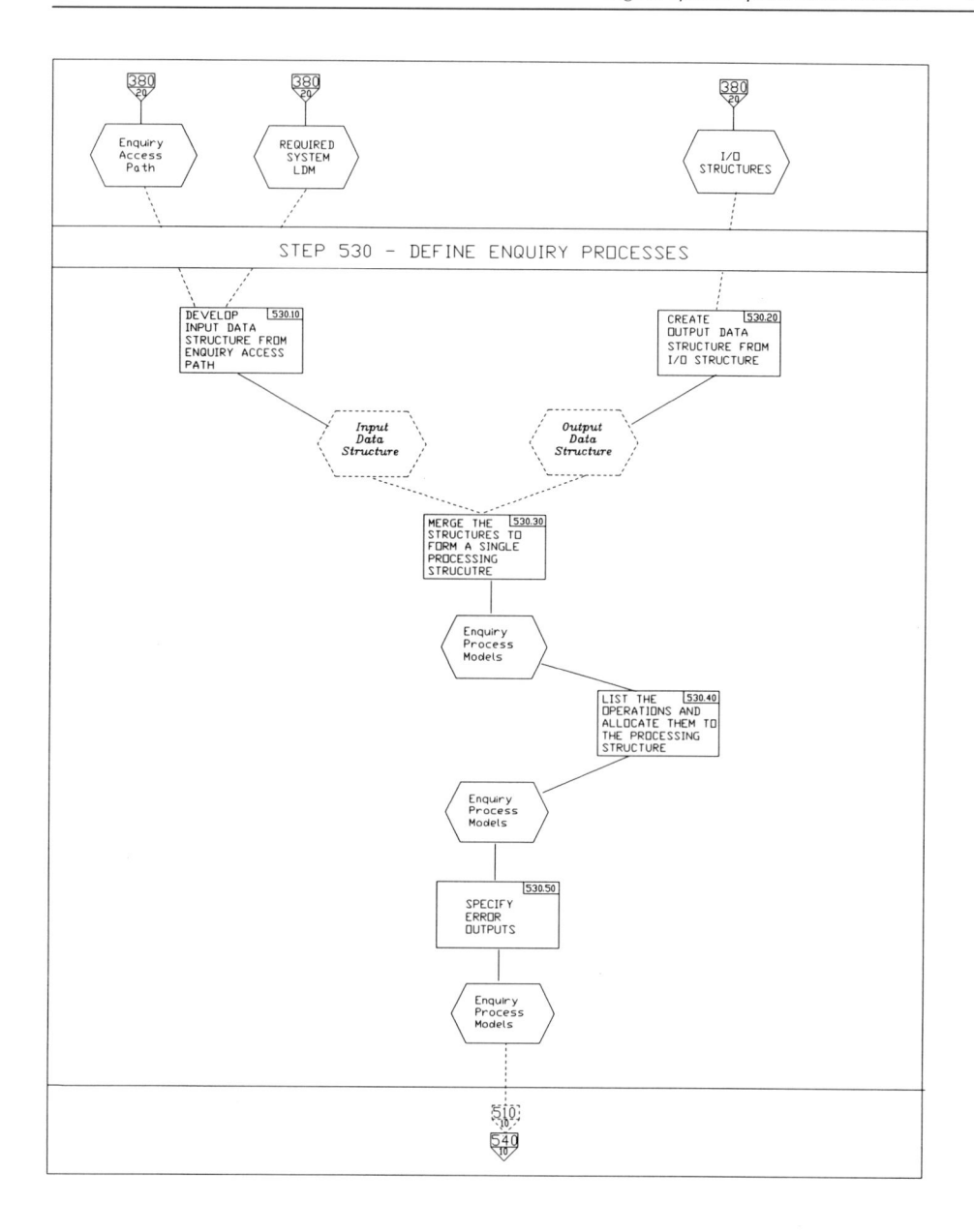

530.40 LIST THE OPERATIONS AND ALLOCATE THEM TO THE PROCESSING STRUCTURE → Enquiry Process Models

530.50 SPECIFY ERROR OUTPUTS → Enquiry Process Models

Outputs to: 510/10, 540/10

Task 40

40.1 List the operations on the Enquiry Process Model, assigning them to the relevant parts of the process structure.

40.2 Allocate conditions on the Enquiry Process Model to govern each selection and iteration.

40.3 Specify integrity error conditions by adding fail conditions to the Operations List after each read operation, and assign them to the relevant parts of the process structure.

Task 50

50.1 Specify and add error outputs to the process structure for each integrity error, thereby completing the Enquiry Process Model.

10.6 Step 540: Assemble Logical System Specification

Objectives

- To ensure the integrity of the products describing the LOGICAL DESIGN.
- To assemble and publish the LOGICAL SYSTEM SPECIFICATION.

Summary

This step is the completion of the Logical System Specification Module, and is concerned with checking the consistency of the products of Stage 5.

Each of the SSADM steps represents a transformation which takes a starting set of products, performs some tasks, and applies quality control to produce a target set of products. Quality management procedures are not part of SSADM, but each of the SSADM products that transports information between steps has quality criteria defined as part of the Product Description (Dictionary Volume). These quality criteria are only those that can be applied to the individual products. The cross-checking of products for consistency is part of this step. The review methods to be used are defined within the quality management procedures.

This step also publishes the formal LOGICAL DESIGN Document, together with the other products that form the LOGICAL SYSTEM SPECIFICATION.

References

None

Products created

Task 10:   LOGICAL DESIGN

Task 20:   LOGICAL SYSTEM SPECIFICATION

Products amended

Task 10:   Dialogue Control Table
Dialogue Level Help
Command Structures
Enquiry Process Models
Dialogue Element Descriptions
Dialogue Structures
Menu Structures
Data Catalogue
Requirements Catalogue
UPDATE PROCESS MODELS
REQUIRED SYSTEM LDM
FUNCTION DEFINITIONS
Common Elementary Process Descriptions

Products included

Task 20:   Application Style Guide
TECHNICAL ENVIRONMENT DESCRIPTION
SELECTED TECHNICAL SYSTEM OPTION
LOGICAL DESIGN

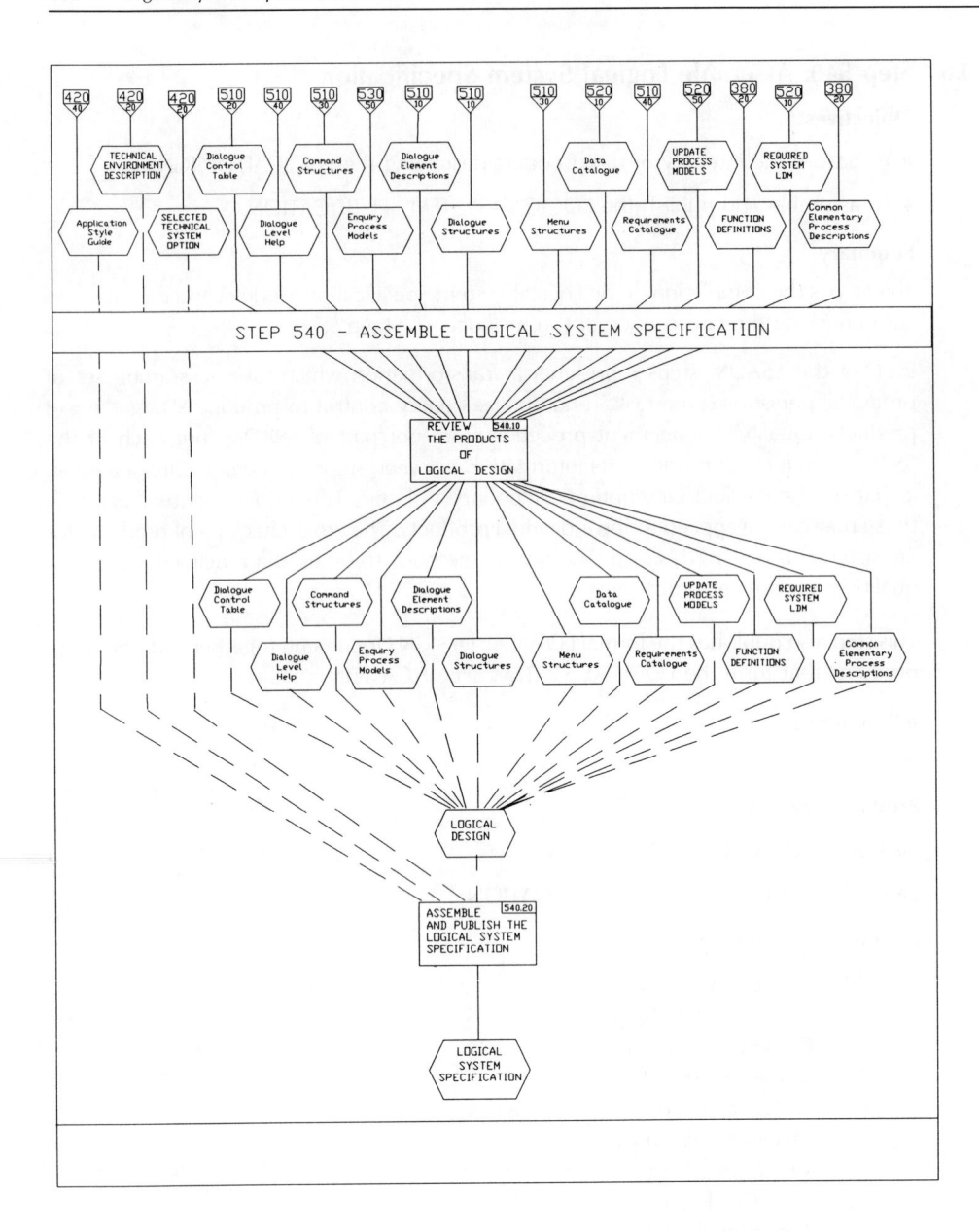

164 *Logical System Specification Module*

Techniques
None

Activities

Task 10

10.1 Review the completeness and consistency of the components of the LOGICAL DESIGN, viz:
- Dialogue Control Table
- Dialogue Level Help
- Command Structures
- Enquiry Process Models
- Dialogue Element Descriptions
- Dialogue Structures
- Menu Structures
- Data Catalogue
- Requirements Catalogue
- UPDATE PROCESS MODELS
- REQUIRED SYSTEM LDM
- FUNCTION DEFINITIONS
- Common Elementary Process Descriptions

Taking each functional requirement in turn from the Requirements Catalogue, check that its entry is complete and consistent. In particular, check that the Resolution element refers to at least one FUNCTION DEFINITION. Check that the FUNCTION DEFINITIONS referred to are complete, and the elements of processing specification referred to are complete, consistent, and fully supported by the REQUIRED SYSTEM LDM.

10.2 Check each FUNCTION DEFINITION to ensure that it refers to a functional requirement in the REQUIREMENTS CATALOGUE.

10.3 Taking each non-functional requirement in turn from the Requirements Catalogue, check that its entry is complete and consistent. In particular, check that the Related Requirements element refers to one or more functional requirements, or if not, ensure that the requirement clearly describes what aspect of the system it refers to.

Note that at this stage it will not be possible to completely verify that service-level non-functional requirements can be satisfied. However, the LOGICAL DESIGN should provide a good indication.

10.4 Amend the LOGICAL DESIGN products, if necessary, as a result of the reviews.

Task 20

20.1 Assemble and publish the LOGICAL SYSTEM SPECIFICATION in accordance with the organization's standards, including the following products:
- LOGICAL DESIGN
- Application Style Guide
- TECHNICAL ENVIRONMENT DESCRIPTION
- SELECTED TECHNICAL SYSTEM OPTION

11 Physical Design Module

This module consists of one stage, Stage 6 — Physical Design, that produces the PHYSICAL DESIGN.

Note that, as discussed in the Technique Reviews for Physical Data Design and Physical Processing Specification, because this stage is not environment-specific it is inevitably of the nature of general guidance. I have therefore included the Product Breakdown Structure, step diagrams and Step Descriptions for interest only, but did not consider that there was any practical value in including a Task/Product Matrix or Activity Network.

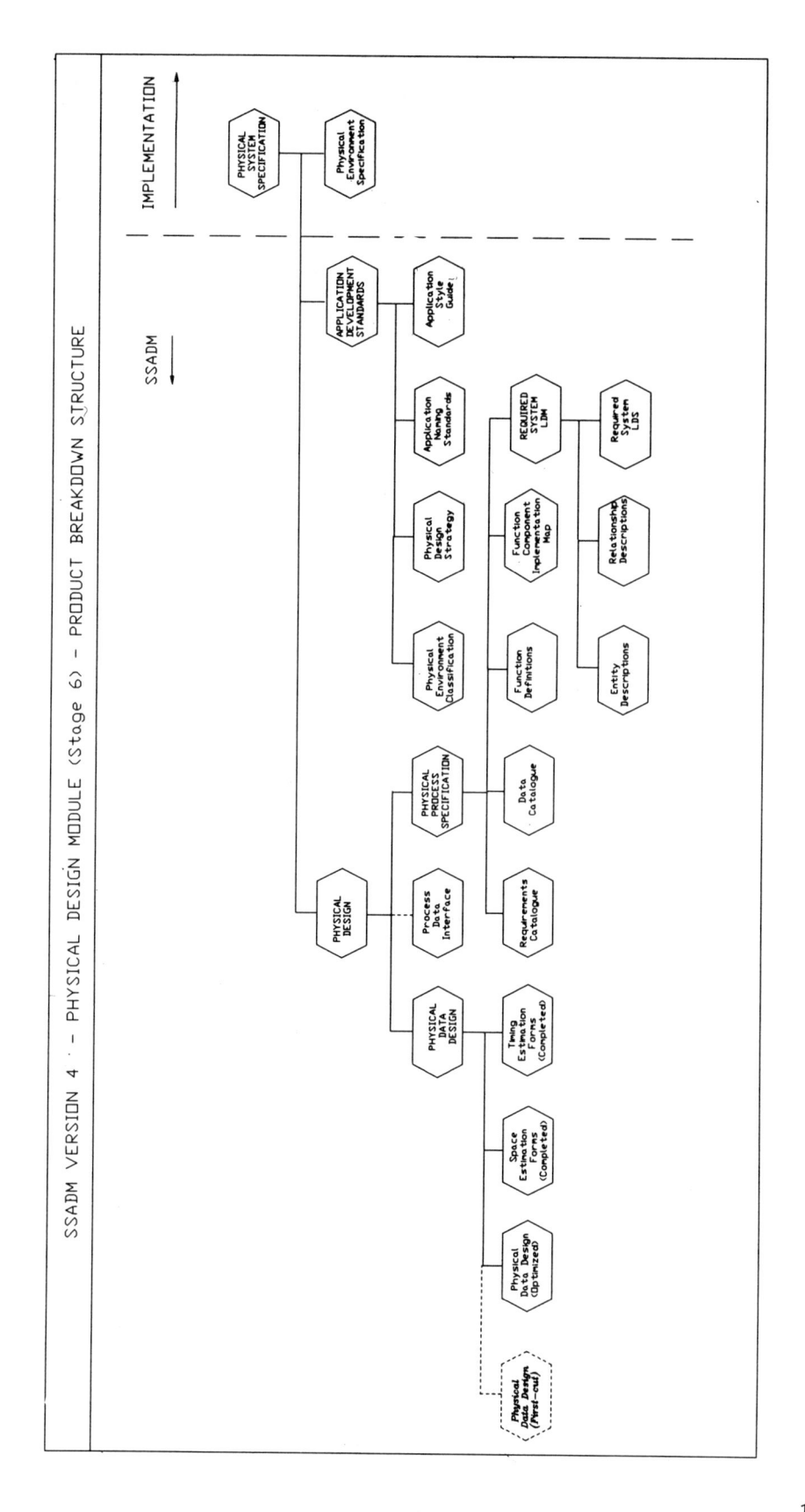

SSADM VERSION 4 - PHYSICAL DESIGN MODULE (Stage 6) - PRODUCT BREAKDOWN STRUCTURE

Stage 6 — Physical Design

This stage consists of the following steps:
- Step 610: Prepare for Physical Design
- Step 620: Create Physical Data Design
- Step 630: Create Function Component Implementation Map
- Step 640: Optimize Physical Data Design
- Step 650: Complete Function Specification
- Step 660: Consolidate Process Data Interface
- Step 670: Assemble Physical Design

11.1 Step 610: Prepare for Physical Design

Objectives

- To gain an understanding of the physical environment in preparation for Physical Design.

- To identify facilities and constraints within the physical environment which will have an impact on the production of the PHYSICAL DESIGN.

- To develop the standards for the use of the DBMS and physical processing system.

Summary

The Physical Environment Classification Scheme is used to categorize the physical environment, as described in Physical Environment Specification. The classification scheme identifies the significant kinds of facility that implementation products can be expected to provide. It covers data storage, performance and processing system characteristics. How these facilities are supported in the physical environment clearly has an effect on the design of the system. The physical environment is classified according to the method(s) by which these facilities are provided. There are two main issues to address in the Processing System Classification: the first is how much of the physical processing can or should be specified in a non-procedural fashion, and the second is how far the logical processes can be directly implemented as physical programs or modules within the physical system.

The Application Development Standards are defined. There are two main tasks involved here:

1. The definition of the standards for the use of the physical processing system.

2. The definition of the program specification standards, i.e. the format of the program specifications.

If a product-specific guide exists, it will contain most of the information required. However, some of the activity within this step may still be necessary to understand and evaluate the options presented in the interface guide.

References

Task 10:   Physical Environment Specification

Task 20:   Physical Environment Specification

Task 30:   LOGICAL SYSTEM SPECIFICATION
             Application Naming Standards

Task 40:   LOGICAL SYSTEM SPECIFICATION
             Physical Environment Specification

Task 50:   Application Style Guide
             Installation Development Standards
             LOGICAL SYSTEM SPECIFICATION

Task 70:   Application Style Guide
             Installation Development Standards
             LOGICAL SYSTEM SPECIFICATION

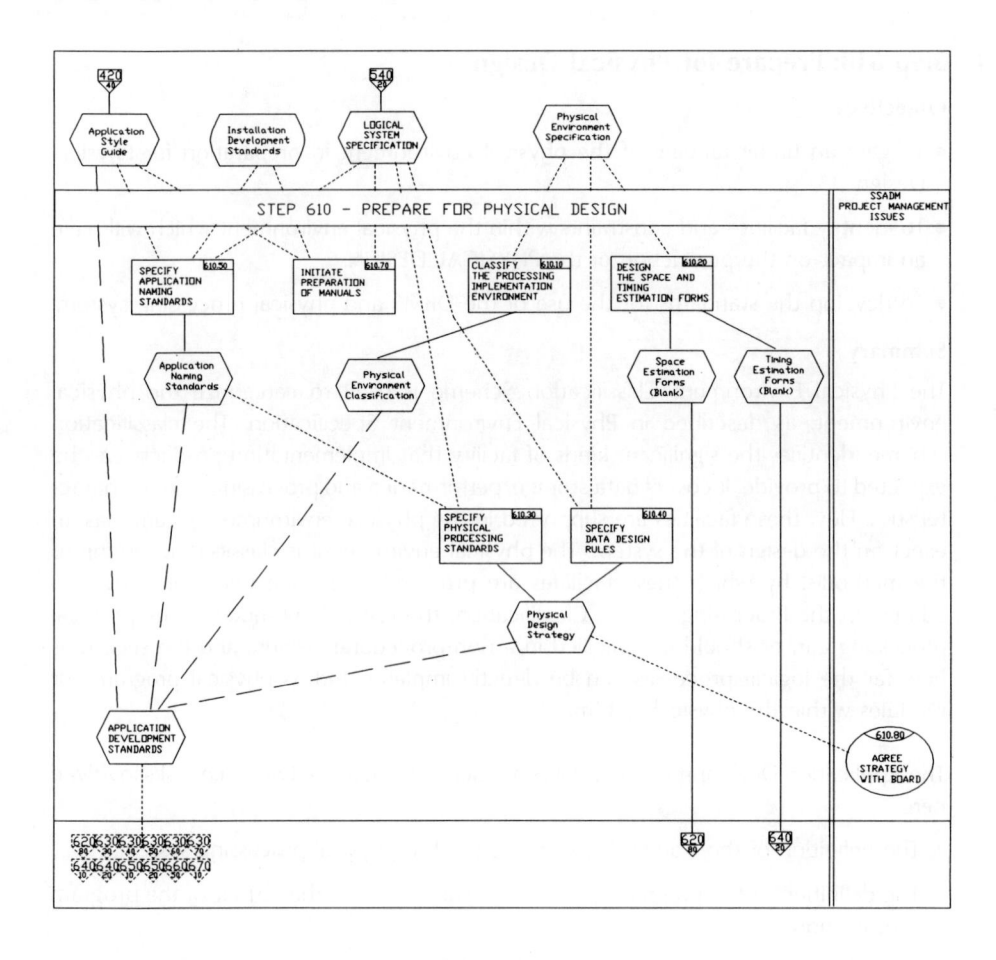

170 *Physical Design Module*

Task 80: Physical Design Strategy

Products created

Task 10: Physical Environment Classification

Task 20: Space Estimation Forms (Blank)
Timing Estimation Forms (Blank)

Task 30: Physical Design Strategy

Task 40: Physical Design Strategy

Task 50: Application Naming Standards

Note that the Application Naming Standards, Application Style Guide, Physical Environment Classification and Physical Design Strategy combine to form the APPLICATION DEVELOPMENT STANDARDS.

Techniques

Project Planning — used at the beginning of this step to create the Module/Stage Plans for the Physical Design Module
Physical Data Design — used in Tasks 10, 20 and 40
Physical Process Specification — used in Task 30

Activities

Task 10

10.1 Classify the processing implementation environment by completing the Processing System Classification.

10.2 Define the DBMS data structuring facilities by completing the DBMS Data Storage Classification.

10.3 Define the DBMS performance characteristics by completing the DBMS Performance Classification.

Note that, in combination, the activities in this task create the Physical Environment Classification.

Task 20

20.1 Design the DBMS Space Estimation Forms and Timing Estimation Forms for the target DBMS.

Task 30

30.1 Specify the standards for the use of the physical processing system and the DBMS facilities.

Task 40

40.1 Specify the product-specific data design rules if not already available.

Note that, in combination, Tasks 30 and 40 create the Physical Design Strategy.

Task 50

50.1 Specify the Application Naming Standards for the application.

Task 70

70.1 Initiate the preparation of user, operation and training manuals. These products will be developed in a separate product lifecycle and may well extend into the construction and introduction phases of the project.

Task 80

80.1 Agree the Physical Design Strategy with the Project Board.

11.2 Step 620: Create Physical Data Design

Objective

- To develop a Physical Data Design that implements the REQUIRED SYSTEM LDM on the target DBMS.

Summary

The REQUIRED SYSTEM LDM is converted via a series of transformations into a *Physical Data Design (First-cut)*.

The strategy for producing the *Physical Data Design (First-cut)* will have been defined in the Physical Design Strategy by identifying which facilities in the DBMS are to be taken advantage of, and the means of minimizing the imposed constraints.

Initially, the REQUIRED SYSTEM LDM is converted into a physical data design based on principles that are common to all database management systems, which determine the detailed requirements for physical data placement and performance. This is then converted to a product-specific *Physical Data Design (First-cut)* using the design rules specified in the Physical Design Strategy.

References

Task 10:   LOGICAL DESIGN
Task 20:   LOGICAL DESIGN
Task 30:   LOGICAL DESIGN
Task 40:   LOGICAL DESIGN
Task 50:   LOGICAL DESIGN
Task 60:   LOGICAL DESIGN
Task 70:   LOGICAL DESIGN
Task 80:   LOGICAL DESIGN
              APPLICATION DEVELOPMENT STANDARDS

Products created

Tasks 10–80:   Physical Data Design (First-cut)

Products amended

Task 80:   Space Estimation Forms

Techniques

Physical Data Design — used in Tasks 10–80

Activities

Task 10

10.1 Identify the features of the REQUIRED SYSTEM LDM that are required for physical data design.

174 *Physical Design Module*

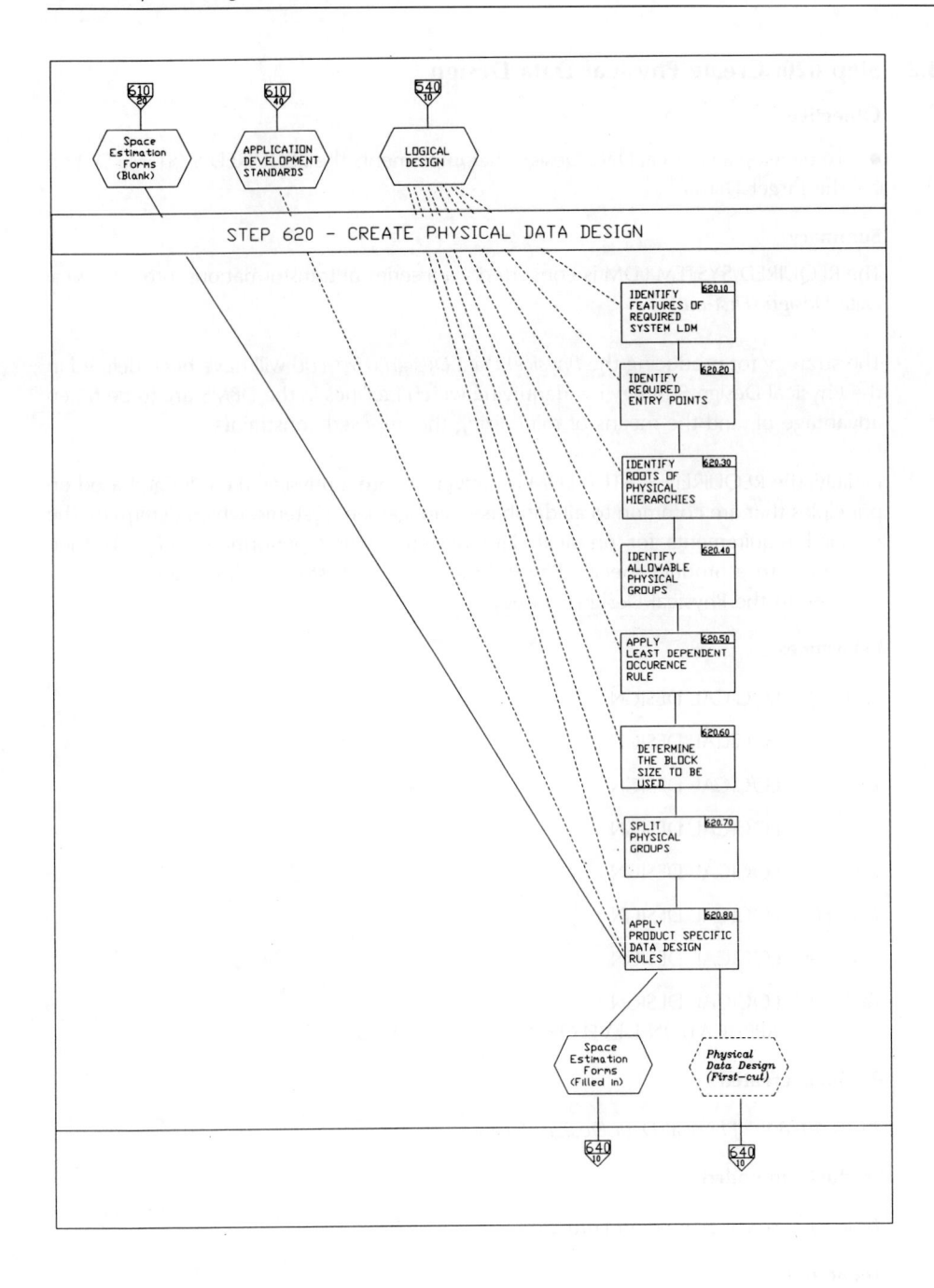

```
┌─────────────────────────────────────────────────────────────┐
│   ⬢610.20      ⬢610.40      ⬢540.10                          │
│   Space        APPLICATION   LOGICAL                          │
│   Estimation   DEVELOPMENT   DESIGN                           │
│   Forms        STANDARDS                                      │
│   (Blank)                                                     │
│─────────────────────────────────────────────────────────────│
│          STEP 620 - CREATE PHYSICAL DATA DESIGN              │
│─────────────────────────────────────────────────────────────│
│                                                               │
│                              ┌──────────────┐ 620.10          │
│                              │ IDENTIFY     │                 │
│                              │ FEATURES OF  │                 │
│                              │ REQUIRED     │                 │
│                              │ SYSTEM LDM   │                 │
│                              └──────────────┘                 │
│                                                               │
│                              ┌──────────────┐ 620.20          │
│                              │ IDENTIFY     │                 │
│                              │ REQUIRED     │                 │
│                              │ ENTRY POINTS │                 │
│                              └──────────────┘                 │
│                                                               │
│                              ┌──────────────┐ 620.30          │
│                              │ IDENTIFY     │                 │
│                              │ ROOTS OF     │                 │
│                              │ PHYSICAL     │                 │
│                              │ HIERARCHIES  │                 │
│                              └──────────────┘                 │
│                                                               │
│                              ┌──────────────┐ 620.40          │
│                              │ IDENTIFY     │                 │
│                              │ ALLOWABLE    │                 │
│                              │ PHYSICAL     │                 │
│                              │ GROUPS       │                 │
│                              └──────────────┘                 │
│                                                               │
│                              ┌──────────────┐ 620.50          │
│                              │ APPLY        │                 │
│                              │ LEAST        │                 │
│                              │ DEPENDENT    │                 │
│                              │ OCCURENCE    │                 │
│                              │ RULE         │                 │
│                              └──────────────┘                 │
│                                                               │
│                              ┌──────────────┐ 620.60          │
│                              │ DETERMINE    │                 │
│                              │ THE BLOCK    │                 │
│                              │ SIZE TO BE   │                 │
│                              │ USED         │                 │
│                              └──────────────┘                 │
│                                                               │
│                              ┌──────────────┐ 620.70          │
│                              │ SPLIT        │                 │
│                              │ PHYSICAL     │                 │
│                              │ GROUPS       │                 │
│                              └──────────────┘                 │
│                                                               │
│                              ┌──────────────┐ 620.80          │
│                              │ APPLY        │                 │
│                              │ PRODUCT      │                 │
│                              │ SPECIFIC     │                 │
│                              │ DATA DESIGN  │                 │
│                              │ RULES        │                 │
│                              └──────────────┘                 │
│                                                               │
│                       ⬢             ⬢                         │
│                    Space          Physical                    │
│                    Estimation     Data Design                 │
│                    Forms          (First-cut)                 │
│                    (Filled in)                                │
│─────────────────────────────────────────────────────────────│
│                       ⬢640.10       ⬢640.10                   │
└─────────────────────────────────────────────────────────────┘
```

Task 20

20.1 Identify the required entry points and distinguish those that are non-key.

Task 30

30.1 Identify the roots of physical hierarchies.

Task 40

40.1 Identify the allowable physical groups for each non-root entry.

Task 50

50.1 Apply the least-dependent occurrence rule.

Task 60

60.1 Determine the block size to be used.

Task 70

70.1 Split the physical groups to fit the required block size.

Task 80

80.1 Apply the product-specific data design rules, using the decisions about the use of DBMS facilities taken in Step 610: Prepare for Physical Design.

80.2 Estimate the space required for the *Physical Data Design (First-cut)* and fill in the Space Estimation Forms.

11.3 Step 630: Create Function Component Implementation Map

Objectives

- To specify the components of functions that are not included in the LOGICAL DESIGN.

- To describe to the physical processing system those function components that can be specified non-procedurally.

Summary

The components of each FUNCTION that are not defined by the end of Stage 5 (syntax error handling; physical input/output formats; physical dialogues) are specified. The creation of the Function Component Implementation Map identifies duplicate and common function components, and defines the relationship between all the function components.

The components of functions that can be specified non-procedurally in the particular physical environment are defined to the physical processing system — with the exception of the database access components.

The specification of the database access components is deferred until Step 660: Consolidate Process Data Interface as part of the development of the Process Data Interface.

References

Task 10:   LOGICAL DESIGN

Task 20:   LOGICAL DESIGN

Task 30:   Function Component Implementation Map
             APPLICATION DEVELOPMENT STANDARDS

Task 40:   APPLICATION DEVELOPMENT STANDARDS

Task 50:   APPLICATION DEVELOPMENT STANDARDS

Task 60:   APPLICATION DEVELOPMENT STANDARDS

Task 70:   APPLICATION DEVELOPMENT STANDARDS

Task 80:   Function Definitions

Products created

Task 10:   Function Component Implementation Map

Task 20:   Function Component Implementation Map

Products amended

Task 30:   FUNCTION DEFINITIONS

STEP 630 – CREATE FUNCTION COMPONENT IMPLEMENTATION MAP

Inputs:
- 540: LOGICAL DESIGN
- 540: Function Definitions
- 610: APPLICATION DEVELOPMENT STANDARDS

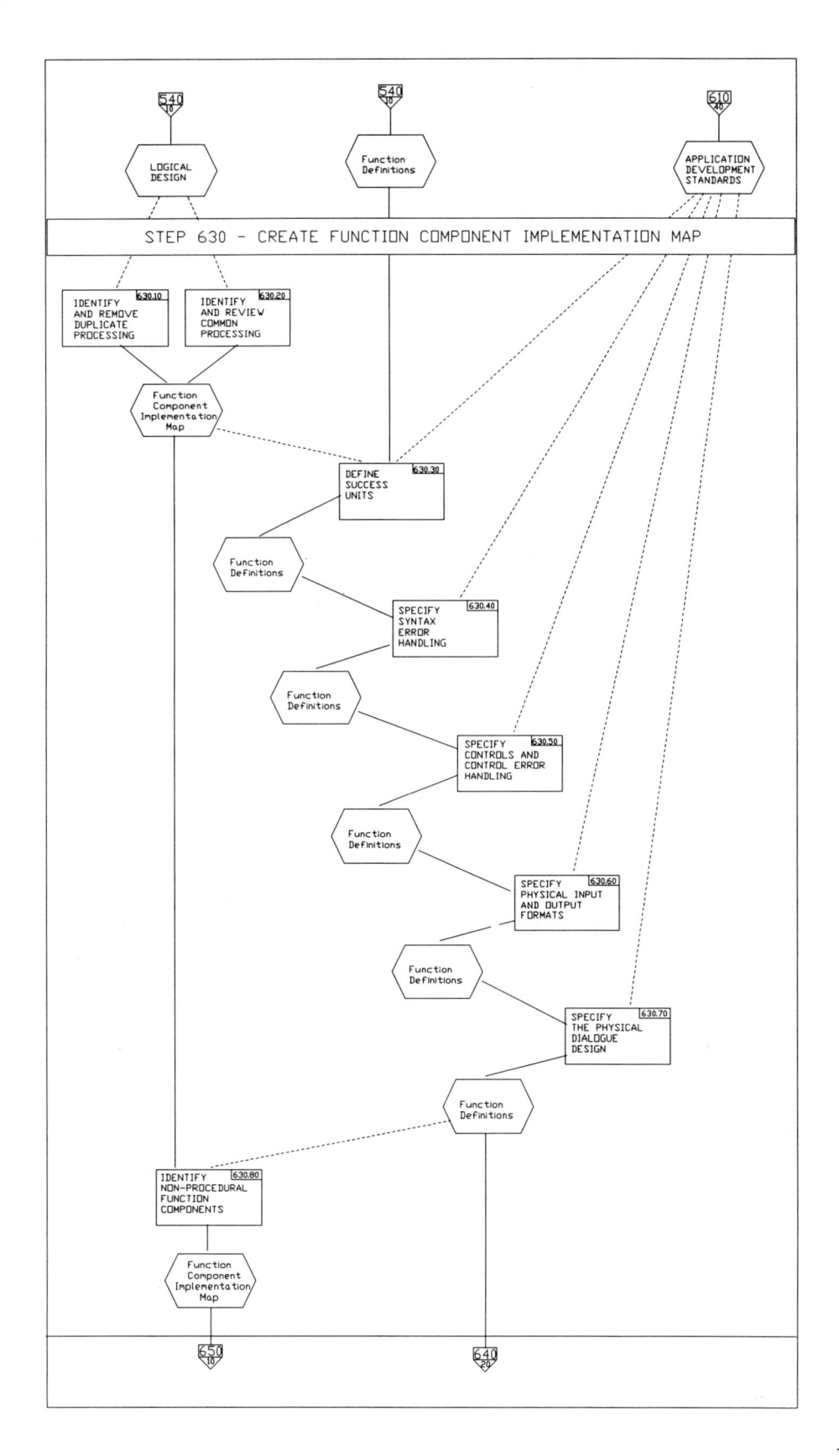

Sub-steps:
- 630.10 IDENTIFY AND REMOVE DUPLICATE PROCESSING
- 630.20 IDENTIFY AND REVIEW COMMON PROCESSING
- 630.30 DEFINE SUCCESS UNITS
- 630.40 SPECIFY SYNTAX ERROR HANDLING
- 630.50 SPECIFY CONTROLS AND CONTROL ERROR HANDLING
- 630.60 SPECIFY PHYSICAL INPUT AND OUTPUT FORMATS
- 630.70 SPECIFY THE PHYSICAL DIALOGUE DESIGN
- 630.80 IDENTIFY NON-PROCEDURAL FUNCTION COMPONENTS

Products: Function Component Implementation Map, Function Definitions

Outputs: 650, 640

Task 40: FUNCTION DEFINITIONS

Task 50: FUNCTION DEFINITIONS

Task 60: FUNCTION DEFINITIONS

Task 70: FUNCTION DEFINITIONS

Task 80: Function Component Implementation Map

Techniques

Physical Process Specification — used in Tasks 10–80

Activities

Task 10

10.1 Identify and remove duplicate processing.

Task 20

20.1 Identify and review the specification of common processing.

Note that, in combination, Tasks 10 and 20 create the Function Component Implementation Map. Tasks 30–80 are performed for each function.

Task 30

30.1 Define success units.

Task 40

40.1 Specify syntax-error handling.

Task 50

50.1 Specify controls and control-error handling.

Task 60

60.1 Specify the physical input and output formats.

Task 70

70.1 Specify the physical dialogue design.

Task 80

80.1 Describe to the physical processing systems those function components that can be specified non-procedurally, except for database access components, and update the Function Component Implementation Map.

11.4 Step 640: Optimize Physical Data Design

Objective

- To develop a PHYSICAL DATA DESIGN that meets the space and timing objectives.

Summary

The *Physical Data Design (First-cut)* is validated against the performance information contained in the FUNCTION DEFINITIONS and Requirements Catalogue. This ensures the earliest possible cross-validation of the two development streams. The *Physical Data Design (First-cut)* is optimized only if the preset performance objectives are not going to be achieved.

If there are any problems with meeting the space objectives, the design is altered to overcome them. The system space objectives are defined in the Requirements Catalogue.

The Timing Estimation Forms are completed for the critical functions and the PHYSICAL DATA DESIGN is altered if necessary. This is done until performance objectives are met, a decision is made to alter the objectives, or it has to become clear that the performance objectives cannot be met solely by data design solutions.

References

Task 10: LOGICAL DESIGN
APPLICATION NAMING STANDARDS

Task 20: LOGICAL DESIGN
APPLICATION NAMING STANDARDS

Products created

Task 10: Physical Data Design (Optimized)

Products amended

Task 10: Space Estimation Forms

Task 20: Timing Estimation Forms
Requirements Catalogue
Function Definitions
Physical Data Design (Optimized)

Techniques

Physical Data Design — used in Tasks 10 and 20

Activities

Task 10

10.1 Estimate the storage requirements and complete the Space Estimation Forms.

10.2 Restructure the data design to fit the storage constraints if necessary, preserving the one-to-one mapping whenever possible.

Physical Design Module

STEP 640 – OPTIMIZE PHYSICAL DATA DESIGN

Inputs:
- Physical Data Design (First-cut) [620/80]
- Space Estimation Forms (Filled In) [620/80]
- LOGICAL DESIGN [540/10]
- APPLICATION DEVELOPMENT STANDARDS [610/40]
- Timing Estimation Forms (Blank) [610/20]
- Requirements Catalogue [540/10]
- Function Definitions [630/70]

640.10 ESTIMATE THE STORAGE REQUIREMENTS

Outputs:
- Space Estimation Forms (Completed)
- Physical Data Design (Optimized)

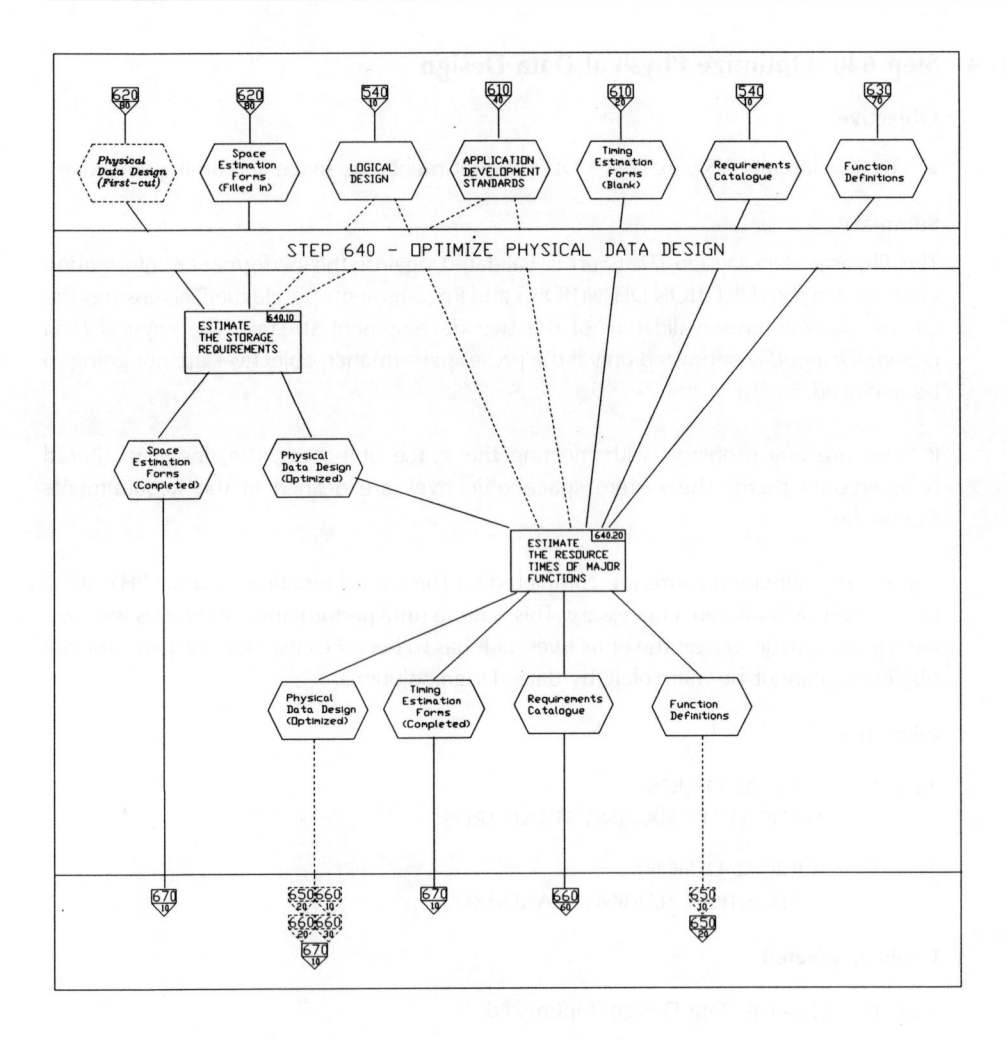

640.20 ESTIMATE THE RESOURCE TIMES OF MAJOR FUNCTIONS

Outputs:
- Physical Data Design (Optimized)
- Timing Estimation Forms (Completed)
- Requirements Catalogue
- Function Definitions

Destinations: 670/10, 650/10, 660/20, 660/30, 670/10, 660/20, 650/20

Task 20

20.1 Estimate the resource times of major functions and complete the Timing Estimation Forms.

20.2 Compare the timing estimates with the performance objectives, which are documented as service-level requirements on the Function Definitions. If the performance objectives are not satisfied, exploit the available mechanisms to improve performance, preserving the one-to-one mapping whenever possible.

20.3 Amend the Requirements Catalogue, Function Definitions, Timing Estimation Forms and Physical Data Design (Optimized) as required.

11.5 Step 650: Complete Function Specification

Objective

- To specify and design the components of a function — except for database access components — that cannot be specified non-procedurally, to the level of detail necessary for a programmer.

Summary

This step is only undertaken if the components of the Function Component Implementation Map must be specified procedurally. If necessary, specific function models are produced to resolve outstanding structure clashes. Program specifications are produced for the function components requiring procedural code.

References

Task 10:   LOGICAL DESIGN
           APPLICATION DEVELOPMENT STANDARDS
           Function Definitions

Task 20:   LOGICAL DESIGN
           APPLICATION DEVELOPMENT STANDARDS
           Physical Data Design (Optimized)
           Function Component Implementation Map

Products amended

Task 10:   Function Component Implementation Map

Task 20:   Function Definitions

Techniques

Physical Process Specification — used in Tasks 10 and 20

Activities

Task 10 and 20 are performed for each function

Task 10

10.1 Identify the logical processes in a FUNCTION that require a specification for procedural code (using a specific function model if the modular structure of the function is not sufficiently defined by the Function Definition).

10.2 Amend the Function Component Implementation Map as required.

Task 20

20.1 Complete the program specifications for those logical processes that require procedural code.

20.2 Update the Function Definitions to include the program specifications.

Physical Design Module **183**

STEP 650 – COMPLETE FUNCTION SPECIFICATION

Inputs:
- 630/80 Function Component Implementation Map
- 540/10 LOGICAL DESIGN
- 610/40 APPLICATION DEVELOPMENT STANDARDS
- 640/20 Function Definitions
- 640/20 Physical Data Design (Optimized)

Tasks:
- 650.10 IDENTIFY LOGICAL PROCESSES THAT REQUIRE PROCEDURAL CODE
- 650.20 COMPLETE FUNCTION DEFINITIONS

Outputs:
- Function Component Implementation Map
- Function Definitions
- 660/50
- 660/10, 660/20, 660/30
- 660/50

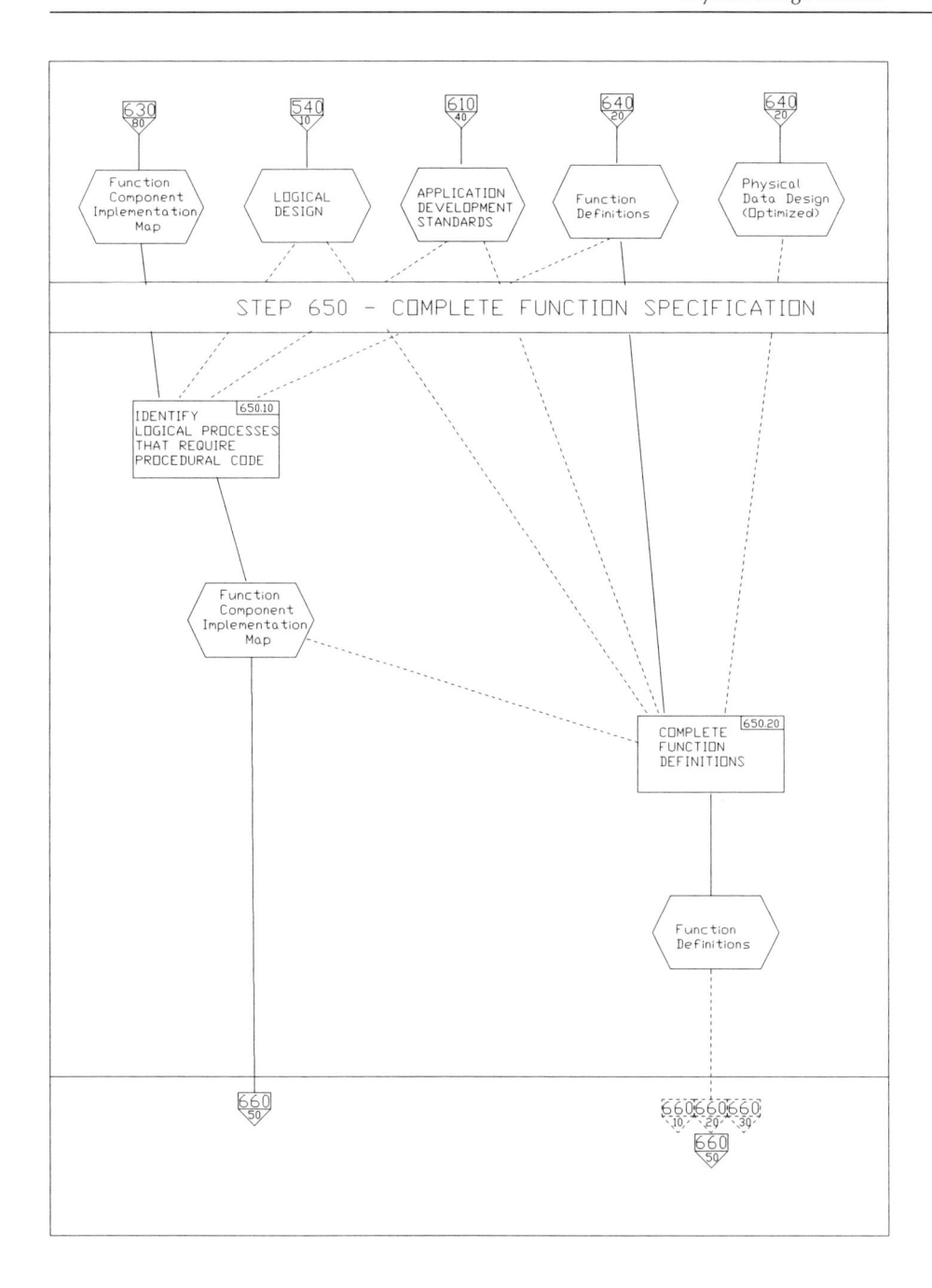

11.6 Step 660: Consolidate Process Data Interface

Objective

- To complete and validate the procedural specification and non-procedural implementation of the mapping between the Physical Data Design (Optimized) and the logical view of the data as seen by users and FUNCTIONS.

The design team's purpose in so doing is:

- To make the best use of language and tool facilities, in accordance with installation data administration policy and taking account of product- and version-specific limitations.

- To maximize the responsiveness of the system design to future changes in both parts of the physical environment and in business requirements.

- To provide additional opportunities for effectiveness, efficiency and economy, by reducing the effort required to make future changes and improvements.

Summary

The Function Component Implementation Map data access components are compared with the Physical Data Design (Optimized) to identify mismatches in 'views' of the data. The Function Component Implementation Map components will 'see' the database as the REQUIRED SYSTEM LDM, but the Physical Data Design (Optimized) — for example in a hierarchic DBMS — may have stored the data with other navigational routes. The mismatches are resolved by identifying first the keys and then the sequence of navigational steps required to deliver the Function Component Implementation Map components with their logical view of the data. This may be done non-procedurally using a data manipulation language such as SQL. In other cases, a specification for a procedural module is prepared according to the installation standards and the approach decided in the Program Design Strategy.

The set of Process Data Interface components is then rationalized as with any other element of the Function Component Implementation Map, and any special maintenance or enhancements requirements are recorded. The Requirements Catalogue may record performance requirements that are not able to be met by data design optimization, and may need to be met by low-level routines in assembler-type language. Also recorded in this way are any syntax validation or other utilities using tool-specific features such as automatic data dictionary validation facilities linked to screen painters. All these tool-specific and special-purpose utilities are catalogued together as the Process Data Interface, to aid impact analysis and to ensure that version- and product-specific features are visible to maintainers and enhancers. Any design compromises are recorded in the Requirements Catalogue against the requirements affected.

Note that, if the REQUIRED SYSTEM LDM can be implemented in the physical environment without change to its structure or definitions, then this step will not be required, and no Process Data Interface will be produced.

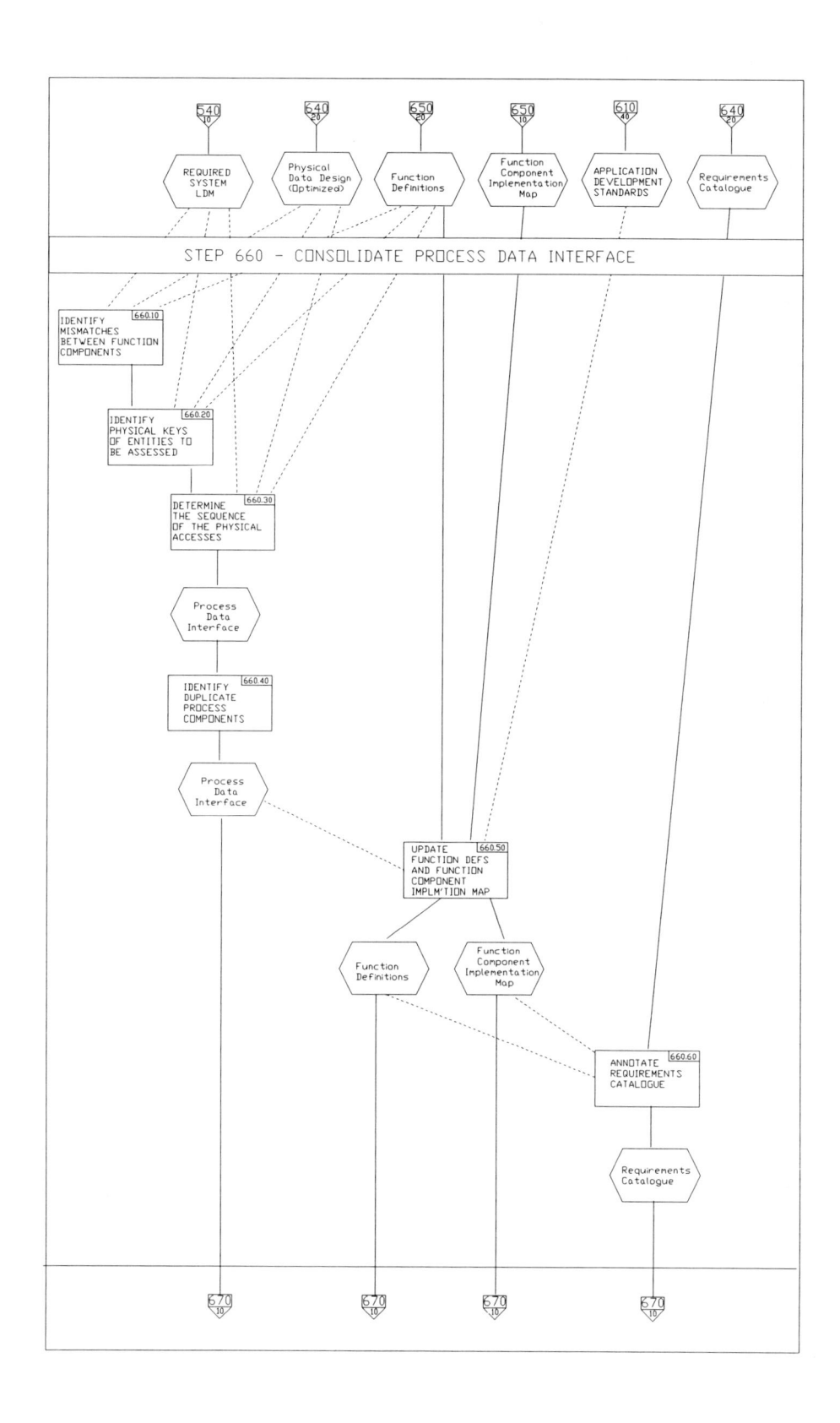

STEP 660 - CONSOLIDATE PROCESS DATA INTERFACE

Inputs:
- 540/10 REQUIRED SYSTEM LDM
- 640/20 Physical Data Design (Optimized)
- 650/20 Function Definitions
- 650/10 Function Component Implementation Map
- 610/40 APPLICATION DEVELOPMENT STANDARDS
- 640/20 Requirements Catalogue

Tasks:
- 660.10 IDENTIFY MISMATCHES BETWEEN FUNCTION COMPONENTS
- 660.20 IDENTIFY PHYSICAL KEYS OF ENTITIES TO BE ASSESSED
- 660.30 DETERMINE THE SEQUENCE OF THE PHYSICAL ACCESSES
- Process Data Interface
- 660.40 IDENTIFY DUPLICATE PROCESS COMPONENTS
- Process Data Interface
- 660.50 UPDATE FUNCTION DEFS AND FUNCTION COMPONENT IMPLM'TION MAP
- Function Definitions
- Function Component Implementation Map
- 660.60 ANNOTATE REQUIREMENTS CATALOGUE
- Requirements Catalogue

Outputs: 670/10 (×4)

185

References

Task 10: REQUIRED SYSTEM LDM
Physical Data Design (Optimized)
Function Definitions

Task 20: REQUIRED SYSTEM LDM
Physical Data Design (Optimized)
Function Definitions

Task 30: REQUIRED SYSTEM LDM
Physical Data Design (Optimized)
Function Definitions

Task 50: Process Data Interface
APPLICATION DEVELOPMENT STANDARDS

Task 60: Function Component Implementation Map
Function Definitions

Products created

Task 30: Process Data Interface

Products amended

Task 40: Process Data Interface

Task 50: Function Definitions
Function Component Implementation Map

Task 60: Requirements Catalogue

Techniques

Physical Process Specification — used in Tasks 10–50

Activities

Task 10

10.1 Identify any mismatches between a function component to handle data access according to the REQUIRED SYSTEM LDM and the Physical Data Design (Optimized). Some of these will have been suggested in the Function Definitions output from Step 640: Optimize Physical Data Design, as compromises are made in optimization which add or remove entities or relationships.

Task 20

20.1 For each mismatch, identify the physical keys of each master and detail to be assessed.

Task 30

30.1 Using either the non-procedural language identified in the Physical Environment Specification or a procedural specification, determine the sequencing of the physical accesses to provide the logical view of the data required by the Function Component Implementation Map database access components, and create the Process Data Interface. It may be helpful to start the process at the top of each hierarchy.

Task 40

40.1 Compare each new processing component thus formed and identify duplicates.

Task 50

50.1 Within the Function Component Implementation Map, fully document the interactions of all access mechanisms, indicating Process Data Interface elements that handle logical–physical mismatches as being the subject of special maintenance and enhancement requirements. Indicate those where special low-level (assembler) service routines may be required for performance reasons, as well as any that use special features in the physical environment.

50.2 Update the Function Definitions as required.

Task 60

60.1 Annotate the Requirements Catalogue to show any design decisions that limit the extent to which requirements have been met.

11.7 Step 670: Assemble Physical Design

Objectives

- To ensure the integrity of the products describing the PHYSICAL DESIGN.
- To publish the PHYSICAL DESIGN.

Summary

This step is the completion of the Physical Design Module, and is concerned with checking the consistency of the products of Stage 6.

Each of the SSADM steps represents a transformation that takes a starting set of products, performs some tasks and applies quality control to produce a target set of products. Quality management procedures are not part of SSADM, but each of the SSADM products that transports information steps has quality criteria defined as part of the Product Description (Dictionary Volume). These quality criteria are only those that can be applied to the individual products. The cross-checking of products for consistency is part of this step. The review methods to be used are defined within the quality management procedures, but the Product Descriptions also contain the recommended qualifications of the review group.

This step also publishes the formal PHYSICAL DESIGN document to the organizational standard, together with any end-of-module management reports.

References

Task 10: APPLICATION DEVELOPMENT STANDARDS
LOGICAL DESIGN
Physical Environment Specification
REQUIRED SYSTEM LDM

Products created

Task 20: PHYSICAL DESIGN

Products amended

Task 10: Function Definitions
Physical Data Design (Optimized)
Process Data Interface
Requirements Catalogue
Function Component Implementation Map
Space Estimation Forms (Completed)
Timing Estimation Forms (Completed)

Products included

Task 20: Process Data Interface
Space Estimation Forms (Completed)
Physical Data Design (Optimized)
Function Definitions
Function Component Implementation Map

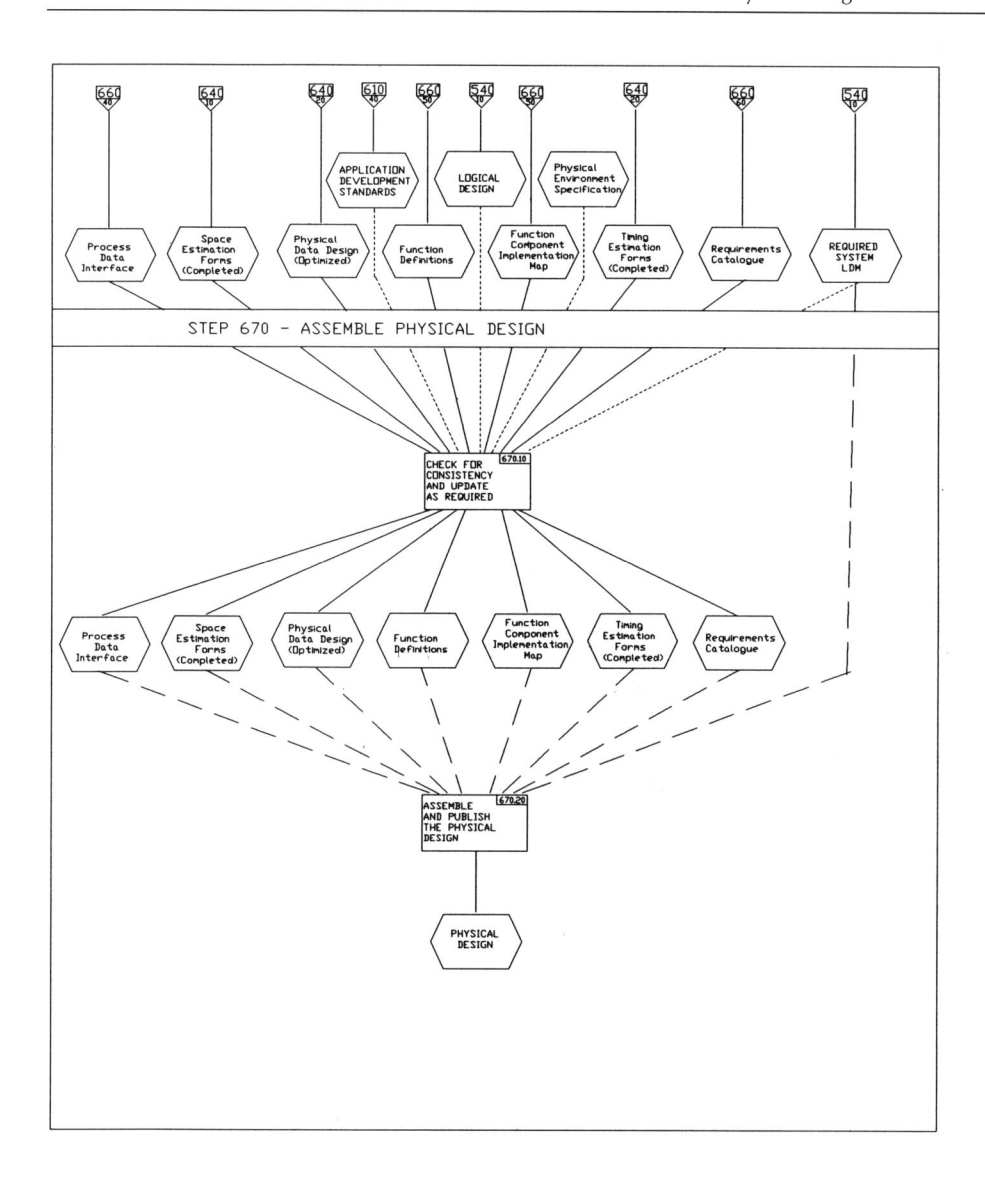

Physical Design Module

STEP 670 – ASSEMBLE PHYSICAL DESIGN

Inputs:
- Process Data Interface (660)
- Space Estimation Forms (Completed) (640)
- Physical Data Design (Optimized) (640)
- Application Development Standards (610)
- Function Definitions (660)
- Logical Design (540)
- Function Component Implementation Map (660)
- Physical Environment Specification (540)
- Timing Estimation Forms (Completed) (640)
- Requirements Catalogue (660)
- Required System LDM (540)

670.10 Check for consistency and update as required

Outputs:
- Process Data Interface
- Space Estimation Forms (Completed)
- Physical Data Design (Optimized)
- Function Definitions
- Function Component Implementation Map
- Timing Estimation Forms (Completed)
- Requirements Catalogue

670.20 Assemble and publish the physical design

→ PHYSICAL DESIGN

Timing Estimation Forms (Completed)
Requirements Catalogue
REQUIRED SYSTEM LDM
Data Catalogue

Techniques

Physical Design

Activities

Task 10

10.1 Referring to the APPLICATION DEVELOPMENT STANDARDS, LOGICAL DESIGN, Physical Environment Specification, and REQUIRED SYSTEM LDM, check the completeness and consistency of the PHYSICAL DESIGN products by reviewing the:
Function Component Implementation Map
Function Definitions
Physical Data Design (Optimized)
Requirements Catalogue
Space Estimation Forms (Completed)
Timing Estimation Forms (Completed)
Process Data Interface

Amend the PHYSICAL DESIGN products, if necessary, as a result of the reviews.

Task 20

20.1 Assemble and publish the PHYSICAL DESIGN in accordance with the organization's standards.

Appendix 1

Techniques — Where they are used, and where they are described

Technique	Described in	Used in
Business System Option	Requirements Analysis	Feasibility Requirements Analysis
Data Flow Modelling	Requirements Analysis	Feasibility Requirements Analysis Requirements Specification
Dialogue Design	Foundation	Requirements Analysis Requirements Specification Logical Design
Entity–Event Modelling	Requirements Specification	Requirements Specification Logical System Specification
Function Definition	Requirements Specification	Requirements Specification
Logical Data Modelling	Requirements Analysis	Feasibility Requirements Analysis Requirements Specification
Logical Database Process Design	Logical System Specification	Logical System Specification
Physical Data Design	Physical Design	Logical System Specification Physical Design
Physical Process Specification	Physical Design	Logical System Specification Physical Design
Relational Data Analysis	Requirements Specification	Requirements Analysis Requirements Specification
Requirements Definition	Foundation	Feasibility Requirements Analysis Requirements Specification
Specification Prototyping	Requirements Specification	Requirements Specification
Technical System Options	Logical System Specification	Feasibility Logical System Specification

Index

Note that the index entries (for products) use the same notation as that used in Section 3, see page 38 for details.

ACTION PLAN
   amended   73
   created   70
   included   73
Activity Networks
   amended   51,54
   included   54
   referenced   51
Additional Products
   created   47
   referenced   47
Application Development Standards
   referenced   175,178,182,190
Application Naming Standards
   created   172
   referenced   179,181
Application Style Guide
   created   150
   included   165
   referenced   155,156,172

Business System Options
       (product)
   amended   102
   created   102
   referenced   103
Business System Options
       (technique)
   review   14
   used   69,70,102,103,105

Command Structures
   amended   137,156,165
   created   126
   included   138,165
   referenced   156
Context Diagram
   amended   87,97
   created   60,81
   referenced   66,84,97
Cost/Benefit Analysis
   created   105
CURRENT SERVICES DESCRIPTION
   created   74,97
   referenced   102

Data Catalogue
   amended   91,94,97,113,114,115,117,
       123,130,131,137,165
   created   87
   included   138,165,190
   referenced   84,88,89,91,94,97,113,
       126,131
DATA FLOW DIAGRAMS
   created   113
Data Flow Modelling (technique)
   review   14
   used   60,66,70,81,87,94,102,113
Data Sub-Models
   created   123
   referenced   123
Dialogue Control Table
   amended   165
   created   156
   included   165
   referenced   156
Dialogue Design (technique)
   review   15
   used   66,114,120,126,155,156
Dialogue Element Descriptions
   amended   156,165
   created   156
   included   165
Dialogue Level Help
   amended   165
   created   156
   included   165
Dialogue Structures
   amended   165
   created   156
   included   165
Document Flow Diagram Network
   created   87
   referenced   87
Document Flow Diagrams
   created   87
   referenced   87

Effect Correspondence Diagrams
   amended   137
   created   130

Index

Effect Correspondence Diagrams (cont.)
    included   138
    referenced   130,159
Elementary Process Descriptions
    amended   91,94,97,113,117,137,165
    created   87
    included   138,165
    referenced   88,97,120,123,130
Enquiry Access Paths
    amended   137
    created   131
    included   138
    referenced   160
Enquiry Process Model
    amended   162,165
    created   160
    included   165
    referenced   155
Entity/Event Matrix
    created   130
    referenced   130
Entity Event Modelling (technique)
    review   16
    used   130,157
Entity Life Histories
    amended   137
    created   130
    included   138
    referenced   130
Entity Life Histories
    amended   159
    referenced   159
External Entity Descriptions
    amended   94,97,113
    created   88
    referenced   88,97
External Entity Descriptions
    created   113

Feasibility Options
    created   70
    referenced   70
FEASIBILITY REPORT
    created   73
    referenced   79,97,102,103
Function Component Implementation Map
    amended   178,182,187,190
    created   178
    included   190
    referenced   182
Function Definition (technique)
    review   18
    used   120,132,134
FUNCTION DEFINITIONS (product)
    amended   120,131,132,
        134,137,165,178,
        181,182,187,190

    created   120
    included   138,165,190
    referenced   121,126,130,178,
        182,186,187

I/O Descriptions
    amended   94,97,113
    created   88
    referenced   88,97
I/O Descriptions
    amended   130
    created   113
    referenced   120
I/O STRUCTURES
    amended   137
    created   120
    included   138
    referenced   121,123,126,130,155,160
Identified Constraints
    created   146
    referenced   146
Impact Analysis
    created   105
Initial Technical System Options
    amended   147
    created   146
Input Data Structure
    created   160
    referenced   160
Installation Development Standards
    referenced   172
Installation Standards
    referenced   47
Installation Style Guide
    referenced   126,150

Level 1 DFD
    amended   66,97,113
    created   66,94
    referenced   97
Level 1 DFD
    created   113
    referenced   113
List of Minimum Requirements
    created   69
    referenced   69
LOGICAL DATA FLOW MODEL
    amended   66,97,113
    created   66,94
    referenced   63,66,94,97
LOGICAL DATA MODEL
    amended   66,91,94,97
    created   66,89
    referenced   63,66,84,87,91,94,97,115
Logical Data Modelling (technique)
    review   19
    used   62,66,70,81,89,91,94,102,115,
        117,123,130,131,134

Logical Database Process Design
(technique)
  review   20
  used   159,160,162
Logical Datastore/Entity Cross-Reference
  amended   97
  created   94
  referenced   94,97,114
LOGICAL DESIGN
  created   165
  included   165
  referenced   173,175,178,179,181,190
LOGICAL SYSTEM SPECIFICATION
  created   165
  referenced   171,172
Logical Grouping of Dialogue Elements
  created   126
  referenced   126
Logical/Physical Datastore Cross-Reference
  created   94
  referenced   94
Lower Level DFDs
  amended   97,113
  created   94
  referenced   97
Lower Level DFDs
  created   113
  referenced   113,120,130

Menu Structures
  amended   156
  created   126
  included   165
  referenced   126,156
Minimum Functional and Non-functional
    Requirements
  created   102
  referenced   102
Module/Stage Deliverables
  created   47
  referenced   47

Normalized Relations
  created   123
  referenced   123

Operations List
  amended   159
  created   159
Outline Business System Options
  amended   70
  created   69,102
  referenced   70
OUTLINE CURRENT ENVIRONMENT
    DESCRIPTION
  amended   73
  created   66
  included   73

  referenced   67,69
Outline Development Plans
  created   70
  referenced   70
OUTLINE REQUIRED ENVIRONMENT
    DESCRIPTION
  amended   73
  created   66
  included   73
  referenced   67,69,70
Outline Technical System Options
  amended   70
  created   70,146
  referenced   146
Output Data Structure
  created   160
  referenced   160
Overview LDS
  amended   66
  created   62,66,81
  referenced   66,89

Physical Data Design (technique)
  review   21
  used   171,173,175,179,181,190
Physical Data Design (First-cut)
  created   175
Physical Data Design (Optimized)
  amended   181,190
  created   179
  included   190
  referenced   182,186
PHYSICAL DATA FLOW MODEL
  amended   66
  created   66
  referenced   63,66
PHYSICAL DESIGN
  created   190
Physical Design Strategy
  created   172
  referenced   172
Physical Environment Classification
  created   171
Physical Environment Specification
  referenced   170,190
Physical Level 1 DFD
  created   60
  referenced   66
Physical Level 1 DFD
  amended   87
  created   81
  referenced   84,87,88,94
Physical Lower Level DFDs
  created   87
  referenced   84,87,88,94
Physical Process Specification (technique)
  review   21
  used   171,178,182,186,187

Index   **195**

Problem Definition Statement
   amended   73
   created   66
   included   73
   referenced   69
Process Data Interface
   amended   187,190
   created   186
   included   190
Process/Entity Matrix
   created   94
Product Breakdown Structures
   amended   47,52,54
   included   54
   referenced   47,51
Product Descriptions
   amended   47,52,54
   included   54
   referenced   47,51
Project Initiation document
   referenced   47,51,60,66,73,79,84,102, 103, 146
PROJECT PLAN
   created   54
Project Planning (the technique)
   described   41
   used   60,82,103,148,171
Prototype Demonstration Objective Document
   created   126
   referenced   127
Prototype Pathways
   created   126
   referenced   126
Prototype Report
   created   128
   included   138
   referenced   137
Prototype Result Log
   created   127
   referenced   127
Prototyping Scope
   created   124
   referenced   126

Quality Assurance Plan
   amended   54
   created   51
   included   54

Redundant Products
   created   47
   referenced   47
Relational Data Analysis
   review   22
   used   89,91,123
REQUIRED SYSTEM DATA FLOW MODEL
   created   114
   referenced   114
REQUIRED SYSTEM LDM
   amended   117,123,130, 131,134,137, 159,165
   created   115
   included   138,165,190
   referenced   113,114,126,130,131,159, 186,190
Requirements Catalogue
   amended   66,73,84,88,91,94,97,117, 127,132,134,137,165, 181,187,190
   created   62,81
   included   73,138,165,190
   referenced   66,69,102,103,117,120, 146,156
Requirements Definition (technique)
   review   23
   used   62,66,81,88,91,94,97,113,115, 127,132,134
REQUIREMENTS SPECIFICATION
   created   138
   referenced   146,147,150
Resource Flow Diagram Network
   created   87
   referenced   87
Resource Flow Diagrams
   created   87
   referenced   87
Resource Plan
   amended   54
   created   51
   included   54

Selected Business System Option
   created   103
SELECTED BUSINESS SYSTEM OPTION
   amended   105
   created   105
   referenced   113,115,137,146
Selected Dialogues and Reports
   created   126
   referenced   126
Selected Feasibility Option
   amended   73
   created   70
   included   73
   referenced   70
Selected Functions
   created   121
   referenced   123
SELECTED TECHNICAL SYSTEM OPTION
   amended   150
   created   150
   included   163
   referenced   150
Shortlisted Business System Options
   created   102

Shortlisted Composite Options
   amended 70
   created 70
Shortlisted Technical System Options
   created 146
   referenced 146
Space Estimation Forms
   amended 175,179,190
   created 171
   included 190
Specification Prototyping (technique)
   review 23
   used 126,127
Step Descriptions
   amended 51,52
   included 54
   referenced 51
Structural Model Diagrams
   amended 51,52,54
   included 54
   referenced 51

Technical Policies
   referenced 47
Technical System Options (technique)
   review 24
   used 70,146,147,148,150
TECHNICAL SYSTEM OPTIONS
   created 147
   referenced 148
TECHNICAL ENVIRONMENT
       DESCRIPTION
   created 150

   included 165
   referenced 150
Timing Estimation Forms
   amended 181,190
   created 171
   included 190

Update Process Structures
   amended 159
   created 159
UPDATE PROCESS MODEL
   amended 165
   created 159
   referenced 155
User Catalogue
   amended 73,97
   created 66,84
   included 73
   referenced 66,69,97,102,114
User Role/Function Matrix
   amended 137
   created 120
   included 138
   referenced 126,132,156
User Roles
   amended 137
   created 114
   included 138
   referenced 120,132,156

Working Products
   created 47
   referenced 47